Studies in Economic Transition

General Editors: Jens Hölscher, Reader in Economics, University of Brighton; and Horst Tomann, Professor of Economics, Free University Berlin

This series has been established in response to a growing demand for a greater understanding of the transformation of economic systems. It brings together theoretical and empirical studies on economic transition and economic development. The post-communist transition from planned to market economies is one of the main areas of applied theory because in this field the most dramatic examples of change and economic dynamics can be found. The series aims to contribute to the understanding of specific major economic changes as well as to advance the theory of economic development. The implications of economic policy will be a major point of focus.

Titles include:

Studies in Economic Transition
Series Standing Order ISBN 978–0–333–73353–0
(outside North America only)

You can receive future titles in this series as they are published by placing a standing order.
Please contact your bookseller or, in case of difficulty, write to us at the address below with
your name and address, the title of the series and the ISBN quoted above.

Customer Services Department, Macmillan Distribution Ltd, Houndmills, Basingstoke,
Hampshire RG21 6XS, England

Economics of Institutional Change

Central and Eastern Europe Revisited

Second Edition

Tomasz Mickiewicz

First published 2005 as *Economic Transition in Central Europe and the Commonwealth of Independent States*

This edition published 2010 by
PALGRAVE MACMILLAN

Palgrave Macmillan in the UK is an imprint of Macmillan Publishers Limited, registered in England, company number 785998, of Houndmills, Basingstoke, Hampshire RG21 6XS.

Palgrave Macmillan in the US is a division of St Martin's Press LLC, 175 Fifth Avenue, New York, NY 10010.

Palgrave Macmillan is the global academic imprint of the above companies and has companies and representatives throughout the world.

Palgrave® and Macmillan® are registered trademarks in the United States, the United Kingdom, Europe and other countries

ISBN 978-0-230-24262-3   hardback

This book is printed on paper suitable for recycling and made from fully managed and sustained forest sources. Logging, pulping and manufacturing processes are expected to conform to the environmental regulations of the country of origin.

A catalogue record for this book is available from the British Library.

A catalogue record for this book is available from the Library of Congress.

10   9   8   7   6   5   4   3   2   1
19   18   17   16   15   14   13   12   11   10

Printed and bound in Great Britain by
CPI Antony Rowe, Chippenham and Eastbourne

for Anna, Danuta, Irena and Lucyna

'Was this progress? Well, it was progress of sorts, because the questions that we are now asking are much smarter than the ones that we were asking to begin with'

—Peter J. Buckley and Mark Casson

Contents

List of Tables

List of Figures

Acknowledgements

I wish to express my gratitude to Maciej Bałtowski, Marek Dąbrowski, Bogusław Fiedor, Christopher Gerry, Dariusz Rosati, Andrzej Wojtyna for comments and criticism, and to the editorial staff of Palgrave Macmillan for their valuable input.

Introduction

This book is about the process of institutional change: its characteristics, determinants and implications for economic performance. Our key area of interest is Central Europe, Eastern Europe and Central Asia, that is a region stretching from Prague in the West to Vladivostok on the Pacific coast in the East. However, the lessons are wider; they relate to other middle income economies that undergo the process of catching up with the high income countries. In other words, our ultimate interest is in the process of development, or more exactly, in its interdependence with institutions.

In most of Central and Eastern Europe the process of institutional change replaced the command economy based on administrative orders, with one relying on private property, free prices, state regulation and policy incentives. Twenty years ago, about thirty nations in Europe and Central Asia embarked on their economic transition path. For some, the outcome was a considerable success. Several others are still struggling to shed the inheritance of the past and to correct more recent policy mistakes. Some are likely to bounce back from the 2008–2009 crisis with energy, others seem to be sliding again into a period of poor performance and fiscal disarray. Why is performance so different? Was democracy a factor that facilitated reforms or, rather, slowed them down? Which reforms matter and why some are so difficult to implement?

In Chapter 1, we discuss the old regime and in Chapter 2 the reasons for the slowdown and ultimate implosion of the command economy system. Chapter 3 introduces institutions and the main components of the reform programme, highlighting some key dimensions to which relatively little attention was given and discusses the interdependence between different elements of the institutional reforms. In Chapter 4 we explore the determinants of reforms and the linkages between the political system, reform and economic growth. We ask whether democracy was good for reform, and for which reform in particular. Chapter 5 continues exploring the political economy themes, focusing on the phenomenon of the 'soft' budget constraint, a micro foundation of many macroeconomic imbalances. In Chapter 6, we ask a fundamental question: why some countries went through a ten-year long recession, while others emerged from the post-communist recessions after a mere two years. What was the relative impact of stabilization policies, liberalization policies and initial conditions? This question is still important today, as it was the negative experience of the 1990s that turned some societies away from the reform path. In Chapter 7 we explore another aspect of performance: the unemployment. We ask why labour market outcomes are so different in the various transition economies. That leads us back to institutions and different labour market institutional configurations that we consider in Chapter 8. In Chapter 9, we turn to the process of privatization, the key aspect of institutional change, which still stirs controversies today (see for instance Gerry *et al.* 2010). The privatization process is far from complete and choices over design, scope and speed are not trivial. The next two chapters focus on private and public finance, respectively. Chapter 10 explores the factors responsible for both the development and the efficiency of the financial sector in the transition countries. In Chapter 11, we explore the impact of the reforms on government expenditure, revenue and fiscal balance. Finally in Chapter 12, we explore the lessons from the 2008–2009 crisis and use this opportunity to compare the countries of our region of interest with others outside.

The book maintains a broad, comparative perspective. There are almost no sections that present single country-based studies of economic policies and our motivation was to avoid duplicating the existing literature. In particular, Gros and Steinherr (1995, 2004) offer good insights into the economic policies and institutional reforms applied in Russia, in Central Europe (in particular, the Czech Republic, Hungary, Poland), in the former Yugoslavia and in East Germany. In addition, while we refer to the economic theory of transition, we avoid replicating the existing mathematical models. In this respect, the book by Roland (2000) is still worth recommending. An earlier, shorter book by Blanchard (1997) focusing on models of reallocation and disorganization, provides an equally stimulating read. We comment on some of these themes in the light of empirical evidence in Chapter 6; it is in that chapter that our own assessment of theories of institutional change is offered.

Following the same logic, we do not cover topics on which we feel unable to add anything new to the existing literature. Gros and Steinherr (2004) present results on the significance of EU markets for all the transition countries, and discuss the argument for trade integration with the EU. Where we expand on that is with reference to the 2008–2009 crisis (Chapter 12); it is the global crisis that sheds additional light on the benefits and costs of internalization. Rozelle and Swinnen (2004) offer an authoritative summary of the results of (either complete or incomplete) liberalization and the introduction of private property rights in the agricultural sector of the transition countries. While we touch on corporate governance in Chapters 3 and 9, hopefully there is far more to be found in our own edited volume (Mickiewicz 2006). Similarly, we leave entrepreneurship aside, recommending Estrin and Mickiewicz (2010) instead. While the book touches on the issues of income distribution and on a related but different and more important theme of poverty in Chapters 4, 7 and 8, no systematic treatment is given. Again, our main excuse is that we saw no realistic chance of adding anything new to the existing research. The book by Milanovic (1998) on inequality and poverty has stood the test of time and still offers very good insights on the subject. Alongside unemployment, poverty should remain a focus of economic policy and institutional design, but with our own discussion of recession and growth performance, we are partly excused by Milanovic's own observation: 'changes in income are the most decisive factor influencing poverty' (1998: 23). Poverty and misguided policies leading to economic decline have been closely related. Some more recent discussion linking poverty to political economy issues can also be found in Gerry and Mickiewicz (2008) and Buccellato and Mickiewicz (2009). However, neither these two papers nor Chapter 4 in this book aspire to offer a systematic treatment of political economy issues in transition. Havrylyshyn (2006) filled this gap very well.

This book project started with an idea of updating my 2005 volume on economic transition, but it soon became obvious that the last five years, including the economic crisis changed a lot. While some old questions remain relevant, some new ones emerge. As a result, about half of material in this book draws from the 2005 with update, but some topics are now excluded, deemed as less relevant today. That relates in particular to the issues around stabilization and macroeconomic policies implemented in the early phase of transition. The stress in current book is on the importance of higher order, constitutional institutions of rule of law, and protection of property rights – its economic component.

However, we also recognize the issues around persistent informal institutions, including the themes of corruption and generalized trust (see also Estrin and Mickiewicz 2010). A new, if only exploratory, chapter relate to discussion of the 2008–2009 recession. A treatment of contemporary issues comes at considerable risk of mistakes; we can only hope that some of it will stand the test of time.

1
Central Planning – Command, Control and Surveillance

Introduction

At the beginning of 1989, Europe was a different place. The continent was dominated by the largest country on earth, which no longer exists: the Union of Soviet Socialist Republics (USSR). It embraced an economic system labelled by different names; 'command economy' being one of the more accurate. Yet 70 years earlier, the USSR had replaced another huge empire, Tsarist Russia, which had collapsed in 1917 near the end of the First World War. Later, towards the end of the Second World War, in 1944–5, a command-type economic system was imposed on several European countries – Bulgaria, Czechoslovakia, the Eastern part of Germany, Estonia, Hungary, Latvia, Lithuania, Poland and Romania.[1] Lithuania, Latvia and Estonia were annexed by the USSR and declared Soviet Republics. The remaining countries preserved varying degrees of autonomy, yet with the monopoly of political power guaranteed to local communist parties.

This international economic and political system collapsed in 1989, a year that began with the official re-emergence of the independent 'Solidarity' trade union in Poland (led by an electrician from the Lenin Shipyards in Gdańsk, Lech Wałęsa), and ended with the fall of the Berlin Wall. The dictatorships in Central Europe were collapsing, either peacefully or violently and, unlike his predecessors, the Soviet leader Mikhail Gorbachev decided not to send tanks to help the native communist parties stay in power. In fact, in some cases he actively supported local liberals against hard-liners. Gorbachev's aim was to reform the Soviet system, not to replace it, yet once the change gathered momentum the social and political dynamics of anti-communist revolution turned out to be impossible to stop.

Economic transformation followed. On 12 September 1989, Poland gained the first non-communist government for 50 years, with the office of Minister of Finance taken by one of the economic advisers of 'Solidarity', an academic from the Warsaw School of Economics, Leszek Balcerowicz. Only three months later, on 17 December 1989, a package of economic reforms orientated towards stabilization and liberalization was introduced in the Polish parliament, and implemented on 1 January 1990 (Balcerowicz 1992). The programme became a benchmark for other post-communist countries, which could learn from both the successes and the mistakes of one of the more fascinating experiments in economic history.

The command economy

To assess the scale of economic change that followed from the fall of communism, one has to appreciate how different the command economy was from the market economy setting in most middle- and high-income countries around the world. While the command economy now seems to be in the remote past, its heritage was a decisive factor in the economic developments which followed the liberalization programmes during the 1990s and is still having an impact in the first decades of the 21st century. In comparative perspective, using the market economy as a benchmark, the command economy has been typically described by four basic dimensions:

(1) property rights,
(2) decision-making rules,
(3) the mechanism of information flows,
(4) the nature of incentives.[2]

Decision rules and property rights are highly related dimensions, as control or decision rights are embedded in property rights; the main reason we distinguish between those is that we follow a presentation style that has became typical for the literature on the command economy. Nevertheless, taken together, the first two dimensions describe the formal institutional architecture of the *Ancien Régime*. In turn, dimensions (3) and (4) present the functional implications of this structure. We discuss all four dimensions below.

In terms of decision-making, the command economy system of production was organized in a centralized, hierarchical way. Enterprises were at the lowest level, industrial conglomerates at an intermediate level and branch ministries and the central planning commission at the highest level, with final authority resting with the Political Bureau (Politburo) and the First Secretary of the Communist Party. From a formal point of view, little discretion was left to enterprises in their decisions on output mix, output-level, prices, choice of trade partners, investment and finance.

This mode of economic organization could be easily contrasted with the market economy, where the choices of enterprises were based on decentralized information conveyed by market prices. In the command economy, the information on which decisions were to be based was passed on by the planning directives, which determined what the enterprise should produce, and how.

However, there were parts of the economy which remained outside the centralized control – i.e. where price information still affected the decisions of economic actors. This kind of systemic inconsistency led to tensions in the overall coordination mechanism. In particular, the margin of freedom related to households which, unlike firms, retained choice in both consumption and labour supply decisions.

In addition, 'unofficial' economic activity was widespread. Kornai (1986) provides an interesting analysis for Hungary. Around 1980, for instance, 42 per cent of new houses were built by individual households themselves (with the help of self-employed construction workers, on many occasions working part-time, i.e. 'moonlighters'). In general, the 'unofficial' economy covered a large section of services.

The inconsistency between household decisions and output decisions by the planning administration was a continual problem. One solution, obviously not very popular, was to impose restrictions on consumer decisions. In some countries, at some periods, consumption was rationed, typically by the use of coupons.

Similarly, freedom of labour was restricted – for instance, where higher-education graduates were told to accept specific jobs. The most infamous example of incorporating labour into the command and planning mechanism related to the vast system of forced labour camps which played a decisive role in the economic development of the USSR, especially in huge infrastructure projects, at least until the mid-1950s. Only after the death of Stalin in 1953 was the Gulag system scaled down.[3]

Restrictions imposed on enterprises in their decision-making were mirrored by the nature of property rights. Private ownership of capital in manufacturing and services was restricted to a limited number of licensed small-scale enterprises operating at the fringes of the economic system. This marginal capitalist sector was allowed to expand in some periods and was next suppressed in others – the cycle started with the liberalization at the beginning of 1920s that come under name of 'New Economic Policy', which lasted until 1928. Similarly, wave of limited economic liberalization reappeared in some Soviet bloc countries in mid-1950s after Stalin's death.

However, the licensed private sector that operated in the Soviet bloc lacked access to wider economic resources. Even more importantly, any rights to (limited) private property were granted arbitrarily by the communist authorities and could be withdrawn at any time. This arbitrariness of any concessions implied that private property was always fragile and never adequately protected; the nature of the government was totalitarian and centralized: there was no independent institution to which a private owner could appeal in a case of unjust expropriation, and the latter was easy to implement, for instance by introducing arbitrary rates of taxation that could instantaneously trigger bankruptcy.

Agriculture was the only sector with a significant share of private production in some of the Soviet bloc countries. In particular, in Poland, private agriculture was restored when a short period of forced collectivization was followed by the concessions made during the wave of post-Stalinist liberalization in 1956. In countries, where private property was not allowed, most of agriculture retained a relatively larger margin of autonomy than industry, in a form of collective farms. There was a structural rationale for allowing private property, or at least some residual autonomy, in agriculture: from the systemic point of view, this is a sector of production, which is particularly ill-suited for centralized decision-making that comes with the state system of production. Performance in agriculture is affected by both random factors (including weather) and by individual skills and effort; these are hard to disentangle and hard to monitor. Rapid liquidation of private property in agriculture in the Soviet Union in early 1930s led to an unprecedented humanitarian catastrophe that costed millions of lives, especially in Ukraine (Conquest, 1987). While situation improved later on, still, the Soviet bloc, which had some of the most fertile soil on earth, remained net importer of food until the end.

Interestingly, while the overwhelming majority of enterprises were not private, their formal ownership status was unclear. It is common to refer to them as 'state-owned enterprises' (SOEs), reflecting the fact that the key control rights remained with the state economic administration; the individual companies were effectively part of the state economic administration. Nevertheless, their formal ownership status was ill-defined; the enterprises were officially declared as 'socialist' – i.e. owned by the people, not by the state treasury, unlike nationalized companies in other parts of the world outside the Soviet bloc. Moreover, in the late communist period, significant control rights were transferred to workers' councils inside enterprises. This change was stipulated in Poland during the first period of the independent 'Solidarity' union (1980–1) and remained in place throughout the 1980s in spite of martial law and political repression. Self-governance was also extended to enterprises in Hungary, and in the USSR in the late 1980s, under Gorbachev. Those solutions drew from the experience of Yugoslavia, a country that remained outside the Soviet bloc and introduced the self-governance model first. In economic theory, the old name of a Roman province (Illyria) was used to label the self-governance model of enterprise as 'Illyrian': it was first described by Ward (1958) in his seminal paper in the *American Economic Review*.

However, even where some elements of self-governance were introduced, enterprises were always subject to continuous surveillance and arbitrary interference. Protection of property rights implies some autonomy given to the economic actors who are endowed with those rights. In that sense, it is not necessarily correct to say that under the command economy private property rights were replaced by state property. Property implies some clearly defined owners and that in turn comes with some long-term autonomy being granted to well-identified economic decision-makers. In contrast, the command economy was characterized by centralization and it was the unwillingness of the top-level decision-makers to accept any constraints on their economic power that is on their ability to interfere in any aspect of economic life at discretion – that both defined the totalitarian nature of the regime, and blurred property rights. With respect to countries where it was not uncommon that the rights to use a property could be transferred as a result of a single phone call by a party official, it is more important to say that the property was not stable and not well defined than to conclude that the property was state-owned.

The aim to centralize the economic power follows from the belief that economic coordination by markets is inefficient and that the economic welfare is best maximized by centralized planning and administration. Assumptions about information are critical here, as if the central planner/administrator is to arrive at optimum decisions on resource allocation, he or she needs to have all the necessary data about the demand and the cost structure in the economy. Market allocation solves this problem by relying on the price system: all information that autonomous decision-makers need for arriving at efficient decisions is contained in prices. In other words, markets are not information-intensive; the coordination problem is solved without a necessity to transfer all the detailed information on individual conditions between the economic actors. It is sufficient to learn about market prices to make rational economic decisions. In contrast, centralized economic decision-making depends critically on collecting low-level information and transferring it up the bureaucratic structures of economic decision-making. That implies extensive administrative structures that transfer information both up from producers to planners and than down from planners to producers in a form of planning directives, or orders, which need to specify in detail what each producer is expected to manufacture and based on which inputs and in which quantities. Not only, the running costs of such a coordination mechanism are high; it is also that some low-level dispersed information is never collected and therefore not used and some of the information becomes distorted when it travels both ways up and down the communication channels within the apparatus of economic administration.

But the problems do not end here. Apart from technological complexity of information transfers and the technical and administrative cost of the extensive system of collecting information, we need to ask if economic actors involved in the process have incentives to pass correct information up or down, or rather, if they may be inclined to distort it. Obviously, if there are incentives to distort information, the transactions costs of the coordination mechanism are increasing even more.

Under a market economy system, where decisions are decentralized following the delimitation of rights assigned by property system, strong incentives result from the right of a private owner to a residual value that can be generated by efficient use of his or her property. The residual value comes typically in a form of profit and the incentives associated with private property rights lead to profit maximization or more exactly to maximization of all current and (discounted) future profits that is of net present value of any economic venture. Again, this is a simple, decentralized mechanism than under conditions of unrestrained competition produces efficient economic outcomes. In contrast, under planning, all economic parameters, and prices in particular, are decided by the planners, therefore profit is no longer a meaningful objective; it can be arbitrary determined from above by shifting around prices of sold goods and prices of inputs. As the system is based on quantities, the low-level objectives must relate to fulfilment (or exceeding) production quotas listed in the planning documents. It follows that appropriate incentives must link managers' remuneration and prestige to the quantity of production. However, while maximization of profits implies economic efficiency, maximization of produced quantities does not. Profits are defined by the difference between revenue and cost. That leads to stress on cost efficiency, which implies that a decision-maker takes into account that any resources used in production have alternative uses: minimizing amount of resources per unit of output implies that those resources are released to be used somewhere else in the economy. In contrast maximizing production creates incentives for excessive use of resources: the easiest way to increase production is by more extensive use of inputs. As an outcome of this, under the command system, there was a continuous tension between the producers and the higher-level economic administrators. The latter aimed to prevent an excessive use of resources by specifying plans for use of inputs. However, the managers had more information about local conditions in their companies and could use this informational advantage (informational asymmetry) to claim that more resources are needed to fulfil the plan. When the planning authorities conceded and granted more resources, the costs were inflated.

In addition, the plan could never be complete. It is simply not possible to specify in detail not only quantities but all specific characteristics of the production expected under the economic plan. As managerial rewards were linked to what was specified by the plan, not to the overall value of production, this generated incentives to neglect elements that were not specified and could not be monitored at low cost. Quality, which cannot be easily and simply specified and is not always easy to assess, was a most characteristic victim of the distorted incentives. But the problem was more general. For instance if a producer of nails was given a production target specified in units of weight, he or she will focus on producing large nails neglecting smaller ones, as those are more difficult to produce.

Ultimately, the problems resulted not from the fact that the planning administrators were incompetent. Rather, they faced a task which was impossible: it is too costly to process and generate all the detailed information in a centralized manner and next to monitor the realization of planning directives based on this information. And on top of this, while questioning the incentives and motivation of socialist managers, we also need to question the motivation of administrators themselves.

Market system simplifies economic coordination task by relying on money and prices. That limits dramatically the amount of information that each of the decentralized producers and consumers need to process in their decision-making. At the same time, profit and monetary incentives create an automatic hard sanction of bankruptcy: those that do not deliver what is consistent with preferences of the buyers can no longer continue to use resources that have more efficient use elsewhere (we will continue on this in Chapter 5). In contrast, the founding father of communism, Karl Marx, envisaged a world without money and profits. In practice however, the system had to rely on monetary income as a main channel determining the access to goods and therefore their final distribution. Wage income and social transfers remained key categories of income, with property income and (official) income from self-employment playing a much smaller role, when compared with the high- and middle-income market economies (Milanovic 1998).

Yet, while the role of monetary incentives was dominant, it was still restricted and was complemented by other distribution mechanisms. First, a combination of administrative prices and free demand decisions by consumers resulted in market dis-equilibria and shortages. The latter implied that money income was a necessity but not a sufficient condition for acquiring goods. For that reason, other distribution mechanisms operated, starting with queuing and – equally important – networking and corruption. Payments in kind for workers were also widespread. Enterprises functioned not only as production units but also as providers of services for workers, including housing, child care, holidays and recreational facilities and health care (Rein, Friedman and Wörgötter 1997). To provide access to these mainly via work was functional from the system point of view, as it gave incentives for higher work participation; indeed, activity rates in all these countries were high.

While discussing the incentive system, one has also to take into account the duality, which was the command economy's defining feature. The administrative hierarchy (all the way up from enterprises to the central planning commission) was always shadowed by the communist party structure, where party officials were expected to act as (supposedly highly motivated) controllers. This vast monitoring system was meant to overcome motivational problems. The party controllers were granted important privileges and offered special access to housing, cars and luxury goods via exclusive distribution channels (vouchers, special shops). According to the official blueprint, all this gratification was only supplementary – the system was supposed to rely heavily on the ideological motivation of the party controllers acting in the 'social interest', i.e. overcoming the 'petty egoism' and 'indifference' of economic actors at various levels of the production process. Until the mid-1950s (the death of Stalin), ideology was always complemented not only by material incentives but also by a reign of terror, and in the case of party apparatchiks it is difficult to disentangle genuine enthusiasm from the disciplining effect of fear: psychologically the latter has as strong effect as the former, as self-delusion is part of human nature. Regardless of the weight we may attach to those two components, it appears that, with time, the appeal of ideology faded away, the era of overwhelming terror ceased, and material incentives to match aspirations proved difficult to deliver. The necessary minimum social support base began to shrink.

Norms, values and the lasting influence of the Soviet system

The account provided above relies primarily on a standard rational choice theory – a cornerstone of any economic analysis. We combine it with institutional analysis, by asking how individual economic actors respond to different rules of the game (different formal institutions), contrasting the impact of the command economy framework with that of the market. However, in this analysis, we take economic actors as uniform: the same people when moved from one environment to another will act differently not because they are different, but because incentives they face change.

Rational choice is a very effective theory, and while simplifying the world it also enables us to form powerful predictions that are confirmed by what we observe in empirical world. However rational choice alone cannot explain all diversity in human behaviour. The way different persons see the world and the objectives they adopt in their behaviour differ in a systematic way and that matters for economic outcomes. In particular, human behaviour is shaped not just by formal institutions (rules) like those we discussed above, but is also driven by rules that come without a specific formal sanction that is by norms and values (Crawford and Ostrom 1995). Those in turn are typically shared across larger communities people live in. Moreover, unlike formal institutions, those cannot be changed quickly by any reform initiated at the top level, say by a change in legislation or even by a more fundamental change in formal constitutional rules: norms and values (informal institutions) become deeply embedded. They are persistent and evolve slowly (North 1990). Accordingly, it is not the legacy of formal institutions but the legacy of informal institutions that make the post-communist countries in Europe and Asia still a distinctive region in some respects, despite the 20 years that passed since the implosion of the Soviet system.

Existing research in sociology of culture documents that communism left a legacy of values and norms that are not conducive to initiative and entrepreneurship; that is there are not compatible with the attitudes that support any market-based system. Sztompka (1996) describes this legacy as 'bloc culture' which comprised priority of dependence over self-reliance, of conformity over individualism, and of rigidity and extremism in beliefs over tolerance and innovation.

He also notes that those norms are subject to generational effect: 'the bridge between the influences of the past and the future is provided by generations; congeries of people who – in their formative years – have happened to be exposed to similar, significant social forces' (*Ibid.,* p. 126). That explains how the change in informal institutions happens and why it may be slow. Similar to Sztompka (1996), Schwartz and Bardi (1997) observe that the differences between the transition and the comparator countries are lower for younger people, both because of the generational effect and to higher capacity of young people to learn and to adopt to new conditions and new cultural influences.

The same theme is developed further and tested empirically by Schwartz and Bardi (1997). They argue that those norms were adopted mostly not as an effect of direct indoctrination during the communist period but as a way of social adaptation to the prevailing economic and social conditions, sometimes in direct contradiction to the official ideology. In particular, while the communist system officially promoted trust and cooperation, the prevailing conditions of massive surveillance and detailed monitoring of citizens led to distrust, which became deeply rooted in values and in resulting social and economic attitudes. In addition, their empirical results confirm that values clustered around autonomy and mastery that are critical for private initiative and entrepreneurship remain much weaker in post-communist societies than in comparator west European societies in mid-1990s.

At the same time, Schwartz and Bardi (1997) detect some differences amongst the post-communist societies. In particular, they observe that countries of the former Orthodox tradition seem to score even less that Central European and Baltics rooted in Protestant and Catholic religious origins. However, the distinction based on religious origin almost overlaps with another based on the length of time spent under communism, therefore one need to be cautious in interpretation. One could note a difference between the transition countries that went through the full long cycle of communism from the end of World War I until late 20th century, including the most damaging Stalinist period (see for instance: Applebaum 2003), as compared with those countries, where communism was introduced only after the end of World War II. The first group of countries relates to most of the former Soviet Union republics, including Russia, Kazakhstan and most of Ukraine and Belarus. The second relates to Central and South East Europe and the three Baltic States. In this second group we find Poland, Czech Republic and Hungary, amongst others.

Thus, it is likely that the differences in informal institutions are driven not by centuries old religious origins of different cultures but by the tens of years old influence of the Soviet (and Stalinist in particular) system.

Schwartz and Bardi's (1997) findings of lack of trust in post-communist countries are confirmed by the results of World Value Surveys, reported by Howard (2000). Lack of generalized trust was partly substituted by private networks, however, later on, in the new conditions of market economy those were no longer efficient as a way of dealing with more sophisticated and larger scale economic activity as that needs to be based more on impersonal (generalized) trust. Economic activity is essentially also a social activity; it is based on cooperation emerging in social milieu. This is important not only for new ventures, but also for bigger firms, as a larger scale of operation relies on a more extensive network of contacts, thereby requiring higher levels of generalized trust. Here, the post-communist countries share a negative heritage of a system based on authoritarian hierarchical organization and detailed surveillance of all citizens. As stated by Fukuyama (1995): 'There are indeed truly individualistic societies with little capacity for association. In such a society, both families and voluntary associations are weak ... Russia and certain other former communist countries come to mind.'

To conclude this section, evidence from existing research suggests that post-communist societies, and the older generation in particular, are characterized by different set of values rooted in the Soviet experience, where autonomy and mastery score lower, and generalized trust is missing. These values not only affect economic activity in a direct way. They may also affect it indirectly via their impact on the way the formal institutions are designed and the way they function in practice. In particular, lack of trust affects expectations and may result in self-fulfilling vicious circle of poor institutional practices and corruption.

Concluding remarks

This chapter does not aim to offer a comprehensive analysis of how the command economy worked in practice. We covered just few key elements: the nature of property rights and decision rights, the structure of information, and resulting incentives that shaped actual behaviour. However, we reached beyond a standard economic analysis to point out to the legacy of norms and values; as these still affect the economic outcomes in those countries, despite 20 years that passed since the end of the communist system.

We left aside details of how the planning administration was organized. We did not discuss how administrative prices were set, and what were the implications of the price system. We did not discuss in detail the allocation of capital and labour. Macroeconomic outcomes were not analysed in detail either. There are two reasons for these omissions. First, outstanding accounts of how the socialist system functioned are readily available (see for instance Kornai (1992) or Gregory and Stuart (1995)) and there is little we could add to it. Second, we will return to some of those details below whenever referring to the past will help us to explain the current economic features of those countries.

But more importantly, it is more interesting to discuss some of the systemic features in a dynamic perspective and see if and what role they played in the implosion of the communist system. This is the issue we turn to next.

2
Decline and Fall of the Soviet System

Why it lasted so long and what went wrong?

As discussed in the previous chapter, control of prices and of production quantities was based on imperfect information and that led to shortages and dis-equilibria. Those in turn resulted in dead-weight cost and inefficiency. Nevertheless, the command economy survived for 70 years in Europe.[1] The system did offer basic economic stability for the population: while on the one hand freedom of labour was restricted, on the other there was no unemployment. Standards of living were not improving fast, yet extreme poverty was eradicated. The premium for education (as, say, measured by the difference between non-manual and manual wages) was minimal, but more education was offered than in countries at a comparable level of income *per capita* (Jackman and Rutkowski 1994; Milanovic 1998; Mickiewicz and Bell 2000). From the political perspective, while episodes of mass repression reoccurred (the Soviet invasion of Hungary in 1956 and of Czechoslovakia in 1968, martial law in Poland in 1982), in most places and for most of the time after the mid-1950s the level of political repression in communist countries was relatively low, especially when compared with many dictatorships in Latin America, Asia and Africa at that time. The interesting question for both economic and political historians is thus what went wrong, and why the system collapsed so dramatically.

It was easier to see the early signs of a crisis from within than for outside observers. More than one generation of Western scholars took the official Soviet growth statistics seriously, and many were impressed with Soviet Union achievements. After all, it was both a military superpower and the only country able to compete successfully with the US in the space programme. But not everybody was misled. A group of UK-based scholars published a book in 1982 with the novel title, 'Crisis in the East European Economy' (Drewnowski 1982): 'There is a spectre haunting Eastern Europe: the spectre of zero growth' the opening sentence by Peter Wiles reads, and he provides a catalogue of likely and unlikely factors that were contributing to economic slowdown and decline (Wiles 1982). Much of that discussion has stood the test of time. Following and expanding it (with the benefit of hindsight), one can distinguish between two inter-related clusters of explanations:

(1) Systemic features of the command economy, which were present from the very beginning but their effects became negative only when they interacted with changing external circumstances;
(2) Non-economic factors.

The first cluster of factors – i.e. the systemic features of the command economy that contributed to economic slowdown – related to inadequate incentives, semi-autarky, structural inertia and the priority that was given to military expenditures. We shall discuss these in turn.

Incentives and innovation

The issue of incentives has been at the centre of the debate on economic efficiency under a command economy. On one hand, Oskar Lange (1936) argued that the efficient prices equivalent to the perfect competition solution might be calculated by the planners. It would mean that along the informational dimension the command economy system could match or even surpass the market economy system.[2] However, Von Mises' reply (1966 [1949]) was that information alone could not be a sufficient condition for efficiency; it would have to be matched by the two parallel dimensions of private property rights and incentives conditioned by them:

> They want to abolish private control of the means of production, market exchange, market prices, and competition. But at the same time they want to organize the socialist utopia in such a way that people could act as if these things were still present. They want people to play market as children play war, railroad, or school. They do not comprehend how such childish play differs from the real thing it tries to imitate. (Von Mises 1966 [1949]: 706–7, emphasis in the original; see also Temkin 1989 for an overview of this discussion.)

Nevertheless, the problem of incentives was recognized much better by central planners than by Marxist economists, and alternative bundles of ideology, intimidation and material incentives were applied to over-come it. In the long run, only the latter proved to have some lasting effect. Even so, the fundamental problem remained: how to shape the objective function on the level of individual economic actors in an efficient way. Rewards for the fulfilment of the plan were relatively simple to implement, but these left many issues outstanding. As argued in the previous chapter, the plan could not cover all contingent states of the world: it had to remain an incomplete contract. In particular, incentives play a critical role in the process of innovation, which is least easy to organize within the framework of a centralized economic administration. By definition, innovation cannot be incorporated into an economic plan.

Inadequacy of the innovation process became a serious constraint in the later phase of the socialist development with both the changing nature of the economic environment (the growth of information tech-nologies, etc.) and the higher level of GDP and therefore more sophis-ticated developmental needs. Over time, those countries were getting relatively closer to the 'technological frontier' as defined by most advanced economies. At that stage, a development strategy should be based more on the innovation, replacing the previous imitation strategies. However, innovation processes remained weak. The paradoxical nature of the science and technology system under the command economy relates to the fact that on the one hand it was orientated towards the needs of enterprises, yet on the other innovation activities had to be incorporated into the economic administration and planning system and therefore remained organized within branch research institutes attached to the correspond-ing branch ministries, with few cross-section links and inadequate diffusion of technology into products:

> As technology is primarily a firm-specific asset, the consequence of this systemic defect was that the links between R&D and production were generally weak. (Radosevic 1999: 283–4)

Semi-autarky

While domestic innovation is important, foreign trade and investment are also the key channels for the transfer of knowledge and technology. After the Second World War, internationalization became one of the key factors of global development, yet the logic of planning adminis-tration prevented the centrally planned economies (CPEs) from parti-cipating fully in the benefits. The openness of these countries remained low, while it grew rapidly elsewhere.

Figure 2.1 illustrates this, using the exports/GDP ratio for 1990,[3] i.e. for the initial point of the transition programmes. As larger economies tend to trade less, the openness (vertical axis) is plotted against the size of GDP (horizontal axis), showing a typical negative correlation. In the lower left corner of the graph we see a group of post-communist economies with very little trade (Albania, Macedonia, Mongolia). The contrast with the outside world would be even more dramatic if it were not for the fact that some former Soviet republics were very much dependent on intra-Soviet Union trade (Kazakhstan, Moldova), which became external trade on the breakdown of the Soviet Union. For Russia, in 1990, 64.4 per cent of its foreign trade was within the former Soviet Union (FSU), and only 35.6 per cent with other countries (Smith 1996). Generally, if CPEs traded, they traded mostly with themselves i.e. within the Soviet bloc. Later on, the capacity to re-orient the trade towards the EU and other developed market economies became an important factor determining economic success.

Semi-autarky was partly a policy choice and partly a systemic feature of the planning system, for which the outside world was an alien, uncontrollable cause of disruption. It was a source for the residual resources that

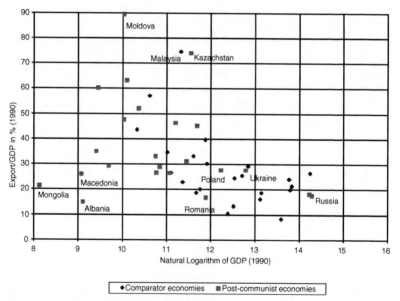

Figure 2.1   Size of the economy and openness

Source: Computed on the basis of World Bank data.

had to be imported to close the material balances of the plan. Exports were generated to pay for them. A related problem was that suitable exports were difficult to find. In 1983, 70 per cent of Soviet exports to the hard currency area were in the form of energy exports, with four-fifths being oil (Schroeder 1986).

Structural inertia

The third related systemic feature, with negative effects increasing over time (i.e. in the later stages of development), was structural inertia. To understand the roots of the problem, one has to look at how the planning mechanism worked in practice. Economic plans were constructed for long periods (five years, sometimes also for three years or seven years), yet in practice the basic tool used in economic administration was the detailed annual plan. The planning process involved three stages: plan development, plan implementation and feedback. The first of those originated with general guidelines provided by the Politburo of the Central Committee of the Party. Those directives were then taken into account by the Central Planning Commission, responsible for establishing provisional production targets. Those production targets (the production plan) had to be linked directly with plans for supplies, employment and transport, and accompanied by the investment plan, the financial plan, the income plan (which decided the wages and other income of the population), the corresponding consumption plan and the trade plan, including both domestic and foreign exchange of commodities. As soon as the draft version of the production plan was ready it was sent down through the corresponding branch ministries and industrial associations to individual enterprises for comment and confirmation of requested inputs.

Next, the details were sent back up the same administrative ladder to the Planning Commission, which had to balance all key inputs and outputs to make the plan consistent. Once that was achieved, the implied production targets were again sent down to individual enterprises as binding law, which became the basis for the subsequent year's production (Kurowski 1991; Gregory and Stuart 1995). Figure 2.2 illustrates the flow of information during the construction of the plan.

The formulation of the plan was thus a time-consuming and complex process with very high informational requirements. Moreover, it implied bargaining between the various levels of the economic administration, where the position of enterprises *vis-à-vis* the higher levels of economic

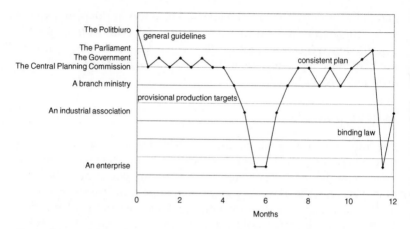

Figure 2.2   Construction of the annual plan: Flow of information

Source: Adapted with some modifications from Kurowski (1991).

administration was strengthened by informational asymmetry (only enterprise managers had full knowledge of the real technological requirements).

From the point of view of the enterprise it was beneficial to have lower production targets, for two reasons. First, some slack in production targets was always beneficial, as supplies of raw materials and intermediate products beyond technological requirements might help to save on effort and minimize a risk of production disruption. Secondly, declaring ambitious production was a strategy which entailed the risk for enterprise managers that this year's achievements could be transformed into higher expectations from the planners next year.[4] In response to the expected slack, rewards were typically linked to over-ambitious production targets. Yet, in turn, the reaction of enterprise was to lobby for increasing the amount of supplies and resources specified by the plan, including labour and capital. A repetitive bargaining game resulted between enterprises and the higher levels of the planning administration. The pressure on increased supplies coming from enterprises, matched with the aim of the planning authorities to maximize production and price controls, led to chronic shortages.

The complexity of the planning mechanism implied that frequently the plan arrived late and enterprises had to rely on provisional figures, with a risk of subsequent disruption. And even if the plan was ready, the logic of the planning mechanism required that much of it was in fact based on an assessment which had a one-year lag built in to it, as this is how long it took to transform the initial data into a coherent plan (see Figure 2.2). In practice:

> The plan for year t was, in effect, little more than a revision and update of the plan for year $t-1$ ... Although it simplified the planning process, it built in considerable inflexibility. (Gregory and Stuart 1995: 275)

Structural change and innovation were the disrupting factors which complicated the task of planning even more. The interests of all involved, including the enterprises, were to expand their own production, with no place left for new entrants (and no exit mechanism). New large firms emerged as a result of centralized investment projects, but even those were primarily oriented towards filling the existing gaps in the material balances of the plan.

In the initial phase of development, growth in the Soviet bloc was fuelled by extensive methods. The increment of working-age population was high and the under-employed labour force in agriculture was transferred to industry. Similarly, production of raw materials and fuels had been expanding. However, all that changed in the later phase, as it did outside the Soviet bloc. Yet, the structural inertia of the system prevented it from adjusting efficiently:

> The extreme sensitivity of the Soviet economy to changes ... is due to its extreme rigidity, including the inability to adjust the system of investment to variations in the rate of growth of the supply of labour and capital ... In other words, the Soviet economy has been able to grow without great difficulty while it was sufficient to produce no matter what and no matter how: labour was plentiful and even waste of capital looked like growth. (Sirc 1981: 74–6)

Thus, the system worked satisfactorily as long as the structures evolved in a predictable way, especially during the early industrialization phase. Problems arose when there was a sudden shift in the relative availability of resources, resulting in a need to switch to new technologies, which could cause an upheaval in the whole complex network of planning balances. An example of such an external shock came at the beginning of the 1970s, and again after 1979, with a dramatic increase in international oil and energy prices. While for the most of the developed economies this implied a long period of structural adjustment, the communist leaders declared the oil crises another sign of the decline of the capitalist system, with no implications for the socialist world. The command economies of Central and Eastern Europe carried on along the old path of energy-intensive development, expanding old technologies, and importing production lines which were just becoming obsolete in the West because of the shift in cost structures. Over time, the gap widened, leaving the command economies with the highest level of energy intensity of production. In 1960, average *per capita* energy consumption in high-income market economies was on average around 3,000 kg of oil-equivalent per year, around 2,000 in CPEs and around 200 kg in market economies at a similar level of income *per capita* (middle-income countries). The latter group is more relevant for comparison, as generally the production/ energy ratio displays a hump-shaped relationship with income *per capita* – for the highest level of income, the energy intensity of consumption increases, counterbalancing the effect of the higher efficiency of use, as exemplified by the US.

Between 1960 and 1980, the rate of growth of energy consumption in the CPE group was visibly faster than in market economics. Moreover, during the 1980s, while the energy consumption in the high-income economies oscillated around the same level, it continued to grow in the CPE group. By the end of the 1980s, it was similar in both groups, approaching 5,000 kg. Yet, in the relevant comparator group of the middle-income market economy, it was only around 1,000 kg – i.e. five times lower (Tolba and El-Kholy 1992: 376).[5]

Figure 2.3 illustrates the closing balance of the command economy period.[6] It is clear from Figure 2.3 that at the beginning of the 1990s the energy efficiency of production was uniformly low in the post-communist economies. The most dramatic cases relate to the former Soviet republics, including the Russian Federation. Similar figures can be obtained for the steel intensity of GDP (see Winiecki 1987, 2002; Winiecki and Winiecki 1992).

The opportunity cost of the growing absorption of energy by the domestic sector came in a form of a low level of exports to developed market economies. This, combined with the necessity of imports from that area for modernization, made the marginal impact of the decrease in exports particularly harmful. Expanding domestic consumption of energy combined with dependence on energy, and more generally on commodity exports to the West, presented a difficult trade-off for the central planners. In the late 1980s, the negative effects were amplified by two additional factors. First, reckless extraction policies led to depletion of some of the most easily available oil pools and ore deposits (Gros and Steinherr 2004). In particular, production of crude oil in Russia levelled

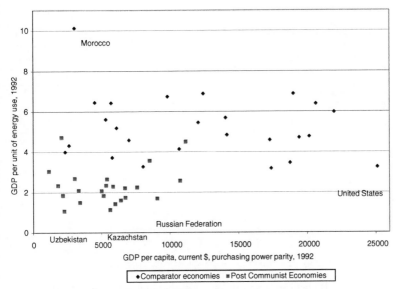

Figure 2.3   Income per capita and energy efficiency of production
Source: World Bank, World Development Indicators.

out, oscillating around 10,000 barrels a day (Gregory and Stuart 1995). Second, the international price of a barrel of oil was slashed by 60 per cent, going down from $29.3 in 1985 to $12.1 in 1986 (constant 1980 $) and remaining at a low level until the end of the decade, which turned out to be the last in the history of the CPEs (Tolba and El-Kholy 1992).

The high energy intensity of GDP resulted both from cost inefficiencies and from distorted production structures. The CPEs were characterized by a high share of steel and heavy industry in the industry sector, and by a high share of the latter in the whole economy. This may be typical for some export-driven economies, but the CPEs were not of this kind, as already discussed. They were rather faced with structural distortion (Mickiewicz 2003). Figure 2.4 illustrates the point.

In Figure 2.4, one may note the three post-communist countries with a particularly high share of industry in employment: Romania, Russia and Ukraine. All three subsequently faced a particularly difficult transition.

Normally we see the hump-shaped relationship between the level of GDP *per capita* and the industry share. Development in poor countries is accompanied by the build-up of industrial employment, transferred from agriculture. The share of industry is highest in the middle-income

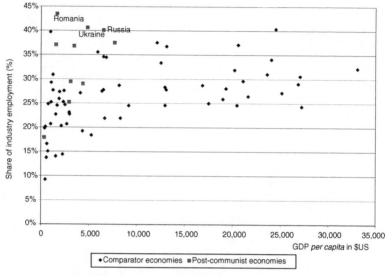

Figure 2.4   GDP per capita and share of industry in employment, 1990

Source: UN Statistical Yearbook (1995) and WIIW database, Vienna Institute for International Economic Studies.

economies and with further development it stabilizes and shrinks, making room for an expanding service sector. In this respect, the initial drive for industrialization in the CPEs was consistent with the standard pattern of development.

Priority was given to both heavy industry and to the primary sector. In Marxist doctrine, this is referred to as 'the law of the priority development of production of producer goods'. It assumed (wrongly) that:

> the production of consumer goods does not grow parallel to that of the whole economy but that initially producer goods are used to produce other producer goods and that only eventually, if ever, there is a switch to consumer good production. (Sirc 1981: 75)

It was the latter which never fully materialized, and the resulting structural distortions increased with time. The problem was that due to structural inertia and maintaining the wrong priorities, the CPEs remained on a track which led them further and further away from an efficient development path based on both consumer goods and modern services. Pulled by the overgrown energy-inefficient industry – the steam engine of the planned economies – the socialist train ultimately came to the end of the line and was derailed.

Military spending

One is tempted to link the high share of steel and heavy industry to the fourth systemic feature identified at the beginning of this section – i.e. to the policy priority given to military spending. However, the input-output data demonstrate that civilian spending, as with civilian construction and civilian durable goods, may have been even more steel-intensive (Leontief and Duchin 1983). Nevertheless, military expenditure always played an important role. The peak of the 'Cold War' was during the first ten years after 1945, with intensive military effort by both the Soviet Union and the US. Yet, while since the mid-1950s, the relative level of spending by the US was reduced, that of the Soviet Union was increased. In 1957, the US share in world military expenditures was 45 per cent and that of the Soviet Union was 20 per cent. By 1978, the former had decreased to 26 per cent, and the latter had increased to 26 per cent (Leontief and Duchin 1983: 6). Yet a similar volume of spending meant a higher share in GDP, given the Soviet Union's much lower GDP level. Moreover, at the

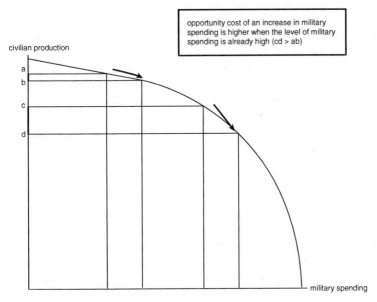

Figure 2.5   Rising opportunity cost of military production

beginning of the 1980s the Soviet Union faced an additional military burden triggered by the decision to invade Afghanistan and the technological challenge from the US 'Space Wars' programme. Arguably, by that time, the marginal opportunity cost of shifting additional resources to the military-industrial complex was already very high and led to disruptions in other parts of the economic system. On the other hand, civilian production did not benefit greatly from technology diffusion. The argument about the rising marginal cost of military spending is summarized by a simple graph (see Figure 2.5).

Public dissatisfaction; investment – consumption trade-offs

The argument so far has focused on the deteriorating economic performance that resulted from the fact that the systemic features and polices became particularly problematic when both external circumstances change and the Soviet bloc countries reached higher stages of development. This deteriorating performance of the command economy system led to the pressure for change, with the latter resulting ultimately in economic transformation. Indeed, there is overwhelming evidence that disillusion with the economic results of the socialist system was a decisive factor behind the pressure for political change, as demands for more political freedom were always mixed with those that were purely economic, as illustrated by the Polish 'Solidarity' trade union movement which emerged in the summer of 1980 and remained active despite repression over the next decade.

The communist leaders fell victim to their own ideological beliefs. The economic superiority of the command economy was a cornerstone of the ideology, and high growth rates were supposed to be its prime manifestation. An ultimate logical implication was to aim at some specific date for overcoming the leading market economies – the US in particular – as for instance declared by Soviet leader Nikita Khrushchev in the mid-1950s. Yet none of those predictions materialized.

Moreover, the liberalization that followed the death of Stalin made the countries of Central Europe more open. In turn, freedom of movement and experience of a higher quality of life in the neighbouring European Economic Community (EEC, the predecessor of the EU) was a dangerous factor undermining the official claims of the superiority of the communist system. By the late 1980s, the Soviet leaders, and Mikhail Gorbachev in particular, were well aware of the necessity for economic reform.

Thus, in the second half of the 20th century, the policy-makers in the Soviet bloc faced a difficult challenge: while economic results were gradually deteriorating, popular dissatisfaction and undercurrent pressure for change was growing. Efforts to revitalize economic growth resulted in macroeconomic cycles of overheating and cooling down, which is ironic given that Marxist criticism of the market economy was too much extent based on the cyclical occurrence of recessions. Kołodko (1979), based at that time at the Warsaw School of Economics, was the author that identified that the command economy was subject to the economic cycle just as much as the market economy (in English: Kołodko 1986, 2002). In the phase of expansion, the investment programme was overstretched and the number of projects mushroomed beyond the capacity of the system to deal with them. Too many investment projects resulted from the coinciding interests of the planning administration and individual enterprises to expand production and remove the bottlenecks in the economic system, with no strong individual interests supporting efforts to match the resulting claims on resources with scarcity constraints. This free-rider problem resulted in the dispersion of investment, long completion times for projects and production gains that came too late and did not match expectations. In the next phase of the cycle, to stabilize the situation, savings had to be made and raiding the private consumption pool was the easiest remedy. A slowdown in the supply of consumer goods matched with administrative prices led to price increases having a socially visible and painful, one-off, discrete character.

However, those adjustment mechanisms became more difficult to implement in the late phase of the system. With time, and with political repression mechanisms being scaled down, adjustment based on periodical suppression of private consumption become more and more difficult to implement politically, as triggering social unrest and protests was now more likely. This led to postponing adjustments and to chronic disequilibria and imbalances that further affected economic performance negatively.

Generally the inefficiency built into the investment processes meant that high growth rates could be generated only by disproportionately high investment rates, at the cost of consumption. This is illustrated by a snapshot of the investment shares in GDP and GDP growth rates in the final period of communism. For the market economies, there is a positive and significant correlation between investment and growth. For CPEs, there is none. Vietnam, with some market reforms already implemented during the 1980s (see Riedel and Comer 1997), enjoyed a period of fast economic growth without an overstretched investment programme. On the other hand, many CPEs were already in recession or near-stagnation, in spite of maintaining huge investment spending

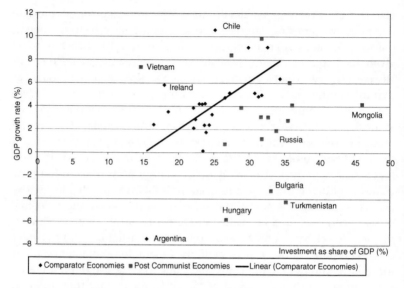

Figure 2.6   Investment and GDP growth, 1989

Source: World Bank, World Development Indicators.

programmes. Mongolia, with a record-breaking 46 per cent of its GDP spent on investment, generated only 4.2 per cent GDP growth, and one may ask how much of that was simply increasing the production of investment goods for future investment in production of investment goods, and so on. At the same time, Chile experienced 10.6 per cent growth, with an investment share in GDP of 25.1 per cent, and Ireland was growing at the rate of 5.8 per cent, spending 18 per cent of its income on investment (see Figure 2.6).

The final stalemate? A political economy perspective

By the mid-1980s, with deteriorating performance, it became more and more difficult to find a balance between the desired level of military spending and the high level of investment required to fuel the chosen pattern of growth on the one hand, and the consumption level that maintained some minimum social acceptance necessary for the system to function without major political unrest on the other. While some CPEs (Czechoslovakia, East Germany, Romania) remained centralized and unchanged until the very end, several CPEs including Hungary, Poland and Russia attempted partial reforms to overcome mounting problems.

It is often argued that the reforms did not produce the expected efficiency gains due to their partial character and inconsistency: a mixed system of economic coordination may be suboptimal not only for a market economy, but also for the classic centralized model of socialism. But the failure of the communist leaders to reform successfully may be also explained from a political economy point of view – one can argue that while reforms were necessary, the communist governments were neither credible enough nor strong enough to face the social cost. The situation resulted in a prisoners' dilemma, which may be illustrated by Table 2.1. For each of the four possible outcomes, the first figure in the brackets

Table 2.1 The prisoners' dilemma: Economic policy stalemate in the last stage of the command economy

Central planner	Strategy 1:	Strategy 2:
	Implement market reform and accept that it will shift production away from central planners' priorities to consumer goods	Do not implement reform; economic inefficiency continues, while traditional economic priorities are retained
Society **Strategy 1:** Accept the initial costs of reforms (prices rise in relation to nominal incomes; some implicit subsidization of basic goods eliminated by changes in the price structure)	*Outcome A:* Successful reform: restructuring of prices and production, some initial social cost (+1, +1)	*Outcome D:* Society is paying for the reform, which is not implemented; savings resulting from decrease in real incomes used to support traditional priorities (–2, +2)
Strategy 2: Social unrest – social costs of reforms not accepted	*Outcome B:* Production is restructured; however, the government continues supporting the level of real incomes (borrowing from abroad?) (+2, –2)	*Outcome C:* Status quo; no reform (–1, –1)

represents a ranking of outcomes from the social point of view, and the second figure that from the central planners' point of view (Mickiewicz 1988).

Successful market reform (Outcome A) is superior to the status quo. However, it is not achieved: reforms are not implemented (Outcome C is a most likely outcome). The paradox can be explained by problems resulting from the time inconsistency of the reform process and the impossibility of a credible commitment by an undemocratic government. To explain this, we may notice that reform can be seen as a two-stage task, where the initial phase of price liberalization has a negative impact on real incomes. After it is implemented, the authorities may carry on with institutional market reforms, measures for freedom of entry, privatization and external openness which should lead to a growth in income (Outcome A). However, alternatively, they can use the resulting stabilization to support traditional systemic priorities (Outcome D). In the latter case, society is paying the costs of the promised reform, which is not implemented; this outcome is the best from the point of view of the authorities and worst from the point of view of society. The government is unable to commit itself credibly to follow Strategy 1; that could be possible only with restoration of democratic control. Given this, the best strategy for society is to refuse to pay the costs of reform, rejecting the economic policy of the government which has no social legitimization and expecting that either the government will find a solution to the problems it has created even if reforms are implemented (Outcome B) or will maintain the status quo (Outcome C), which from the social point of view is still superior to Outcome D.

Thus, in this world of a non-cooperative game, the rational strategies of all involved lead to a stalemate and aborted reforms, even if a movement from C to A would be Pareto-efficient. In most communist countries the game was implicit, not explicit. There was not enough social representation to negotiate with the government, nevertheless the threat of social unrest was real. In Poland, the pattern can be identified in the negotiations between 'Solidarity' and the government in 1980–1, and again in 1987–9. During the latter episode, the authorities decided to hold a referendum, proposing to introduce economic reforms, with initial social costs implied by price increases. The proposal was accepted by a small section of population only, as the dominant strategy was a simple boycott leading to invalidation of the referendum due to low attendance. Both in 1981 and in 1987, 'Solidarity' was criticized by outside observers for 'irrational' behaviour. The interpretation given above (Mickiewicz 1988) shows that it was perfectly rational to reject 'price reforms' introduced by a government lacking political legitimization. This interpret-ation was confirmed two years later, when the new non-communist, 'Solidarity' government was able to introduce much further-reaching reforms, without provoking social unrest.

If the above interpretation is correct, it could point to the imposs-ibility of reform or change of a command economy system without political change. Yet change was becoming a necessity, given deterior-ating economic results. This led the authorities to negotiate political reforms, and 'round table' discussions between the government and inde-pendent social representation became the trademark of the peaceful polit-ical transition implemented in Central and Eastern Europe during 1989. The aim was no longer to reform, but to transform the system.

While above we stressed a difficulty to reform a command economy without a political change, there is a strong, mutual link – that is inter-dependence between the economic and political spheres. It is precisely the control over employment and over wages of the whole population, either in the state sector or in the licensed private sector, that preserves foundations of the totalitarian state and of the political power of the ruling communist party, even when mass terror is no longer applied. Once this economic control is being relaxed, political liberalization is more difficult to block as well.

An alternative perspective: Democracy, the level of development and the future of communism

An alternative interpretation of the link between political reform and the economy can be derived from Barro (1997). According to this, the implosion of the communist system can be seen as a spectacular histor-ical event, yet one which is still consistent with global trends. Political freedom can be seen as a 'luxury good' – i.e. one for which demand appears only at some specific level of income. There is not much need for political freedom in poor countries, where basic material necessities take precedence over civic liberties. This reasoning is based on the empirical link between income *per capita* and political freedom. Indeed, at the beginning of the 21st century, the command economies which remain rigid both in terms of political repression are also those which have failed in terms of economic development: Cuba and North Korea.

Consistent with this perspective, as long as the local governments in developing countries deliver some elementary stability and some econ-omic performance, the pressure for any regime change is contained. Where the governments fail, a resulting change often does not result in

Table 2.2 The opening balance – post communist economies in 1990

Country name	GNI, PPP (current international $ million)	Population, total	GNI per capita, PPP (current international $ million)	Industry, value added (% GDP)	Exports, goods & services (% GDP)	External debt/GDP (%)	External debt/Exports (%)	GDP/Energy use
Albania	9,025.64	3,282,000	2,750	48.2	14.9	16.6	111.6	4.719837
Armenia	12,211.40	3,545,000	3,440	52.0	35.0			1.853619
Azerbaijan	36,882.73	7,159,000	5,150	47.2	46.3			1.501622
Belarus	73,132.41	10,200,530	7,170	51.3	33.1	52.4	158.3	1.74408
Bulgaria	46,718.37	8,718,000	5,360	41.6	17.5	15.6	88.9	2.075735
China	1,594,130.69	1,135,185,024	1,400	48.8	45.2			2.334284
Czech Republic	119,093.91	10,363,000	11,490	49.7	60.3	18.3	40.5	2.569731
Estonia	12,713.20	1,571,000	8,090	39.1	31.1	0.9		1.613445
Hungary	93,979.91	10,365,000	9,070	44.6	74.0	64.1	205.9	3.562825
Kazakhstan	103,755.80	16,266,250	6,380	35.8	29.2	0.1		1.141505
Kirghiz Republic	16,205.51	4,395,000	3,690	46.2	47.7			2.686325
Latvia	22,737.57	2,670,700	8,510	30.9	52.1	0.5	1.1	2.348068
Lithuania	31,891.45	3,722,000	8,570	46.7	25.9	0.4	0.8	2.208035
Macedonia	8,732.91	1,903,000	4,590	33.3	89.4			
Moldova	22,843.50	4,362,000	5,240	40.6		0.4		2.094474
Mongolia	3,387.48	2,106,000	1,610					
Poland	205,162.68	38,118,800	5,380	48.3	21.4	80.7	292.2	2.300305
Romania	145,538.53	23,207,000	6,270	50.0	27.6	3.0	17.8	2.65555
Russia	1,497,556.06	148,292,000	10,100	48.4	16.7	10.2	56.4	1.698988
Slovak Republic	47,649.59	5,283,000	9,020	59.1	18.2	13.0	48.9	2.245187
Slovenia	24,232.73	1,998,100	12,130	45.6	26.5			4.5096
Turkmenistan	21,713.72	3,668,000	5,920	29.6	63.1			1.838056
Ukraine	358,724.37	51,892,000	6,910	44.6	27.6	0.6	2.2	1.433306
Uzbekistan	51,356.68	20,420,000	2,520	33.0	28.8			1.074833
Vietnam	64,536.84	66,200,000	970	22.7	26.4	359.6	1361.0	3.049592

Source: World Bank Development Indicators.

Notes: (i) for the former republics of USRR, data on external debt relate to 1992; (ii) for Estonia, Kazakhstan, Moldova and Slovenia export data relate to 1992; (iii) Energy/GDP: PPP $ per kg of oil equivalent, 1992.

Table 2.3 The opening balance – comparator countries in 1990

Country name	GNI, PPP (current international $ million)	Population, total	GNI per capita, PPP (current international $ million)	Industry, value added (% GDP)	Exports, goods & services (% GDP)	External debt/GDP (%)	External debt/ Exports (%)	GDP/ Energy use
Argentina	241,277.70	32,527,000	7,420	36.0	10.4	44.0	425.0	6.729418
Austria	145,056.28	7,725,700	18,780	30.9	39.6			6.378514
Brazil	801,898.23	147,940,000	5,420	38.7	8.2	25.8	314.4	6.416394
Chile	61,495.80	13,099,000	4,690	41.5	34.6	63.4	183.1	5.187386
Egypt	128,738.17	52,442,000	2,450	28.7	20.0	76.4	381.1	4.321693
Finland	86,674.75	4,986,000	17,380	29.2	22.8			3.176463
France	1,019,410.12	56,735,000	17,970	26.5	21.2			4.709553
Germany	1,536,286.26	79,433,000	19,200	33.1	26.3			4.761975
Greece	118,081.96	10,161,000	11,620	25.5	18.5			5.447119
Indonesia	333,337.33	178,232,000	1,870	39.1	25.3	61.1	241.1	3.993804
Ireland	41,099.46	3,505,800	11,720	31.8	57.0			4.839881
Italy	977,699.80	56,719,000	17,240	30.8	19.7			6.870801
Japan	2,476,708.20	123,537,000	20,050	41.2	10.7			5.968128
Korea, Republic	382,138.74	42,869,000	8,910	43.1	29.1	13.8	47.6	4.144351
Malaysia	83,004.57	18,201,900	4,560	42.2	74.5	34.8	46.7	3.719639
Mexico	515,859.68	83,226,000	6,200	28.4	18.6	39.8	213.7	4.58916
Morocco	67,062.85	24,043,000	2,790	32.4	26.5	94.7	358.1	10.12036
Portugal	110,437.83	9,896,000	11,160	28.7	33.2			6.876195
South Africa	281,336.45	35,200,000	7,990	40.1	24.4			3.274795
Spain	500,099.87	38,836,000	12,880		16.1			5.683627
Sweden	150,715.63	8,559,000	17,610	28.1	30.1			3.453745
Tunisia	30,871.57	8,156,000	3,790	29.8	43.6	62.6	143.6	6.44978
Turkey	274,817.09	56,126,000	4,900	29.8	13.3	32.8	246.8	5.606571
UK	955,583.50	57,561,000	16,600	31.4	24.0			4.589401
US	5,876,806.58	249,440,000	23,560		9.7			3.244226

Source: World Bank Development Indicators.
Notes: (i) for Germany data relates to 1991 (i.e. post-unification); (ii) Energy/GDP: PPP $ per kg of oil equivalent, 1992.

establishment of a stable democracy, but just in exchange of one dictatorship by another.

However, while the empirical link is hard to question, the under-lying factors are likely to be more complex than just the strength of democratic aspirations as envisaged by the 'luxury good' argument. Generalized trust, which we discussed in the previous chapter, may be critical for stable democratic outcomes. Where trust is missing, edu-cation is inadequate, civil society is non-existent and the individuals do not have resources needed to organize themselves (and some of those resources come with personal property and wealth), change is difficult. This implies in turn that exit from a communist dictatorship, which is based on massive repression, poverty and little personal resources avail-able, may be particularly difficult. For example, at time of writing, North Korea remains an unprecedented economic failure, facing recurrent waves of hunger, as collectivized agriculture is unable to feed the local popu-lation. Yet it is certainly not the economic performance but massive apparatus of terror and economic control that prevents North Korea from change.

In contrast, if we accept the link between development and democracy based on the 'luxury good' argument, we could argue that the political change in Central Europe and the Soviet Union was triggered by the rela-tive success of the command economy system there, not by its failure. Even if the system were not able to converge with the advanced market economies, it was still producing satisfactory rates of economic growth (Tables 2.2, 2.3). In the longer run, the standard of living improved, and that both amplified demand for political change and created means for individuals to achieve it. An alternative view is that even if those econ-omies were growing, so was the gap with the West, and it was becoming more and more obvious that the system could not deliver the success that it promised for 60 years.

3
Institutions; Institutional Reform

Introduction: economic objectives

Following the wave of (mostly) peaceful political revolutions that started in mid-1989, the new governments in Central and Eastern Europe and Central Asia faced an immediate task to fix the ailing economies. The West, which unlike the Soviet bloc achieved prosperity and economic stability, was an obvious point of reference. That implied replacing the command economy with the markets; that is with the conditions of economic freedom. Freedom of economic contracts and fully protected private property rights were expected to change the incentives: with rights to residual value, the profit motive – the anathema of the socialist system – was reintroduced. At the same time both price controls and state support for companies was to be removed leading to pressure on cost efficiency, including energy efficiency. Competition was to be reintroduced, replacing cosy socialist monopolies and sellers' markets with buyers' markets, that is exchanging planners' sovereignty for consumers' sovereignty. It was hoped that responding to new incentives, the economic actors will reallocate the resources from old to new activities, the latter being consistent both with real structure of costs and with consumers' preferences. The reallocation was to be achieved both by restructuring of surviving old firms and by emergence of new players.

In the language of the previous two chapters, economic transition from plan to market consisted of changing the system of control and property rights, leading to changes in information flows and incentives in an economy. In socialist enterprises managers had control rights and it was unclear to whom the residual claims could be attributed so that the property rights were blurred. Private property rights restored a link between control rights and residual claims, making the motivation of economic agents consistent with the aim of value maximization. As discussed in Chapter 2, one important element of efficiency relates to flexibility: unlike the inertia that characterized the command economy, under the market conditions, the producers should adequately respond and adjust to changes (1) in the real structure of costs (scarcity), and (2) in the set of preferences of buyers. However, it is not only the behaviour of producers, but also of other economic agents, that matters: households should be motivated to save money instead of hoarding goods, and investors to choose the long-term best value-adding projects. ·

In addition to the institutional change discussed above, macro-economic outcomes as represented by budget balances, external balances and inflation needed urgent attention. In fact as we will argue later on, institutional change and macroeconomic policies are intertwined; yet to cope both with the reform of institutional frameworks and introducing new macroeconomic policies was a considerable challenge.

The main components of the reform programme and speed of reforms

Following Balcerowicz (1995: 239), with some slight modifications, we may distinguish between the three main components of reforms that characterized the transition process as implemented in Central and Eastern Europe:

(1) Liberalization (First-stage institutional reforms)
  • Microeconomic liberalization of prices (elimination of price controls)
  • Currency convertibility and removal of all major quantitative restrictions (QRs) on foreign trade; removal of external barriers to entry
  • Removal of internal barriers to entry (i.e. to developing and setting up new private enterprises)
(2) Second-stage institutional reforms (changes in existing institutions; privatization of state enterprises, reorganizing the state administration, reform of the tax system, financial system reform)
(3) Macroeconomic stabilization policies

Both liberalization and stabilization policies can be introduced immediately. Liberalization is equivalent to the removal of existing barriers. It is very easy in technical sense, even if not necessary easy in political economy sense – some special interests of economic actors may be affected, and opposition is likely to emerge. On the other hand, what is labelled above as 'second stage' reforms corresponds to preparing a new legal and organizational framework. It takes time to implement.

It may be useful to present a more detailed mapping of the key components of institutional reforms. The standard list of indicators is produced for all transition economies by the European Bank for Reconstruction (EBRD) and Development and published in the annual Transition Reports (EBRD 1995–2009). The list was expanded in 2003 to add legal and infrastructure indicators, which we do not discuss here. The core set of eight indicators is presented below; for each indicator, the tasks are presented in order from the less to the more complicated (EBRD 2001, 2003; Falcetti, Raiser and Sanfey 2002):

(1) Internal price liberalization   The definition of this measure was modified in 2003 (with corresponding scores adjusted for previous years). At present, it focuses entirely on the removal of administrative prices and price controls and the phasing out of state procurement at non-market prices, and excludes utility tariffs. In the original version, it also included utility pricing – i.e. the relation of prices to economic cost and generally adequate regulation of utility prices. At present, the latter issue is treated separately under a new heading of the 'infrastructure index'.

(2) External liberalization (2a)   Foreign trade: Removal of most quantitative and administrative restrictions on import and export (agriculture being a typical exception); removal of high export tariffs; abolition of direct involvement in exports and imports by the state administration and state-owned foreign trade companies – foreign trade monopolies no longer granted to the latter, no barriers in access to foreign exchange, uniformity of custom duties for non-agricultural goods and services, membership in the World Trade Organization (WTO), which implies meeting the standard criteria of the international trade system; (2b) Foreign exchange: No multiple exchange rates, full current account convertibility.

(3) Competition policy   Unrestricted entry to most markets; competition and anti-trust institutions and legislation; enforcement actions to counteract any abuse of a dominant market position and to strengthen competition, break-up of monopolies.

(4) Large-scale privatization   Here, progress is measured by the percentage of large-scale enterprise assets being transferred to private

owners, with 25 per cent, 50 per cent and 75 per cent being used as threshold levels for assessment; the subsequent criterion is the quality of governance of these enterprises.

(5) Small-scale privatization and freedom of entry   Complete privatization of small companies resulting in ownership rights that can be transferred with no restriction; effective tradability of ownership rights for land, freedom of entry for new enterprises.

(6) Enterprise reform (governance and enterprise restructuring)   'Hard' budgets: tight credit and subsidies policies; enforcement of bankruptcy legislation; effective corporate governance provided by capital markets and banks; active owners and investors; well-functioning markets for corporate control; evidence of efficient restructuring and investment.

(7) Bank reform and interest rate liberalization   Full interest rate liberalization; no preferential access to cheap refinancing; banking laws and regulations consistent with Bank for International Settlements (BIS) standards related to capital requirements, supervision and market discipline (Basel Committee on Banking Supervision 2004); availability of a full set of banking services; financial deepening; significant provision of lending to private enterprises, privatization of banks.

(8) Securities markets and non-bank financial institutions (NBFI)   Fully developed NBFI (collective investment schemes, private insurance and pension funds, leasing companies); substantial market liquidity and capitalization of the stock exchange; substantial issue of securities by private enterprises; convergence of securities laws, regulations and practice with international standards set by the International Organization of Securities Commissions (IOSCO) (IOSCO 2003); protection of minority shareholders and, generally, all other customers of financial services; fair, efficient and transparent organization of financial markets, minimizing systemic risk, secure clearance and settlement procedures.

Each EBRD indicator can be attributed to one of the two categories discussed at the beginning of this chapter. Internal and external liberalization and small-scale privatization are all components of liberalization. They can be introduced relatively quickly. The remaining five dimensions (privatization of large enterprises, competition policy, corporate and financial governance) rely on introducing new institutional, legal and administrative frameworks, a process that is time-consuming and more difficult to implement. Indeed, there are marked differences in the speed with which the particular elements of reforms were introduced. Figures 3.1 and 3.2 below contrast the individual countries scores for the key first-stage reform (price liberalization) with the scores on one of the important second-stage reforms (governance and restructuring), from the most recent period available. The range of all EBRD transition indicators is from 1 (no reform) to 4.33 (as defined by best existing practice amongst developed market economies).

Price liberalization is registered at the level compatible with developed market economies in more than half of the transition economies. It is not lagging behind in most of the other. In contrast, the governance indicators show a very different picture. None of the transition countries score on the highest level compatible with the developed market economies. Moreover, differences between the transition countries are much larger. While few new EU members score relatively high, in Turkmenistan no sign of reforms is noticed. Also, little was done in some CIS countries and in some of the former Yugoslavia republics (albeit the situation in the Balkans is likely to change with all economies including Serbia now aspiring to EU membership).

While the two graphs illustrate the distinction between liberalization and second-stage institutional reforms, we may ask another, related question: which components of reform were typically implemented jointly? Is the empirical pattern consistent with the distinction we introduced above?

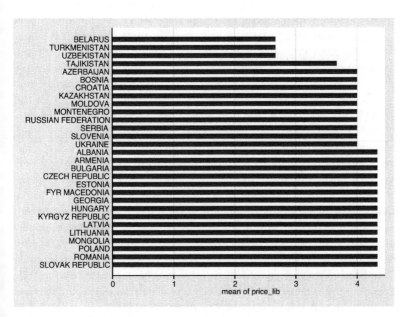

Figure 3.1 Price liberalization (EBRD Indicator, 2008)

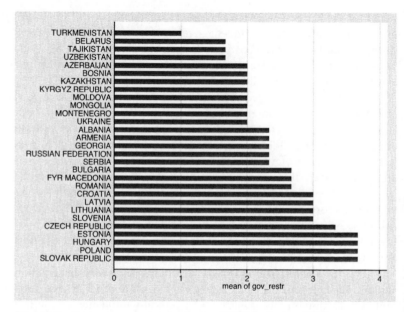

Figure 3.2   Governance and restructuring (EBRD Indicator, 2008)

Indeed, it is not difficult to verify that the individual reform indicators are correlated, which suggest that they were in fact implemented together. To understand better this structure of correlation one may apply data reduction techniques. Below we report results of such exercise; more technical details can be found in Mickiewicz (2005). We used a sample which included 340 available scores from the set of thirteen annual data points over 1990–2002 for 27 countries.[1] The correlation matrix for the EBRD indicators reveals that the pair of indicators with the highest correlation is 'Bank reform' and 'Governance' (0.916). The strong link between corporate governance and the quality of the financial system is not a surprise, as corporate governance is nothing else but a system that protects the providers of finance (Shleifer and Vishny 1997), and any deepening of the financial system is difficult to achieve without it. Descriptive statistics for all indicators are given in Table 3.1.

It is interesting to note that both price liberalization and competition policy indicators have the lowest standard deviation, albeit for very different reasons. As illustrated with Figure 3.1 above, elementary price liberalization was introduced early in practically all the transition countries (and the average of this indicator is the highest). That confirms the intuition which will be discussed in more detail later on: price liberalization is a first and indispensable element of the transition programme.

Table 3.1 Descriptive statistics: EBRD indicators, 27 countries, 1990–2002

Indicator	Mean	Standard deviation
Freedom of entry and small-scale privatization	3.01	1.17
External liberalization (trade and exchange rate)	2.97	1.29
Internal price liberalization	2.63	0.70
Large-scale privatization	2.30	1.01
Bank reform	2.04	0.88
Governance and enterprise restructuring	1.88	0.74
Competition policy	1.79	0.69
Securities markets and non-banking financial	1.75	0.73

In addition, the mean values of institutions indicators are also high for both external liberalization and freedom of entry and small-scale privatization. All three were traditionally merged in research into a composite measure of liberalization, consistent with our classification above. At the other end of the spectrum, we find competition policy and non-banking financial institutions – here, the mean indicator (and standard deviation) are the lowest, indicating that those two components of reforms were the most difficult to implement. Generally, in terms of standard deviations, external (trade) liberalization stands apart as the element of reform where policy differences are most clearly visible. These differences are likely to be linked to the political dimension. As will be shown in the next chapter, this is the dimension of reform that is most affected by the quality of the mediating institutions of democracy, as trade liberalization effects considerably change the balance of costs and benefits for the various groups of economic actors.

To confirm empirically which components of reforms were introduced jointly, principal component analysis (PCA) was applied as a factor-extracting technique (again, see details in Mickiewicz 2005). The results of rotated solution are summarized in Table 3.2. To make the analysis clearer, we retained only values above 0.4.

The three indicators chosen to represent liberalization – (1) Price liberalization (2) External liberalization and (3) Small-scale privatization and freedom of entry – are indeed all included in one component (2), where they play the dominant role. However, we find that progress in banking reform has also run typically parallel to basic liberalization.

Table 3.2 The pattern matrix: Liberalization and institutional reforms

Indicator	Component 1: Institutional reforms (2nd Stage)	Component 2: Liberalization
Internal price liberalization		1.007
External liberalization		0.778
Free entry and small-scale privatization		0.654
Banking reform	0.606	0.424
Large-scale privatization	0.626	
Governance and enterprise restructuring	0.709	
Competition policy	0.976	
Securities markets and non-banking	0.985	

On the other hand, the first principal component relates to those institutional reforms that are more difficult to implement. The most important elements here are capital market reform and competition policy.

Overall, the results suggest that the groupings financial sector institutions obtained cut across the groups of indicators identified by the EBRD (1995–2009) and split naturally into two groups with an easy intuitive interpretation: Component 1 may be labelled 'Second-stage institutional reforms' and Component 2 'Liberalization'. In the long time span encompassing most of the transition perspective, there is more variation in second-stage institutional reforms than in liberalization policies – the first component explains more variance in reform indicators that the second.

Figure 3.3 presents the same information graphically. Price liberalization dominates the second principal component, and is practically absent in the first. At the end of the spectrum we find competition policy and NBFI reforms ('securities'), which play a dominant role in the first component, being practically absent in the second.

We may also use the results, to illustrate the pattern of reforms for different countries. Figures 3.4 and 3.5 illustrate the progress of reforms for the six largest transition economies. Again, it is interesting to notice the different dynamics of the liberalization and institutional reform processes. Figure 3.4 shows that liberalization was typically introduced quickly over a period of one or two years. Hungary and Poland were already liberalized in 1990, so the moment of liberalization is not illustrated on the graph; for all other countries, the moment when the liberalization programme was introduced is easily identifiable. This illustrates the approach adopted earlier in this chapter and also a concept to which we

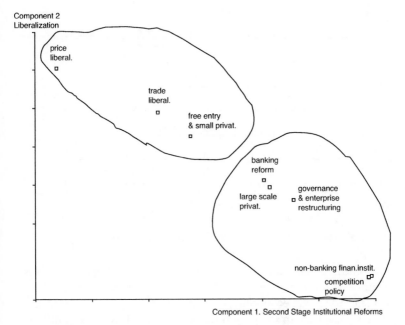

Figure 3.3 Component plot in rotated space: Liberalization and second stage institutional reforms

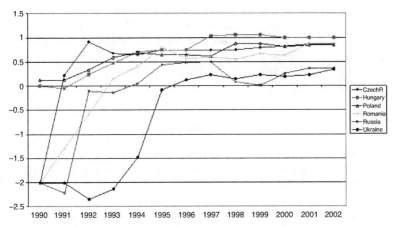

Figure 3.4 Liberalization, 1990–2002 (second principal components scores)

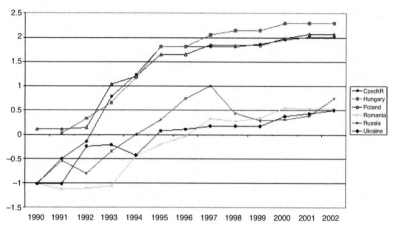

Figure 3.5   Institutional reforms, 1990–2002 (first principal component scores)

will come back later in this book, where the threshold level of reforms is identified and based on the basic liberalization indicators. Comparing the six major transition economies, one may see that while the liberalization process started late in some countries, the end result is not very different. In particular, the convergence of Romania towards the level of liberalization observed in the three Central European (CE) economies is noticeable (in 2001 in particular, following the earlier reversal of liberalization in 1996). Reversal of economic liberalization in Russia (after the 1998 rouble crisis) may be seen as temporary, as liberalization measures were reintroduced after 2000.

In contrast with liberalization, the time path of the institutional reform indicator is slower, and the differences between the three CE economies and the two major CIS economies and Romania are more substantial. No clear pattern of convergence can be detected, and reversal of institutional reforms in Russia in 1998 has a more lasting effect than the reversal of basic liberalization, albeit some reforms were reintroduced in early 2000s.

Determinants of the speed of reforms

A more general question is which were the factors that affected the speed and completion of reforms? Here we may distinguish between three clusters of variables:

(1) Initial conditions, including initial level of development and structural characteristics, geography, history

(2) Initial political set-up around the time reforms were first attempted
(3) Initial transition policies

We will discuss briefly these three categories. The key historical dimension that comes under the label of initial conditions is time spent under communism. As we discussed in Chapter 1, there is evidence that norms and values (informal institutions) differ in countries depending on the amount of time those societies remained under the communist regime. In Central Europe and the Baltic States, in 1989 there was still a generation with a memory of market economies. In most of the former Soviet Union there wasn't one. Legal (second stage) reforms in the first group of countries could be built on business law that was already developed before the Second World War; in contrast, there was very little to build on in the second group of countries. Again, as mentioned in Chapter 1, these differences coincide closely with the religious origin of the respective culture, with a fault line running between the Western and Eastern (Orthodox) Christian tradition. If taking this perspective, most of the Balkan peninsula is shifted to the second group. Cultural dimension is also related to ethnic homogeneity. The reason for the importance of the latter is that – as will be discussed in more detail in the next chapter – reforms may be blocked when special interests of some social or economic groups diverge too much from the general interest (are not 'encompassing' to use Mancur Olson's (2000) terminology) and those groups can impact policies and institutional design. When some societies are fragmented, ethnic identification may serve as an easy device for discrimination and group-specific gains from this discrimination may be larger for a given dominant group than their gain from reforms, even if the overall gain is larger.

Two cluster of factors, describing the economic structure may indicate a potential of special interest that could block reforms. First of those relate to sectoral composition: the inherited share of industry, share of heavy industry and share of the military production. As those are sections of the economy that are likely to shrink as a result of reforms, strong special interests in these branches may block the reforms. For example, Czech and Slovak nations spend exactly the same time under the communist regime. However, Czech industry was one of the most developed in Europe at the time of communist takeover. Slovak was not: the industry was built according to the Stalinist blueprint from late 1940s onwards. And it turned out that the reforms were met with far more difficulties in Slovakia as compared with the Czech Republic after being started in the 1990s.

Second, natural resource endowment may be not only a blessing but also a curse. It becomes a course when the wealth generated in the sector becomes a source of entrenchment of special interests, as for instance in Russia (see Buccellato and Mickiewicz 2009 and further references therein).

Culture (informal institutions) are also affected by neighbourhood and external influences. Nations learn from their neighbours, especially if those neighbours are successful. To capture potential institutional learning, variables like distance of a capital city from Brussels can be used. Similarly landlocked status as contrasted with access to see may be another proxy for intensity of contacts with outside world and institutional learning potential.

In addition, the latter may also not only depend on cultural factors, but also on the quality of individual human capital as captured by education.

Overall level of development as captured, say, by GDP *per capita*, is a convenient composite measure that may capture many of the dimensions just discussed. Institutional quality is highly correlated with the level of development and causation runs both from human capital and informal institutions (values, norms) to development and from the level of development to institutions via both human capital and education and associated values and norms.

Economic reforms may also be explained by political frameworks at time those reforms were first initiated. The links between politics and economic reform will be the subject of next chapter: we will argue that political and economic liberalization are related. In addition, wars and civil conflicts that emerged in some of those countries at the time the communism fell were detrimental to reforms: war effort implies concentrated economic decision-making, as we already discussed this is not quite compatible with markets. This can be linked back to the ethnolinguistic fragmentation, which becomes a problem where a tradition of peaceful conflict resolution had not become embedded in cultural norms and values.

Finally, there may be path dependence in reforms, therefore initial choices in sequencing and in speed could be critical. As we will discuss in more detail in the next chapter, some authors would argue that a point of no return could be created provided that the reforms were introduced quickly. Other doubt if this could be possible without a political framework supportive to reforms. In addition, there may be a self-enforcing mechanism linking stabilization and liberalization. We will return to it in more detail soon.

Beyond EBRD indicators: Institutional variables at the constitutional level

There are some rather obvious omissions on the EBRD list of indicators we just discussed. It is easy to justify the omission of stabilization policies. Stabilization outcomes may be assessed using the macroeconomic indicators, and there is no need for special transition indicators here, as standard measures of inflation, the budget deficit, the current account balance, unemployment and GDP growth apply. Nevertheless, there is a direct link between macro stabilization and micro liberalization (see Mickiewicz 2005). Subsequently, we shall also discuss 'hard' budget constraint – an issue that we will argue is central to the success of transition programmes – and which cuts across several dimensions. Another important omission among this set of indicators relates to fiscal reform. This links with 'soft' budgets and subsidies – and appears under dimension (6) (Governance and enterprise restructuring), yet the reform of both government revenue and expenditures is a wider issue, key to the success of the transition programme, and deserving more attention. Tax and expenditure reform is not just short-term policy, it is also an institutional reform, to which we will come back later on (in Chapter 11). The omission is partly explained by the fact that macroeconomic assessment is treated separately by the EBRD, with the focus on the budget deficit. Yet, the structural aspects of the fiscal sphere deserve more attention on their own and cannot be reduced to the issue of government balance. Both reform of the distortionary tax structure and introduction of an efficient and effective pattern of social spending is crucial. On the revenue side, Schaffer and Turley's (2001) work offers a useful supplement to EBRD indicators; they calculate ratios of effective to statutory taxation, low values of which can be taken as measures of problems with tax compliance and collection, many of which are related directly to 'soft' budgeting by firms.

Finally, labour market reforms are also not included despite the fact that they are critical for labour market outcomes. Again, we will come back to it later on, in Chapter 8.

Despite those limitations, and despite measurement problems (Campos and Horváth 2006), EBRD reform indicators became immensely popular, because they offer a unique opportunity to follow the institutional reform process from the very beginning to the present time. However, they tell us little about a deeper level of institutional frameworks. As argued by Olson (2000) efficient institutions are conditional on stable, solid constitutional frameworks. These 'higher order', constitutional features, which are probably best captured by the concept of the rule of law (Hayek 1960) and its economic sub-component of protection of property rights (North 1990). We already argued this point in Chapters 1 and 2. Protection of property rights relate to two key dimensions (Acemoglu and Johnson 2005):

(1) effective constitutional constraints limiting arbitrariness in the executive branch of the government, and
(2) constitutional order, which implemented in practice, guarantees an independent and reliable judicial system

The first of those two dimensions is more critical than the other. Any judicial system will not function well and will not protect individual economic rights, where it is subject to arbitrary intervention.

The importance of protection of property rights relates to the fact that the command over means of production is necessary for any economic venture and it is not necessary access to own property, but wide access to other resources via contracts that matters most (Hayek 1960). In general, risk of expropriation discourages any form of investment and is detrimental to economic performance. Inefficient public protection of private property rights implies that valuable resources are sunk into private protection of property, which is inefficient as it suffers from dis-economies of scale (protection of property has public good characteristics).

While those are standard economic arguments, based on rational choice model, the quality of property rights also impacts on norms and values: 'the institution of private property ... has an important psychological dimension that enhances our feelings of ... internal control ... and it thereby promotes entrepreneurial alertness' (Harper 2003). In terms of the language we introduced in Chapter 1, stable private property are associated with values of autonomy and mastery, and those in turn lead to attitudes that can realize all potential offered by formal institutions of markets.

Measuring institutions is still a relatively new enterprise, and discussions on measurement continue. Property rights protection is assessed as one of the indicators published annually by Heritage Foundation and *Wall Street Journal*. Below we present the latest available scores for transition economies. However, instead of presenting raw scores, we filter them taking into account the level of development. The underlying idea is that as higher GDP *per capita* is associated with better institutions, it is more useful to present 'net assessment', where the impact

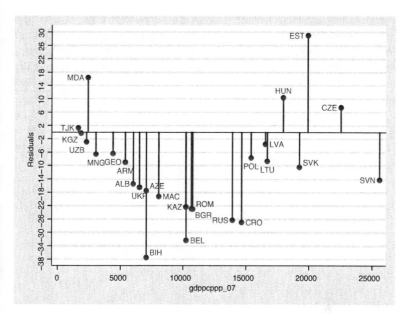

Figure 3.6 Regression of property rights (2008) on natural logarithm of GDP per capita, purchasing power parity (2007). Residuals for transition economies

Sources of data: GDP pc PPP in constant 2005 US dollars from World Bank, World Development Indicators, Property rights from 2008 Economic Freedom indicators by Heritage Foundation and *Wall Street Journal*.

of the level of development is neutralized by focusing on the residuals from regression of property rights measure on the level of GDP *per capita*. That is the results illustrated by Figure 3.6 above which presents how much protection of property rights differ from the level expected for a given level of income *per capita*.

The horizontal line represents expected score for property rights protection based on worldwide sample mean effect. The fact that most of the transition countries score below this line indicates that almost 20 years after the reform programme was implemented, the quality of deeper level constitutional foundations remains deficient in the transition economies as compared with countries with similar level of economic development. The message we get here is slightly less optimistic compared to that based on the EBRD indicators, which are of lower order in terms of institutional hierarchy (Williamson 2000). For instance, in terms of freedom of price setting the transition economies are no longer that different from the advanced market economies (see

Figure 3.1). However, where private property rights are not secure, price liberalization may not be sufficient to generate strong incentives leading to economic dynamism, stable growth paths and high economic performance. Some disappointment with reform results may relate to the fact that either those fundamentals were neglected by policy-makers or proved far more difficult to improve.

4
Political Economy of Reforms

On the 12th of June 1991, Boris Yeltsin became the president of Russia, as a result of the country's first presidential elections. Two months later, in response to the communist putsch of August 1991, Yeltsin – risking snipers' fire – climbed a tank addressing the crowd at the front of Russian Parliament. The putsch failed. That was 19th of August 1991, probably the high point of the democratic revolution in Russia. Yet, only two years later, it was Yeltsin who sent tanks against the same parliament building. The parliament, which opposed Yeltsin, triggering constitutional crisis, was elected in quasi-democratic elections, so its legitimacy could be contested. However, it is not the nature of elections that define democracy. It is the willingness of all key players to reach consensus instead of using force against each other. Yeltsin consolidated power, which could arguably be used to complete the reforms – the reforms which proved partial, inconsequential, chaotic and producing little results over the previous year. Did suppressing democracy help the economic reform process? Or was 4th of October 1993 another turning point in Russian history, from which neither political nor economic liberalization fully recovered until today?

This chapter discusses the link between political freedom and reform. However, we will not present any overview of parallel political and economic developments in Russia or in other transition economies. Our primary interest is in analytical concepts that could help us to understand both the past and the present directions of change in institutions and policies. We observe first that the gains from reforms may be unevenly distributed. That leads us to conclude that the democratic institutions within which the economic actors mediate may facilitate consensus and remove obstacles to reform. In addition to political democracy, the institutions of a civil society, free media in particular – may have an important role to play. Low-cost access to information may help to alleviate economic policy capture by special interests.

We then go into more detail. We discuss key reforms, to see which of them are likely to affect both income distribution and special interests. This leads us to form empirical hypotheses about the relative role of democracy in facilitating particular reforms. We discuss the results of tests of those hypotheses, and finally draw some brief conclusions.

Preliminaries: Transition as a welfare issue

Our intention here is to discuss the reforms from the point of view of political feasibility. What are the framework conditions that may facilitate reforms, stall them, or result in a policy reversal?

We need to recall a few basic notions. A more detailed discussion may be found in any advanced microeconomic text. Here, we draw from Varian (1992) and Gravelle and Rees (2004).

First, 'allocation' will denote a matrix which describes how much of each good produced in the economy is consumed by each consumer. When we simplify, assuming just one composite good (say, equivalent to real income), the allocations become vectors with the number of components representing the number of consumers. More importantly, to make a graphical illustration easier, we will consider two representative consumers (are also voters) representing some two major socio-economic groups (say, we call them workers and entrepreneurs). From now on, feasible allocations will be denoted by $x^0, x^1, \ldots, x^n$.

After defining allocation, we recall the concept of Pareto-optimality (the Pareto-criterion), the fundamental measure of economic efficiency. An allocation x^* is said to be Pareto-optimal if there is no other feasible allocation x^0 which would be preferred by everybody to x^*. In other words, while some economic agents may be better off with a different allocation, it would never be preferred by everybody, so no change away from x^* could be achieved by unanimous voting. Also, in the case where there is an allocation x^*, which is preferred by everybody to x^1, we say that it is Pareto-preferred.

The Pareto optimality condition is perfectly rational, but weak. For instance, we may think about a move from the initial allocation x^0 to some allocation x^*, which could lead to a great benefit for a large number of economic agents, with the cost paid by a small number of people. Some of the reforms introduced as part of the transition programme may bear that characteristic. Still, the Pareto-criterion is too weak to distinguish between the two outcomes. Then, the interesting issues are: when can x^* be seen as 'superior' to x^0 in a broader sense (a welfare economics issue) and when may we expect a move from x^0 to x^* (a political economy issue)? The compensation criterion aims to answer the first question:

> 'x^1 is potentially Pareto preferred to x^0, if there is some way to reallocate x^1 so that everyone prefers the new reallocation (x^2) to the original allocation x^0. More formally: x^1 is potentially Pareto preferred to x^0, if there is some allocation x^2, with $\sum_{i=1}^{n} x_i^2 = \sum_{i=1}^{n} x_i^1$ (i.e. x^2 is a reallocation of x^1) such that $x_{i'}^2 > x_{i'}^0$ for all agents i' (Varian 1992: 405).

The compensation principle is illustrated by Figure 4.1. Take allocation x^0 as a starting point. An economic reform results in a new allocation x^*. However, this is not acceptable for a representative consumer I (a worker): in terms of utility she is now worse off than at the beginning of the reforms. Now, curve F' represents a set of allocations that all amount to the same aggregate output as x^*. This curve is called a utility possibility frontier.[1] If we can modify the post-reform allocation x^* to compensate the losers, without output loss, we arrive at a point such as x^1, which makes everybody better off as compared with the pre-reform situation.

However, there is one problem with the compensation criterion. Defining the utility possibility frontier is not the same thing as assuming that movement along the frontier is feasible. The criterion has practical relevance only if we can use some non-distortionary and costless taxation to redistribute – i.e. to move between the points on the frontier. However, 'the first rule of public finance' tells us that 'there is no such thing as a lump-sum tax' (Gravelle and Rees 2004: 303). Thus, to make the framework more realistic, we have to complement the utility possibility frontier with a 'utility feasibility frontier showing the utility combinations achievable from the original endowments by varying the level of non-lump-sum transfers' (2004: 304). This is shown as curve f' on Figure 4.1. Here, the reforms followed (accompanied) by compensation (redistribution) result in a move from x^0 to x^* and then to x^2, as the move to x^1 is not feasible due to the dead-weight loss resulting from fiscal intervention.

Thus, we may think of transitional reforms as a move from one economic allocation to another. Allocation x^0 corresponds to the old economic regime, and allocation x^1 and the utility feasibility frontier associated with it relates to the post-reform situation. The ideal case of non-controversial reform, with no need for compensation, would correspond to a direct move from x^0 to x^1. While, theoretically, reforms

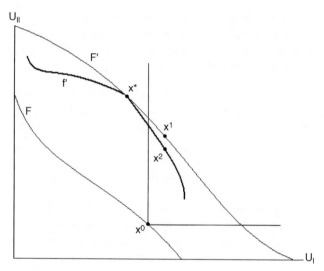

Figure 4.1   Welfare gains from reforms and redistribution

benefiting everybody are possible, in reality it is unlikely that there will be no losers. We will explore why in the next section. The losers, denoted by agent I may not be a large economic group, but a minority. However, if that minority is strong enough to block the reform (as it represents some embedded special interests), a possibility to negotiate compensation (subsequent move from x^* to x^2) becomes a critical issue. Moreover, it is more realistic to see transition as a cluster of reforms, each of them modifying the economic regime with different allocational shifts. In each case, a different group of economic actors is affected and different compensational issues may arise. This leads to the interesting possibility that the allocational effects of some reforms may balance each other, alleviating the need for *ex post* compensation. For instance, it is likely that, for the low-income households, the gains from price liberalization may be lower. However, at least part of that group may be compensated with a particular design of the privatization scheme, where either workers in low-wage occupations (typically, low-capital-intensive branches of industry and services) or the population at large (voucher privatization) are given shares in the privatized companies. A more general example relates to reforms that may result in unemployment being accompanied by the introduction of a social safety net system.

Compensation schemes may be difficult to negotiate and prepare. This argument may lead to the conclusion that, from the political economy point of view, as much as possible should be done immediately during the first move (say from x^0 to x^* on Figure 4.1), leaving the subsequent reallocation to be sorted out later (a move from x^* to x^2). That eliminates the risk that the transition process stalls before the start. The problem with this argument is its reliance on the assumption that voters are myopic. If not, then expecting problems with compensation (the high transaction cost of negotiating the subsequent move from x^* to x^2), they may block the reforms in the first place (see Roland 2000, for a theoretical modelling of this issue). Alternatively, this becomes an argument against democracy. In this latter version, the initial reform decisions should be taken by a group of technocrats and more democratic procedures allowed only after the move from x^0 to x^*. Is there a contradiction between democracy and the speed of reforms? Not necessarily. The transaction costs of negotiating appropriate compensation may imply that the latter may be a time consuming-task. On the other hand, given the unravelling crisis of the old regime (see Chapter 2), the costs of postponing the reforms may also be high. In this respect, acceptance of fast and far-reaching reforms may crucially depend on the expectation that the appropriate compensating transfers can be negotiated later via democratic institutions. Thus, even if voters accept that the initial reforms will be implemented by knowledgeable technocrats, it may only be because the voters do not expect the technocrats to retain power later. If true, the hypothesis implies that democratic institutions will facilitate the reforms, because they facilitate negotiating and correcting the allocational outcomes after the implementation of the reforms.[2]

We may extend the argument by referring to the Coase theorem (Coase 1960). This says that the efficient allocation of resources is always achieved if it is possible to carry out negotiations at little or no cost. In the course of the negotiations, the relevant parties will take proper account of the effects on all other parties of moving from one allocation of resources to another (from one economic regime to another). The outcome will be efficient, regardless of which party is endowed with the right to block the change (i.e. with property rights).

However, the cost of the negotiations will be small only if the mediating institutions are efficient, the number of well-identified parties is small, full information is available and it is feasible to create a credible contract between the parties. In the context of reforms, we can relate all those characteristics to a developed and well-functioning political system. As argued in the previous chapter, in the CEE countries, the initial conditions differed in this respect. Some of these countries inherited elements of a civic society which could be developed to represent a variety of interests and ideas. In others, the totalitarian regimes had a far more radical atomizing impact. From this point of view, the fault line may be between (1) Central and South East Europe and the three Baltic states, and (2) the other former republics of the Soviet Union. The latter group came through a far longer period of demolition of civic and democratic institutions, in particular during the long reign of terror under Stalin. In that group, at the onset of transition, there was no generation of an active age with a memory of any kind of alternative political system.

While democratic institutions and political freedom in general may facilitate mediation and therefore make reforms easier, it is not necessarily the case that democracy will always result in efficient outcomes. One important characteristic of the political process, which is associated with lower efficiency, is its susceptibility to special interests – i.e. issues that generate substantial individual benefit to a small minority while imposing a small average cost on all other voters. In total, the cost to the majority may exceed the net benefits to the special interest group. However, each member of the majority has no interest in becoming active, while the members of the minority group have such an interest. The special interests problem is typically more acute because of the 'rational political ignorance' effect (Tullock 1967). This relates to the fact that most citizens recognize that their vote is unlikely to determine the outcome of an election. As a result, the citizens have little incentive to seek costly information that will help them cast an informed vote. This attitude leaves an opportunity for special interest issues.

Seen from this perspective, it is not only the formal institutions of democracy, but also the availability of low-cost information, which becomes critical. Even if individual voters are not sufficiently motivated to acquire knowledge on all relevant issues, the free, independent and diversified media may play a pivotal role in making the voters more adequately informed, and limiting government capture by special interests. Free and independent media are thus not only the key element of civil liberties, but also a necessary condition for the adequate functioning of the formal institutions of democracy.

For different reforms, the distribution of (relative) losers and winners will vary. The negatively affected minorities may differ considerably with respect to their bargaining power. Compensation schemes may be easy to design in some cases and difficult in others. In the next section, we shall focus on the effects of liberalization, distinguishing between different markets and different sets of winners and losers. Which reforms are more likely to be blocked? In which cases will the role of mediating institutions be most critical?

Reforms: Winners and losers

We shall organize the analysis of reforms around the four simple models of internal and external liberalization adapted from Gros and Steinherr (1995: 115–17) with some minor modifications. Their analysis is mostly in terms of welfare effects. Building on their work directly, we extend the discussion towards political economy issues.

In all the examples below, we shall rely on consumer surplus and producer surplus as measures of welfare. These are approximations based on simplifying assumptions. Nevertheless, they are widely used. Their advantage is that via demand and supply they can be linked to empirical research (assuming that we can overcome the standard identification problems for simultaneous equations in demand and supply systems).

If $x(p)$ is the demand for some good as a function of its price (illustrated in a standard Marshallian way, with price on the vertical axis and quantity on the horizontal axis), then the gain in consumers' surplus associated with a price decrease from p^0 to p^1 is equivalent to the area left of the demand curve between p^0 and p^1. However, the consumer surplus is a precise measure of welfare change only when the consumer preferences in the p^0 and p^1 range can be approximated by a quasi-linear utility function, $u(p, m) = u(p) + m$, where m relates to income. This functional form implies that there is no interaction between the effects of price change on utility and the effects of income on utility. In particular, the income effect of price change is zero. In other words, it is useful to bear in mind that consumer surplus becomes a poor analytical tool when we analyse the price changes in a product where demand is sensitive to income (Varian 1992: 164–6). Similarly, if we have a supply (marginal cost) curve as a function of price (again drawn in a traditional Marshallian way), and the price increases from p^0 to p^1, then the area to the left of the supply curve between p^0 and p^1 can be interpreted as an increase in producers' surplus.

Price liberalization

Figures 4.2–4.5 below describe four cases of price liberalization. Each differs in the characteristics of supply, demand, degree of potential integration with the world market and the nature of initial administrative intervention.

Figure 4.2 illustrates the first, most fundamental case of a representative consumer product market characterized by disequilibrium and shortages.

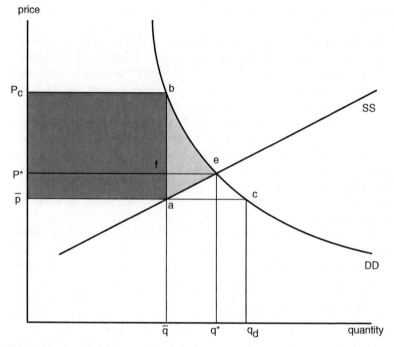

Figure 4.2   Price liberalization

This first model also assumes that the net effect of opening the market to international competition is relatively small and does not affect the main conclusions. We also assume that the domestic supply is price elastic.

Initially, the administrative price is set at $\bar{p}$, and the corresponding supply is $\bar{q}$. There is excess demand ac, given by the section of the price line p between the supply curve SS (i.e. to the right of the vertical $\bar{q}$ line) and the demand curve DD (point c).

Given the administratively set level of supply $\bar{q}$, removal of price controls alone will result in a jump in market price to p_c, driving demand back from qd to $\bar{q}$. However, with price controls, goods are not allocated via the price mechanism. In that void, some other means of competition between buyers is needed to re-establish the match between their claims on the product and restricted supply – i.e. decide the final distribution, eliminating the excess demand by adjusting it to $\bar{q}$. The simplest and most common example of such a mechanism is queuing. Each consumer pays an additional time cost, which drives up the real consumer price from $\bar{p}$ to p_c. Thus, the real price paid by consumers consists of two components:

(1) p, which is the monetary, nominal price paid for the product, plus
(2) disequilibrium dead-weight cost, which may have both a monetary and a non-monetary component.

In the case of queuing, the cost corresponds to the opportunity cost of time lost by consumers. However, it may have some additional components. Time cost may relate not only to queuing, but also to market search. The monetary component may reappear in the case of corruption, where scarce products are first acquired by those with privileged access (members of a communist nomenklatura, employees of the retail trade), who realize economic rents by reselling above the official price. In the latter case, the difference between p_c and $\bar{p}$ may come with lower dead-weight cost, the latter being replaced by a transfer of income from one group of economic agents to another. However, before concluding that privileged access and resale is economically more efficient than queuing and search, one has also to take into account both the transaction costs, which are likely to be high in the case of resale, and also the negative external effects of corruption. Corruption, while providing some form of allocation mechanism (a popular saying under the command economy was 'corruption is the human face of socialism'), comes with a strong negative external cost: as already argued in Chapter 1, the heritage of the social attitudes developed under communism is still haunting Central and Eastern Europe.

Full liberalization amounts to the removal of controls over price and production decisions. Ultimately, supply and demand adjust to the market equilibrium point given by e. Both consumers and producers gain. Consumers gain from saving on disequilibrium costs (the area p^*fbp_c) and from the net value of additional consumption (*feb*). Producers gain from higher prices (the area $\bar{p}afp^*$) and from the surplus generated from increased production (*aef*). The net welfare gain of both groups of economic agents is given by the area: $\bar{p}aebp_c$. Within it, the area above the equilibrium price line represents the consumer gain; producer gain is shown below the equilibrium price line. Thus, apparently, everybody gains from price liberalization and reforms should be greeted with overwhelming support. However, this conclusion hinges critically on the homogeneity of economic agents, consumers in particular.

First, the opportunity cost of time may differ. Those with a high income gain more from restoring equilibrium, while those with a lower income gain less. Therefore, liberalization has an element of redistribution built in, with an uneven impact on various economic groups. One important example relates to the retired. Their incomes are not work-related and their opportunity cost of time may be relatively low. For that very reason, one of the sad features of the command economy was that within households the oldest people had typically to 'specialize' in queuing. They were also the group unlikely to transform the time gained from eliminating disequilibria into some income-generating activity. This may partly explain why, in spite the protection of the real value of pensions, this group was particularly vocal against the reforms. In a more general perspective, the redistributional aspect of price liberalization implies that democratic institutions may have an important role to play in mediating the compensation mechanisms, including the introduction of a social safety net.

Second, the assessment of price liberalization by consumers may be ambiguous, in spite of the welfare gains, if the initial low price (p) is perceived as equivalent to claims on government. We discussed that issue in Chapter 2, describing the prisoners' dilemma resulting in a reform stalemate during the last period of the command economy. Increasing the price to a market equilibrium level does not decrease real incomes as it replaces non-monetary disequilibrium cost by its (lower!) monetary equivalent. In addition, there are gains from increased supply. The situation differs, however, if there is an expectation that the market could be equalized at the initial price p. The problem is that with informational asymmetry between the consumers and policy-makers, consumers may not be sure if the new equilibrium price does not contain a hidden element of taxation (resulting in some unwanted redistribution of income), so that price adjustment is used as an opportunity to suppress real incomes. From this point of view, both civil liberties (in particular, the freedom of the media) and political freedom are important. Here, the issue of concern is not redistribution between some income-defined social groups (poor versus rich), but rather between those who may benefit from being close to the power centre (old nomenklatura) and those who may not. Because of the nature of the distribution under the old regime, this second classification will only partly overlap with income distribution. For a similar reason, the reforms were more credible when they were introduced by policy-makers not perceived as linked to the old regime.

External liberalization: Imports

With Figure 4.3, we move to external liberalization. We have a tradable good. This time, the initial administrative price (p) is not below but

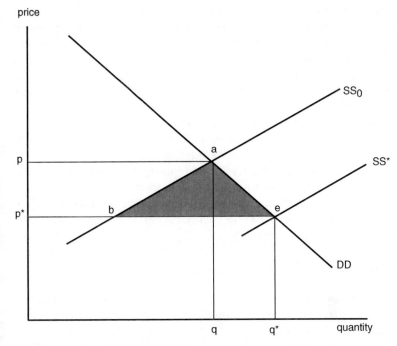

Figure 4.3 External liberalization: Imports

above the equilibrium level (the world market price). For simplicity, we assume that no imports are allowed initially (a more general inter- mediate case with tariff barriers and some imports is discussed in most trade and/or public finance texts; see, for instance, Cullis and Jones 1992). When imports are liberalized, the price decreases to p^* and con- sumption expands. Both effects result in consumers' gain (represented by the area $paep^*$). However, in this case, the domestic producer loses: the market price is now lower and some domestic production is crowded out by imports; the producers' loss is represented by the area p^*bap. Comparing the two areas, we arrive at a net gain *abe*.

Here, the risk of blocking the reforms results from special interest prob- lems. While aggregate consumer gain is substantial, it may be small *per capita*. A typical case, not unique to the transition economies, relates to agricultural products. The irony is that food prices are precisely those which have the strongest impact on the poorest stratum of consumers, for which food represents the most substantial share in their spending. The reintroduction/preservation of import barriers for food was a typical effect of special interests at the beginning of the 1990s. However, the net impact of liberalization of international exchange in agricultural products may well be positive. While some products may indeed face competition from abroad, for many others new export opportunities may dominate. Indeed, in mid-2004, when the old EU finally widened access for the agricultural production of the new members, it caused a positive average price effect on the domestic prices of food in the latter group, because of export opportunities.[3]

However, the problem reaches far beyond agriculture. In general, while (internal) price liberalization brings in partial adjustment, the full effects emerge only when prices move towards the world market level, which in turn is triggered by opening foreign trade and liberalizing exchange rates. Moreover, the effects of the removal of import barriers for consumer products works in the same direction as the removal of export barriers for producers of raw materials and energy, an effect which is discussed in detail by McKinnon (1993).

External liberalization: Exports

Again, drawing from Gros and Steinherr (1995), we may now illustrate the liberalization of exports, focusing only on those welfare effects which are relevant from the political economy point of view, with the intention of finding out what special interests may possibly stall the reform process. We again face a product where the effect of external liberalization is important. However, contrary to Figure 4.3, the initial market price is below equilibrium. And, unlike Figure 4.2, the government is implicitly subsidizing consumption by forcing producers to sell on the domestic market instead of exporting (Figure 4.4). Some energy-related products such as oil may be the most important illustration for this example. This is a tradable product, with domestic supply being inelastic in the short run and given by the vertical line $\bar{q}$. Initially, the domestic price is below the equilibrium price, consumption is subsidized and domestic consumption has priority over exports. Producers are discouraged from exporting; instead they sell cheaply to domestic users of energy, due to some form of export restrictions. To simplify this example (without undermining our general conclusions), we assume that all domestic production is absorbed, leaving no room for exports. The initial level of consumption is thus $\bar{q}$.

After liberalization, the domestic price adjusts to the world market level p^*. Domestic consumption falls to q^*, as domestic users of energy are forced to restructure and shift to new energy-saving technologies. The welfare outcome of liberalization is thus exactly opposite to the

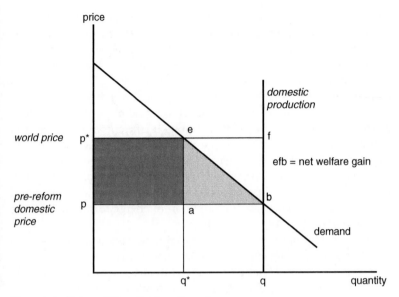

Figure 4.4   External liberalization: Exports

previous one: consumers lose and producers gain. Producers gain from new export opportunities and from higher world market prices amounting to $(q - q^*)(p^* - p)$ and from higher domestic prices amounting to q^* $(p^* - p)$. On the other hand, the loss to domestic users of energy amounts to *pbep**. Subtracting the latter from the former we arrive at the net welfare gain, which amounts to:

$$efb = 1/2(q - q^*)(p^* - p).$$

The political economy problem results from the fact that the users of energy may represent a strong special interest group. In an economy where cheap energy is a cornerstone of industrial policy, changes may be difficult to implement. The empirical example may come from Russia, a country particularly rich in energy resources, where increasing domestic consumption in the late communist period systematically drove down exports (see also Chapter 2). At the beginning of the liberalization programme, full adjustment in energy price was blocked by the special interests of energy users. On the other hand, the producers of energy were also compensated with 'soft' tax regimes and a substantial share in the under-priced transfer of assets during the privatization period. Gros and Steinherr (1995) calculate the rough approximation of area *efb* – i.e. the welfare loss from maintaining low domestic prices of energy. Given the initial world market price premium of 150 per cent above the domestic price and the long-run price elasticity of demand of about 0.5, they arrive at a spectacular figure of loss, due to the low domestic price of energy and export controls, equivalent to 5–10 per cent of FSU GDP in 1990. As pointed out by McKinsey (1999), an additional negative effect, which continued during the 1990s, was that efficient domestic users were hurt by the prevalence of non-payment among inefficient users. In the steel industry, the providers of energy resources had far more leverage over the large most efficient producers with a direct network connection and vulnerable to the threat of blocked supply. On the other hand, smaller, older technology, less efficient producers were far less easy to control, and it was difficult to disentangle the provision of energy for them from the provision of heating for local housing.

The important point to note here is again that various components of the liberalization programme are interdependent. The change in relative energy prices is insufficient to trigger real adjustment if 'soft' budget channels are present. In fact, the prices of energy resources were to some degree adjusted during the 1990s towards the world market level, yet one could still detect two layers of subsidization, first of domestic producers and to a lesser degree of some CIS recipients (Belarus in particular). Both energy prices below the world market level and 'soft' budget channels via non-payment for energy imply that producers were forced to subsidize domestic consumption, and that their investment in both production facilities and transport infrastructure (critical for any increase in exports) suffered. The impact on industrial users of energy was that restructuring to increase energy efficiency slowed down. The comparison of the time paths of the use of energy and GDP shows that the former adjusted far less to production in Russia than in those transition economies that were most advanced in reforms.[4]

The difference between the relative domestic price of energy and the world market price was possibly the most important nominal distortion under the command economy. Adjustment towards world market prices made a significant share of industrial production far less profitable. Some of it could even emerge as value-subtracting – i.e. where the cost of resources was higher than the value of final production. McKinnon (1993, ch. 12) provides a model which illustrates how price distortions may be maintained by both import and export restrictions. Both have a similar impact in a general equilibrium perspective. Liberalization leads to price adjustment and reveals that much industrial production may be value-subtracting unless it is restructured. Empirical estimates of the extent of value-subtracting activities at the starting point of the reforms are provided by Hughes and Hare (1992). They classify industries into four categories:

- Industries already in long-run competitive equilibrium (a ratio of value-added at domestic prices to that at world prices – 1)
- Very competitive branches at the global level (a ratio of value-added at domestic prices to that at world prices < 1). Those were branches which were implicitly discriminated against under the command economy
- Branches protected from foreign competition (a ratio of value-added at domestic prices to that at world prices > 1)
- Value-subtracting branches (a ratio of value-added at domestic prices to that at world prices < 0, because the nominator is negative).

Hughes and Hare's (1992) estimates are reproduced in Table 4.1. Poland looks particularly good; however, that can be easily explained by the early start of the transition process there. In 1992, Poland was already in its third year of reforms, the Czech Republic was into its second year, while the timing for Hungary is more difficult to determine. Nevertheless, the clear outlier is the FSU group, when compared with the three CE countries mentioned above. In the FSU group, 1992 was the first year of reforms, and those were not fully implemented. Thus, comparing Poland with FSU, in a sense, we compare the pre-reform and post-(full) reform outcomes.

The indicators are based on average value-added in branches of industry. They may be misleading, as they do not tell us much about the potential for restructuring. In some industries classified as value-subtracting, the

Table 4.1 Industrial competitiveness, selected transition economies, 1992 (percentages)

	Czech Republic output	Czech Republic employment	Hungary output	Hungary employment	Poland output	Poland employment	FSU output	FSU employment
DRC < 1[a]	20.59	36.35	18.18	12.95	17.65	2.67	16.13	13.90
DRC > 2	26.47	22.39	18.18	13.09	5.88	0	38.71	18.36
DRC < O	23.53	3.20	12.12	3.44	0	0	25.81	50.99

Note:
[a] DRC = domestic resource cost = a ratio of value-added at domestic prices to that at world prices

Sources: Hughes and Hare (1992); ILO (1996). with external flows after liberalization playing a less significant role.

majority of companies may be just below the break-even point, in some others the exit and bankruptcies of many firms may be unavoidable. In addition, in some cases restructuring may be achieved with little investment, by reorientation of production on more value creation, in some other far more financial resources are needed. Comparing results for Poland and the two other Central European economies with those for the former Soviet Union may suggest that fast progress, achieved mostly by reallocation, without significant investment effort was possible.

Enterprise governance reform: Elimination of subsidies

We now discuss the final example of the effects of reforms. Unlike the previous case we now focus on a 'second-stage' institutional reform, in particular on elimination of subsidies that comes under heading of 'enterprise (governance) reform' (see both previous chapter and the next chapter). Elimination of subsidies also links directly with the fiscal dimension (see Figure 4.5), with taxpayers as another group of economic agents affected by the reform. Unlike the case of price liberalization, supply is now modelled as elastic.

Initially, price is below the equilibrium price. However, instead of market disequilibrium, this time production is subsidized, and therefore supply is maintained at the market-clearing level. Subsidy is equal to $(p_p - p_c)\bar{q}$, i.e. to area $p_c abp_p$. Here, we consider the effect of the removal of subsidies. As a result, the price increases to p^*, and the quantity produced decreases to q^*. Both producers and consumers lose, but the taxpayer gains. Consumer loss is equivalent to the area p^*eap_c and producer loss to p^*ebp_p. However, both of those taken together do not exceed the savings by taxpayer and the resulting net welfare gain is *abe*. In reality, the gain is even higher, as we should add the elimination of the administrative cost of handling the subsidy, influence costs and distortionary cost of tax used to finance it – subsidy does not represent just a pure income transfer based on lump sum tax effortlessly collected.

It is interesting to compare this case (removal of subsidization, Figure 4.5) with that illustrated with Figure 4.2 (straightforward price liberalization). In the latter case, we have both average producers and average consumers benefiting from liberalization (albeit we pointed out that the gains may not be evenly distributed among consumers). In the former case, those directly interested in the particular market lose, and the gain is acquired by the most dispersed group in the economy – i.e. taxpayers. From the political economy point of view, one should expect a far stronger presence of special interests in case of subsidies than in the case of disequilibria.

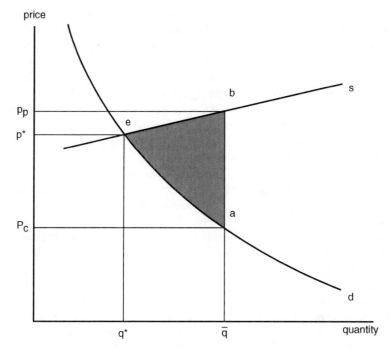

Figure 4.5 Governance reform: Removal of subsidization

In other words, it is more difficult to eliminate the subsidies than to liberalize prices where no direct subsidies were present.

Winners and losers: Other reform components

We argued above that while internal price liberalization should be met with relatively little opposition, the external liberalization is likely to run across some special interests and may therefore be more difficult to implement, and may be more critically dependent on the quality of mediating, intermediary political (democratic) institutions.

In particular, an component of first-stage reforms (see Chapter 3) relates to freedom of entry/small-scale privatization. Here, domestic new entry comes mostly at a form of newly created small enterprises. Incumbent producers lose and dispersed consumers and new entrepreneurs gain. One may expect opposition to reforms from both the state-owned (or privatized) firms or from the 'old', licensed private sector, where it existed. However, at the beginning of reforms the incumbent producers may lack organization and political leverage to stall the reforms.

It is only over time, that the interests of incumbent may become consolidated, at the same time the expansion of the new private sector may pose a more direct threat to them. Therefore, opposition to new entry may grow in later phase of transition (see also: Aidis *et al.* 2008). This case can be again illustrated by Figure 4.3 above. New entrants will shift the supply curve to the right, eliminating the rents enjoyed by 'old' producers, as the price declines. Thus, even if we did not discuss this case in more detail, the conclusions are fairly obvious: again, special interests may still potentially stall the reforms, especially if the reform was not introduced early on.

With respect to second-stage reforms, we already discussed governance (the enterprise reform) and argued that removal of subsidies may be challenging from the political economy point of view. In Chapter 3 we also noticed that banking reform is closely associated with enterprise governance reform: cheap credit to incumbent firms is one of the widespread forms of implicit subsidization. Thus, banking reform may also face political economy obstacles.

In contrast, introduction of a formal capital market (non-bank financial reform) does not present an immediate threat to any special interests. Similarly, competition policy (anti-monopoly regulation) does not result in immediate threat to most of incumbent producers – the number of companies affected is typically very small, and the regulation creates possibilities for those affected to defend their interests.

Finally, large-scale privatization is an interesting case. Privatization of industrial assets leads to enormous transfers of wealth. However, it is also relatively easy to identify and compensate the losers – especially, the insiders (the incumbent workers and managers). Existing employees are exposed to a risk of labour-shedding, but may be compensated with shares (Aghion and Blanchard 1998).

Conclusion

We are now able to summarize the political economy conclusions derived from this section.

In Chapter 3 we focused on the distinction between first-stage (liberalization) reforms and second-stage institutional reforms. That was based on differences in technical difficulty of implementation: the contrast between removal of obstacles to economic freedom and the active building of legal frameworks supporting the markets. Here we focus on another factor along which the reforms differ: the degree to which interests of various groups of economic actors are affected by reforms, which in turn determine the political economies difficulties in implementation. This second cross-section cuts across the first stage – second stage distinction. For instance, while price liberalization may meet little opposition, external liberalization (imports, exports and the exchange rate) is likely to result in the largest distributional effects, and in removing significant economic rents enjoyed by economic actors who are likely to be influential in political terms. Yet, both are first-stage reforms, easy to implement from purely technical point of view. The redistributional effects are also strong in the case of enterprise reform (removal of subsidies). The latter may be difficult to implement, due to the fact that the removal of subsidies produces concentrated losses and dispersed larger gains. It may not be only for technical reasons, therefore, that enterprise reform took longer to implement than price liberalization (see comparison in Chapter 3).

From this perspective, there are two main reasons why political freedom (democracy) may facilitate reform implementation.

First, democracy and political rights may result in the creation of mediation institutions. These may facilitate negotiating compensating transfers between the various parties affected by reforms. Given this possibility, no economic group attempts to stall the reforms. However, an equally or even more important effect relates to the guarantee that the democratic institutions give against the possibility that the costs of reforms are paid by the general public, while the benefits are acquired by the nomenklatura – i.e. the main beneficiaries of the old regime.

Second, civil liberties are also important. Not only are democratic institutions unlikely to function well without civil liberties, but the latter have an important direct role to play. In particular, acute special interests effects may be most likely where the informational barriers are most significant. This implies that low-cost quality information may be a most efficient method to prevent the reforms being either stalled or captured by special interests. A free media, a key component of civil liberties, is likely to facilitate reforms.

Empirical results on the link between political freedom and reforms

The link between democracy and an aggregate indicator of reforms was tested empirically by Falcetti, Raiser and Sanfey (2002). Using both three-stage least squares (3SLS) estimation of joint growth and reform, a two-equation system and an ordinary least squares estimator, they found robust positive effects of democracy on reforms. Mickiewicz (2005) builds on their work, extending it in two ways. Falcetti, Raiser and Sanfey's measure of reforms is an average of the EBRD indices of the three key components of reforms: (1) Internal price liberalization, (2) External liberalization of foreign trade and the exchange rate, and (3) Freedom of entry and small-scale privatization. Mickiewicz (2005) tested for all eight basic reform indicators available from the EBRD. In addition, those tests allowed for the possibility that the link between political freedom and reforms is non-linear: the incremental impact on the reforms of achieving a basic threshold of political freedom could be higher than the influence of moving between an average and high degree of political freedom.

Variables, empirical models and results are discussed in detail in Mickiewicz (2005). The standard set of measures of political freedom is available from Freedom House. It includes the ranking of political rights, the ranking of civil liberties and a composite measure which combines both categories in a joint ranking of political freedom status, dividing countries into three categories: 'not free', 'partly free' and 'free'. A detailed description of the criteria used to build each index is available from http://www.freedomhouse.org. We argued in the previous section that political rights have slightly different implications for reforms than civil liberties. The former are directly relevant for democratic mediation mechanisms. The latter may have a critical role in containing the influence of special interests by facilitating access to information, via free media in particular. However, both indices are highly correlated. As noted by Freedom House (New York), civil liberties are a typical prerequisite for political rights. Both are highly correlated and empirical results were not sensitive to either choice. The results obtained by Mickiewicz (2005) were consistent with the discussion above. In particular, as expected, external liberalization, while not difficult from the technical point of view, creates the most serious challenge (in terms of both wide distributional effects and special interests). Indeed, it stands apart as being most facilitated by the quality of democratic and civil society institutions.

Next, democracy proved to be important for internal price liberalization, freedom of entry and small-scale privatization, governance and enterprise restructuring and bank reform; for all four reforms, coefficients have the expected signs and were significant. The intuition behind the first two results is as described above – both price liberalization and freedom of entry imply distributional effects. To understand why 'enterprise reform' may be conditional on democracy, one has to take into account that the indicator includes the elimination of the 'soft' budget constraint at the enterprise level, a reform that also has a strong distributional impact. Finally, the link between bank reform and democracy can be interpreted in the same way. As established by PCA in Chapter 3, bank reform and enterprise restructuring are correlated; moreover, the elimination of the 'soft' budget constraint is an important phenomenon which creates a link between the two.

In contrast with the significant results for the five reforms described above, the link with democracy is insignificant for competition policy, NBFIs and large-scale privatization. The first two results are very intuitive. The impact of competition policy is limited to a few narrowly defined sectors. Similarly, the stock exchange plays a limited role in the financial systems of the transition countries, and strong redistributional effects are unlikely.

On the other hand, the insignificance of the link between democracy and privatization of large firms may be seen as puzzling. A likely explanation is that while the effects on wealth distribution are important here, the transaction costs of compensating the conflicting claims may not be high. As already discussed, the corresponding compensation schemes for insiders were relatively easy to design (Blanchard and Aghion 1996; Aghion and Blanchard 1998; Mickiewicz and Bałtowski 2003).

Finally, there were also clear-cut non-linear effects. The general result was that the effect of the difference between regimes which are 'not free' and both 'free' and 'partly free' is far more significant than the difference between 'partly free' and 'free'. There is thus some indication of diminishing returns to democracy. To reach the elementary threshold of political freedom has a more important incremental effect on reforms than a further improvement in the quality of the democratic institutions.

From this perspective, again the two reforms we highlighted above – external liberalization and governance (enterprise) reform – stand apart as most significantly (positively) affected by reaching a threshold level of democracy. While the results discussed so far were based on multivariate dynamic panel estimation (Mickiewicz 2005), the intuition behind may also be illustrated by simple cross-sectional correlations. The latter are presented by Figures 4.6 and 4.7 below, which correspond to the two reforms we found as most sensitive (most facilitated) by political freedom.

The threshold effect we discussed above is more visible for external liberalization, while enterprise governance seems to be correlated with the political rights index in a more linear way.

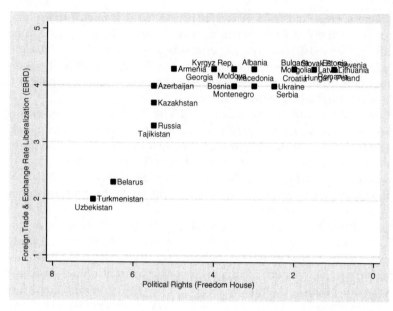

Figure 4.6   External liberalization and index of political rights (2009)

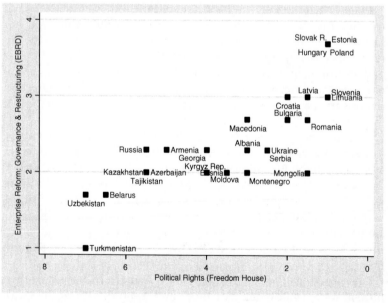

Figure 4.7   Enterprise reform (governance) and index of political rights (2009)

Conclusion

In the previous chapter we argued that economic and political institutions are connected at the fundamental, constitutional level: in particular effective protection of property rights may be seen as a subset of the rule of law. Both assume that there are effective constraints imposed on the arbitrary power of the executive branch of the government. In this chapter we follow another link between politics and economics. We argue that from the dynamic perspective, a critical advantage of a stable democratic order is that it facilitates the process of institutional change and the process of reform. Moreover, reforms vary in the degree to which they affect incumbents' interests, therefore they vary in the degree to which mediation and credible compensation schemes are important.

The Chapter 3 and Chapter 4 perspectives are not mutually exclusive. For instance, good frameworks of enterprise governance may be conditional on both political mediation at time of implementation and on underlying 'higher order' institutional frameworks (Mickiewicz 2009).That correspond to two different questions: the likelihood that reforms are initiated and implemented, and the likelihood that they prove sustainable.

For any policy-makers, dictatorships are tempting as they offer apparent technical freedom of action. Yet, in the longer run, dictatorships and political oppression that typically follows are not good for reforms. Democratic institutions may facilitate mediation between economic actors, while dictators risk more than just losing elections if the reforms fail, which may inhibit them from implementing institutional change. In addition, free media and other components of civil liberties may facilitate access to information and limit the extent of state capture by special interests.

The institutional framework of political freedom matters most for reforms for which distributional and special interests effects are large, the effects on income distribution are complex and it is not easy to build compensating effects directly into reforms. As confirmed by empirical results, external liberalization seems to be a prime example of such a situation. On the other hand, while privatization results in spectacular shifts in wealth distribution, it is relatively easy to build the privatization programmes in a way which compensates the losers, insiders in particular. For such reforms, the importance of democratic institutions may be smaller.

5
Hard Budget Constraint

In 1992, Russia embarked on the liberalization program, coordinated by Yegor Gaidar. At the same time, Bank of Russia led by Viktor Gerash-chenko continued to channel massive amount of money to inefficient large state firms via the banking system (Gros and Steinherr 1995). Inflation reached 2,520 per cent. Resources that could be spent to provide direct welfare safety net for the population, were wasted instead. Supported by easy credit, large state firms felt no immediate pressure to change their production programme or to release resources that could be use more efficiently elsewhere. With soft budgets, liberalization did not work and Russian people became disappointed with reforms.

In the previous chapter we argued that eliminating subsidization is an economic reform, which is particularly difficult to implement from the political economy point of view. At the same time, subsidization is part of a wider phenomenon of soft budget constraint. The latter will be the focus of this chapter. We will argue that where present, the soft budget can make other reforms ineffective. We also highlight the link with the macroeconomic outcomes: government budget deficits and macroeconomic destabilization have their microeconomic roots, and those can be described under the heading of soft budgeting. Fiscal imbalances, which typically lead to inflation, are signs of weak government: from the economic point of view, the weak government is the one that cannot mediate and align different claims on resources efficiently. The issues we discuss are more than of historical interest: In some transition countries, soft budget proved to be a persistent feature, it has been typical not only for 1990s, but remains so in early 2000s.

The soft budget channels and its sources

We discuss what happens when the budget constraint is not binding, being 'soft', in the sense that the economic agent can reach beyond it. The question is, under what circumstances does the budget constraint cease to be effective – when it is not determining economic agent behaviour? While quantitative constraints which are more harsh than the budget line are typical for consumers (under price controls), the opposite case of a 'soft' budget normally relate to enterprises. However, the two problems are strictly related. If the financial constraints are not binding, some others have to be. It is likely that where all economic agents are not restricted by finance, they will ultimately face quantitative constraints. The 'financial veil' hides the fundamental scarcity of resources: when it is torn, the latter are faced directly.

The 'soft' budget constraint is not just replacing one set of constraints with another; in that case, it would not be 'soft' in any sense. A strong element of redistribution is involved. From the general equilibrium perspective, making the budget 'softer' for some economic agents implies that constraints are becoming more severe for others.

As stated by Kornai (1986):

> The concept of 'budget' ... is of a general nature and serves to denote the plan for revenue and expenditure of any economic unit: household, enterprise, government agency or non-profit institution. (Kornai 1986: 33)

Kornai made the issue of the 'soft' budget the cornerstone of his comparative system analysis (1979, 1980, 1986). The 'soft' budget situation may result from one of the following circumstances (Kornai 1986):

(1) Firms are price-makers, not price-takers; in a pure competitive model, a company is not able to transfer any idiosyncratic increase in costs onto its customers via increasing prices, as its sales will fall to zero; thus control over prices always introduces some slack, even if the demand curve is not vertical.

(2) The tax system is 'soft': 'formulation of tax rules has been influenced by the firm, the firm may be granted exemption or postponement as an individual favour; taxes are not collected strictly' (1986: 41).

(3) Subsidies exist, that may come in the form of contributions to investment funding with a financial cost below opportunity cost,

or weak repayment obligations, some continuous production subsidies, or ad hoc subsidies to cover a one-off loss.

(4) The credit system is 'soft': availability of credit is not linked to the
net present value (NPV) of a project, the terms of the financial
contract are not always enforced and there is a built-in expectation
that they may not be followed at the time the credit is granted.

(5) External financial investment is on 'soft' conditions, similar to
point (4); this channel is relevant where equity markets exist. In
the case of the command economy there was uniform ownership
of enterprises, which had no separate equity.

If the budget is 'soft', firms with negative NPV may survive, and growth
opportunities are no longer correlated with the value of the firm. From
the general equilibrium perspective, this situation implies the transfer of
resources from value enhancing producers to those which may generate
little value-added or may even be value-destroying. The firm shares the
risk with the government; the additional profits may be skimmed off, but
losses may also be shifted onto somebody else. The structure of incentives
is affected. Instead of a 'real economy', it becomes more profitable
for managers to focus on the 'control sphere' (Kornai 1986) – i.e. on lobbying for decisions and administrative, fiscal and financial actions of
corresponding decision-makers (supporting organizations) to 'soften'
the budget constraints. The corollary is that the budget constraint is not
uniformly 'soft' for all firms, as it depends on their lobbying potential.

Here, we may focus on the role of social networks. We discussed the
role of private networks substituting for generalized trust in Chapter 1.
These networks, where they encompass government officials, may result
in soft budgets. Alternatively, we may model sources of soft budget
in terms of bargaining, and list the possible threats available to budget-
constrained organizations seeking finance, including disruptive strike
action. The budgeted organization is represented by managers bargaining
with the supportive organization. However, the strike action may have
the tacit support of managers, where it is targeting the supporting organization (say, a branch ministry in the case of state-owned firms). Generally, any kind of disruption with external effects creates a credible threat
– we may think about large infrastructure companies, such as public
transport. Always, the informational asymmetry between the budgeted
organization and the sponsor (supporting organization) will also strengthen
the position of the former.

The parallel perspective is that the extent of the 'soft' budget will
also depend on how attractive it is for the supporting organization

(typically the government administration) to intervene to relax the constraints. For this reason, the budget may be relatively 'softer' for the largest companies, for which the political cost and external economic effects of bankruptcy may be the strongest. Shleifer and Vishny (1994) and Boycko, Shleifer and Vishny (1996) take labour spending as an example of a situation where the preferences of the sponsor (the supporting organization) may differ from those of the managers of the budget-constrained organization. The politicians may prefer higher spending than that resulting from profit maximizing choice, to maintain either higher employment or higher wages, which may be linked to either 'patronage jobs' which lead to individual exchange of favours, or to electoral and political support. To motivate the managers, they have to be compensated. This is easier in state-owned companies than in private companies, because the private owners are full residual claimants, and more costly to compensate. It follows from this line of analysis that the extent of a 'soft' budget should be positively correlated with the extent of state ownership of the productive assets (see also Kornai, Maskin and Roland 2003).

Wider and narrower concept of soft budget

Kornai, Maskin and Roland (2003) argue convincingly that it is not just any support (typically by the government) for some economic agents (typically producers) that creates a situation of soft budget constraint. Some subsidization may be economically efficient, for instance in case of low (and decreasing) marginal cost of operation combined with large fixed costs of investment, as in some network industries. They argue that at the core of the soft budget situation we find the problem of time inconsistency. This can best be explained with a simple example taken from elementary game theory. Consider Figure 5.1 below.

The initial decision is made by the sponsor (say, the government), who may provide the sponsored organization (say, a large state-owned manufacturing company) with a subsidy. This typically comes with some conditions attached. Say, the sponsored company is expected to implement some restructuring programme. If the subsidy is granted, than the sponsored organization decides if it is going to comply with conditions under which the subsidy was given. In practice the choice may not be between full compliance and no compliance, but between partial compliance and no compliance. The sponsored organization may decide not to comply and after a while to come back to sponsoring organization asking for more funds. It is here, when the problem becomes interesting. At this

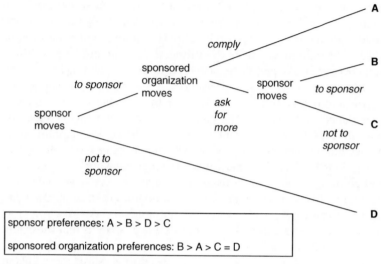

Figure 5.1   Soft budget constraint

point the sponsor may decide to punish the sponsored organization refusing to provide more funds. However, this decision would be sub-optimal from his/her point of view, i.e. given the order of preferences as listed on Figure 5.1. For instance, refusing to provide additional funding would result in bankruptcy of an industrial enterprise, which restructuring programme was already generously sponsored by the government, a worse case scenario, as the government faces both economic and political cost (outcome C). Faced with this alternative, the government provides additional funds creating a soft budget situation (outcome B).

This situation would not arise, if the government could credibly commit itself to implement scenario C, in case the sponsored organization does not comply. It is the anticipation of the sponsor choice B that triggers a choice of non-compliance by the sponsored organization However, with credible commitment, the sponsored organization would face a more narrow choice between outcomes A and C. As a result it would comply and the soft budget situation would not arise.

Seen from this perspective, soft budget is an example of a wider class of problems that come under the headings of post-contractual opportunism: initial sponsoring contract implies some specific behaviour of the sponsored organization, however the latter breaks the contract conditions. The soft budget solution arises, because at that stage the sponsor has no incentives to punish. Considering soft budget in terms of contractual opportunism helps to understand why we followed EBRD and identified the soft budget as the key problem of enterprise governance reform: the area of governance relates to contractual obligations.

We may also notice that while informational asymmetry (more information on its real conditions being available to sponsored organization than to the sponsor) always amplifies the problem, still it is not necessary condition for the problem to arise. As long as the outcome B is preferred to outcome D by the sponsor, he/she can offer a subsidy, even anticipating the problems resulting from opportunistic behaviour by the sponsored organization. If there is disrupted information in this game, it comes mostly from the uncertainty about the degree of opportunism and therefore about uncertainty of behaviour of the sponsored organization.

Implications of soft budget

Under a 'soft' budget, the responsiveness and adjustment to changes in the economic environment is lower. In particular, the firm is not compelled to adjust fully to external prices (Kornai 1986). The objective of liberalization is to achieve a situation where the decisions of economic actors result in efficient adjustment to the structure of real costs (scarcity) and consumer preferences, as revealed by liberalized prices. Restoring market price equilibrium establishes a basic set of price information, which may guide enterprises in an efficient direction. Transformation of the corporate control sphere (including ownership reform, as will be discussed later on) may align the motivation of economic agents with the incentives offered by the economic environment. However, our discussion of 'soft' budget implies that changes in corporate control (which implies re-introduction of the profit incentive) is not a sufficient condition for successful liberalization: even if the economic agents who control the firm are driven by the profit motive, this does not in itself determine their behaviour completely; the characteristics of the economic environment also matter. Only when profit incentives are combined with a 'hard' budget constraint are efforts directed towards 'real actions' (adjusting quantities, technological decisions, etc.). Combining profit incentives with a 'soft' budget constraint gives at least an equal or greater role to the manipulation of the control sphere: financial variables, price increases, lobbying for government subsidies, etc. In fact, in this respect, more not less disruption may result: as with the profit motive, the incentives for lobbying are now much stronger. This idea is illustrated by Figure 5.2 below.

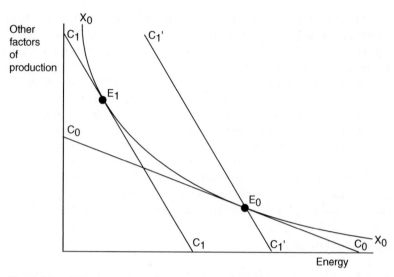

Figure 5.2 Adjustment to a shift in cost structure: Technological adaptation versus soft budget

We may think about Figure 5.2 in terms of the soft budget problem emerging between the government and the large firms in need of restructuring. We consider a major shift in relative prices of energy triggered by price liberalization. As relative prices change, so does the slope of the isocost line – which is defined as a line which representing a given level of producer's cost (expenditure, budget) – by construction it remains the same alongside any isocost line. In particular, on Figure 5.2, an old isocost representing high availability of cheap energy (C_0C_0), now shifts to a new position (C_1C_1). If producer considers this new cost structure as binding (hard), so he/she is constrained by the same maximum level of costs/expenditure, he/she restructures towards new less-energy intensive technology, which represent a different combination of factors of production. That corresponds to the move from E_0 to E_1. The level of production represented by isoquant X_0X_0 remains the same, but the real value added determined by the difference between the costs and revenue increases considerably, as new prices reflect the opportunity cost of resources better than before.

However, the government may not be credible enough to induce the effort needed to restructure (to the move from E_0 to E_1). The large enterprises may choose not to comply. Instead they come back to the government asking for subsidies. With an implicit threat of large-scale bankruptcies, the subsidies are likely to be granted. Instead of restructuring production and shifting technology to E_1, a large inefficient firm continues operating at E_0. The only gain from price liberalization is that implicit subsidization via distorted price structure may now become more explicit. This gain in transparency however may or may not materialize. It is sufficient to take another look at alternative channels of soft budget listed above to realize that subsidization may still be easily hidden as low collection of due taxes or cheap bank credit by state controlled or influenced banks.

In fact, it is this multidimensional nature of soft budget that makes it difficult to be translated into exact empirical measures. Direct EBRD operationalization of a 'hard' budget is more narrow than that used by Kornai (1986). It is included under the heading of 'Governance and enterprise restructuring' and relates to government subsidies and 'soft' credit. However, other aspects of the 'hard' budget are dealt with; but they are spread over several indicators. The indicator of banking sector reforms is a good measure of the quality of credit systems and the elimination of that channel of the 'soft' budget. We argued already that those two are related. Price-setting is dealt with under 'competition policy'. And prices may

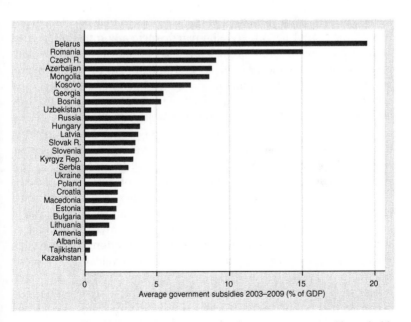

Figure 5.3 Budgetary transfers and current transfers to enterprises and households excluding social transfers (% GDP)

become an element of the 'soft' budget in another way, namely where there is state procurement of the firm's products at non-market prices. This is included under the EBRD indicator 'Internal price liberalization'. Thus, not just 'enterprise governance' but at least four of our eight EBRD indicators cover various aspects of the 'soft' budget issue. Again, not accounting for taxes remains a major omission.

Belarussian government, which we already identified as an outlier in terms of its low implementation of market reforms, spends about 20 per cent of its GDP supporting selected industrial enterprises. (Figure 5.3 above). It is more surprising to find Romania, a most recent EU entrant, transferring about 15 per cent of its GDP to producers that are unwilling or unable to restructure adjusting to market prices. In other transition countries subsidies remain below 10 per cent and one should not attach too much significance to the relative position of each country. Again, as can be argued, transforming some distorionary government intervention like price controls into open subsidies may actually be a first step in the right direction.

Too soft, too hard

More generally, while the extent of the 'soft' budget may be dramatically reduced, it cannot be entirely eliminated where any forms of external finance are present. This complication results from the ambiguity built into any form of finance. A time lag is always present between any provision of finance and repayment, and so is imperfect information and an element of risk. For that reason, any finance has a potentially 'soft' element: it may be subject to renegotiation or default without the full consequences being borne by the receiver of the finance. This deficiency is unavoidable due to the fundamental issue of time inconsistency (Kornai, Maskin and Roland 2003) we already discussed: in many situations it is not possible for the sponsoring (supporting) organization – i.e. the provider of finance – to commit credibly at the time the financial contract is signed. The reason is that in subsequent periods it may be beneficial to both parties to renegotiate, when the initial financial investment becomes sunk cost. Anticipating this, the budgeted organization, which has an informational advantage, may propose that negative value-added projects be financed. A corollary is that eliminating any possibility of a 'soft' budget will come at a cost, as it is not always possible to separate good and bad projects – the budget can also be too 'hard' in some cases.

The latter case follows from what Kornai (1986) defined as a pure case of a 'hard' budget constraint, where all external finance is eliminated. In that case, the firm's survival depends exclusively on the proceeds from sales and on the costs of inputs, which bear an element of risk which is not related to the internal efficiency of the firm. As a result, in the short term the firm may have to build excessive cash reserves to smooth cash flow over time. Moreover, growth and technical progress depend on the same factors: the financial resources necessary for expansion of the firm are created exclusively by internal accumulation. That becomes a serious problem for the economy where scope for structure change is high, and some bottlenecks cannot be sorted out quickly based on internal finance alone. Calvo and Corricelli (1992) promoted the point of view that the credit constraint was an important factor which contributed to initial recession in the transition economies. Indeed, there is no reason why the initial distribution of relative price shocks across enterprises and the resulting distribution of shocks to revenue should be closely correlated with the forward-looking (after-adjustment) NPV of companies. From this perspective, the availability of finance for restructuring becomes the key issue. If the financing was missing, some valuable capital could be destroyed in the process of initial change, leading to an overall output loss (see Chapter 6). However, as always, there is a trade-off. At the onset of transition, the state banks were not prepared for the task of efficient credit allocation and commercial lending. We will discuss it in more detail later on in Chapter 10. As argued by McKinnon (1992, 1993) forcing enterprises to rely on internal cash flow as a predominant source of finance may be a second-best solution, given the initial inadequacy of the financial system. The risk of a financial crisis following the opening of an easy channel of 'soft' financing and accumulation of bad loans may be too serious relative to the cost of restricting finance opportunities to enterprises.

Transition to hard budget

Kornai (1995) illustrates the transition from the 'soft to 'hard' budget using survey data, where Hungarian firms were asked to state what were the main barriers they faced to an increase in production. Figure 5.4 plots Kornai's data on the graph showing the category of firms pointing to the given obstacle (the answers may sum to more than 100 per cent, due to multiple choices).

The survey identified six categories of barriers. Four are characteristic of quantitative constraints on the supply side (shortage of materials and labour, the typical command economy phenomena that we discussed in Chapters 1 and 2) and two are constraints that are more typical for the market economy: consumer demand and finance. There is a striking time

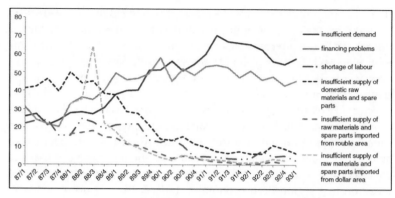

Figure 5.4 Impediments to production, Hungarian survey, 1987–93

Source: Kornai (1995, Table 4).

pattern, where all the quantitative, supply-side constraints become marginal while demand and finance become most important about the same time.

In general, quantitative constraints and 'soft' finance are two sides of the same coin. Where the financial barrier does not hold, the economy falls back on the more fundamental quantitative constraints, where shortages replace the price coordination mechanism. The financial constraint is restored by the liberalization process: companies compete for revenues from consumers and finance from external investors.

Another interesting indicator comes from Berg (1994), who compares profits (1) before and (2) after taxes and subsidies for the 500 largest enterprises in Poland. The simple correlation between the profits before and after taxes and subsidies in 1987 was zero. It had increased to 0.38 in 1989, after the first elements of reform had been introduced. In 1991, one year into the full transition programme, it had increased further, to 0.71. The link between the cash flow generated from sales and the final financial position of companies broken under old regime – was restored by the transition programme. One should note however that both examples come from countries, where reform processes were relatively consistent. We cannot imply similar consistency in reforming with respect to other countries.

Concluding remarks: Soft budget and the global financial crisis

A mark of a good analytical concept is that it can be applied in many settings. While many empirical examples discussed in this chapter are drawn from the transition process and from its early phase, the phenomenon of soft budget is not the thing of the past. A casual inspection of Figure 5.3 demonstrates that subsidization is still commonplace in Central and Eastern Europe. However, as already emphasized, direct subsidization is just one dimension of the soft budget. There are two more that are particularly important at the time of writing that is at time of the global financial crisis.

Firstly, soft budgets on micro level often feed into and result in budget imbalances at macro level. And, while it was not the only factor, the countries that were characterized by most acute budget imbalances prior to the crisis found themselves facing troubles when the global crisis led to a further deterioration of fiscal position (e.g. Hungary, Latvia, Ukraine, albeit to different degree).

Second, while in our examples we focused on manufacturing, with respect to financial crisis it is the banking sector where soft budget becomes the key issue. Over 2008–2009 massive amount of money was offered to the banking sector. Typically, restructuring conditions have been attached to this finance, and at least some of it is expected to be returned back. Yet, with bankruptcies in the financial sector being almost unheard of, the credibility of sponsors remains low. This is exactly the problem illustrated with Figure 5.1 above. Without any credible threat, the risk that (some) banks will behave opportunistically and come back asking for more money is very real.

Therefore, our discussion on soft budget does not finish here. We will come back to it when discussing both to private and to public finance later on.

6
Liberalizations, Partial Liberalizations and Recessions

Recessions examined

In this chapter, we explore the determinants of the post-communist recessions – i.e. the recessions experienced during the 1990s by the 30 countries that emerged from the Soviet bloc. As will be discussed, most of transition theory focuses on the related but different concept of the 'transitional recession' (Kornai 1995) – i.e. the recession following the implementation of the liberalization programme. Transitional recession is often assumed without closer empirical scrutiny, yet actual evidence of it is mixed at best. Accordingly, we will stress that analytical focus on transitional recession is misleading: 'Once one makes allowance for the likelihood that the counter-factual – no reform – produces even worse results in the short run, the consequences of reform actually look pretty good' (Rodrik 1996: 29). This captures the key idea of this chapter: to understand what happened in 1990s we need to compare countries that introduced market reforms with those where the reform process was slow or partial.

Moreover, the empirical estimations that suggests 'J-curve' path of output following the liberalization, or even apparent negative impact of reforms, neglect an important technical point. All reform measures are constructed in such a way that they are restricted from above. Over time, as the countries most advanced in reforms approach this upper limit change is slowing down. This time series pattern in data is easy to detect but neglected by most researchers (with a notable exception of Falcetti *et al.* 2006). It implies that relying either on first difference of reform coefficients or on current and lagged coefficients produces spurious results (Rzońca and Ciżkowicz 2003; Mickiewicz 2005). In essence, where evidence was found suggesting that slower pace of reforms is associated with better results, it neglects the fact that this slower pace produces better performance in the period when there is less to change, as fast reforms were already implemented earlier.

Nevertheless, even if its association with reforms is not clear or more likely just spurious, the post-communist recessions were a real phenomena. At the same time, the differences between the countries are striking. In Poland, the recession was two years long; in neighbouring Ukraine (and in Moldova), it took ten years for economic growth to recover.

The key point is that the timing of recessions did not coincide with the introduction of the core liberalization programme. Out of 27 former command economies in Central Eastern Europe and the FSU, 12 went into recession in 1989, 12 more joined in 1990 and virtually all the post-communist economies were in recession in 1991 (see Table 6.1, below). More importantly, these were not 'transitional' recessions: 25 economies went into recession *before* the stabilization or liberalization programmes had been implemented. The only two exceptions were Hungary and Poland. In Hungary, GDP growth reported for 1989 was close to zero (i.e. 0.4 per cent). The stabilization programme was introduced in March 1990 and the economy went into recession in the same year. However, the level of liberalization corresponding to the Polish reforms of 1990 was reached in Hungary only two years after the recession started (i.e. in 1992).[1] That leaves us with Poland as the only example where the beginning of the recession coincided with introduction of the full liberalization and stabilization programmes. Indeed, in 1989, Polish GDP seemed still to be growing at a rate of 2.8 per cent,[2] albeit inflation was soaring and it is disputable how long the growth could last. The stabilization and liberalization programmes were introduced in January 1990, and the economy immediately went into recession, which lasted for just over two years: as it turned out later, the shortest period as compared with any other transition economy. This account is intended to reiterate what was already discussed in Chapter 2. The command economies were already in crisis in the late 1980s. The liberalization introduced in early 1990s was a response to this crisis. Still, the nature of this response differed, and which policies were chosen had clear impact on subsequent economic performance.

In the next section, we shall consider theoretical explanations for the link between systemic reforms and the output path. In the subsequent section, we wish to focus on the empirical analysis: which set of factors explains the length and depth of recessions experienced by the group of post-command economy countries ('post-communist' recessions)? As will be argued, it is not transition and stabilization but the absence of them

Table 6.1 Timing of recession, liberalization and stabilization programmes

Country	Liberal-ization date	Stabil-ization programme date	Beginning of recession	Last year of recession	Length of recession	Lowest output/ 1989 value
Central Europe and South Eastern Europe						
Albania	1993	1992	1990	1992	3	0.604
Bosnia	1998	1997	1989	1994	6	0.120
Bulgaria	1994	1997	1990	1997	8	0.632
Croatia	1991	1993	1989	1993	5	0.595
Czech Republic	1991	1991	1990	1992	3	0.846
Estonia	1993	1992	1989	1994	6	0.608
FYR Macedonia	1991	1994	1989	1995	7	0.551
Hungary	1992	1990	1990	1993	4	0.819
Latvia	1993	1992	1991	1995	5	0.510
Lithuania	1993	1992	1990	1994	5	0.533
Poland	1990	1990	1990	1991	2	0.822
Romania	1994	1993	1989	1992	4	0.750
Serbia	2001	1993	1989	1993	5	0.400
Slovakia	1991	1991	1990	1993	4	0.750
Slovenia	1991	1992	1989	1992	4	0.820
Commonwealth of Independent States						
Armenia	1996	1994	1990	1993	4	0.310
Azerbaijan	1998	1995	1989	1995	7	0.370
Belarus	not yet	1994	1990	1995	6	0.627
Georgia	1996	1994	1989	1994	6	0.254
Kazakhstan	1995	1994	1989	1995	7	0.612
Kyrgyzstan	1994	1993	1991	1995	5	0.504
Moldova	1995	1993	1990	1999	10	0.317
Russia	1993	1995	1990	1998	9	0.553
Tajikistan	2000	1995	1989	1996	8	0.392
Turkmenistan	not yet	1997	1989	1997	9	0.420
Ukraine	1996	1994	1990	1999	10	0.365
Uzbekistan	not yet	1994	1991	1995	5	0.834

Notes:
(i)   Liberalization: year when the average of the three EBRD liberalization indicators (price liberalization, external liberalization and small privatization) takes value of 3 or higher (with price liberalization indicator based on pre-2003 EBRD definition, adjusted where necessary to preserve compatibility). *Source*: EBRD (1995–2004) and Falcetti *et al.* (2002).
(ii) Stabilization: year when successful stabilization programme was introduced (i.e. for countries with recurring high inflation episodes, the second date is reported; example: Bulgaria). *Source*: EBRD (1999–2004).
(iii) Timing of recession: based on EBRD (1995–2004) and World Bank, World Development Indicators (2001 dataset).
(iv) Lowest value of output (depth of recession): based on EBRD (1995–2004).
(v)   At time of writing, Georgia is no longer a member of CIS.

that imposed the most serious economic costs on the group of countries we consider.

The theoretical literature on 'transitional recession': Impact of full versus partial reforms

As already discussed, empirical evidence that suggests liberalization triggered the 'transitional recession' is far from obvious. Yet liberalization introduced dramatic changes in the economic environment and therefore did affect performance. The positive effects of liberalization were implicit in our discussion of Chapter 2; while the command economy systems were ailing, dismantling them was an obvious recommendation. Reintroducing economic freedom led to stronger incentives and better use of dispersed knowledge by economic actors. That in turn was associated with better performance. In contrast 'transition recession' literature seeks to focus on potential short-term costs of reforms. And even if the empirical link between liberalization and fall in output may be spurious resulting from specification errors, this still does not prove that those negative effects were not present. What could happen in fact is that positive effects of liberalization were to some extent initially counterbalanced by the short-term negative effects. This complex, multidimensional nature of how reforms worked is difficult to disentangle. But the exercise is fruitful. What we will argue as a conclusion of this chapter is that while the 'transitional recession' models make claims which seem too bold, they are particularly useful in helping us to understand what happened under partial reforms conditions, when negative short-term effects are strong and positive effects are weak, producing a negative net balance.

Coming back to distinctions we introduced in Chapter 3, liberalization could be introduced immediately and also had much faster impact. In contrast, second stage institutional reforms took more time. The concept of partial reforms relate to either a situation where liberalization was partial, or liberalization was introduced, yet second stage reforms did not follow in due time. Moreover, the expectations matter as well. What counts for the behaviour of economic actors is not only the implementation of reforms but also an expectation that those reforms will be introduced. This may already trigger a positive change in behaviour. For instance, as we will discuss later on, it is expectation of privatization that may already affect the behaviour of managers of state firms in a positive way.

Before discussing the theories of 'transitional recessions', it is worth noting two additional themes which feature in the literature.

First, stabilization (disinflation) typically brings positive not negative effects (Rodrik 1996); a corollary of this is that high inflation or hyperinflation distorts economic environment and is associated with output loss. It is only some specific types of stabilization programmes that may have a temporary negative impact on GDP growth, for instance when the programme aims at fast disinflation combined with fixed exchange rate (Christoffersen and Doyle 2000). Here, the experience of the transition economies does not differ from that of other middle-income market economies, Latin America in particular. The transition countries inherited monetary overhangs resulting from initial price controls, which implies that liberalization could result in a one-off price jump which could trigger a policy response in the form of stabilization programmes. While the macro disequilibria to be addressed were deeply rooted, yet regardless of those initial conditions, the stabilization programmes were qualitatively not very different from those applied in any other market-type economy. Thus, generally, it is not in macro policy where the transition experience has some unique features.

Secondly, the foreign trade shock was real, but should not be related to individual liberalization programmes. The disappearance of trade structures coordinated by the Soviet Council of Mutual Economic Assistance (CMEA) and the disruption of intra-Soviet trade within the FSU (15 out of the 30 transition countries were Soviet republics in 1989) led to trade shocks. This explanation is consistent with the empirical results: the more within-Soviet-bloc-trade-dependent countries were more affected by recessions (Christoffersen and Doyle 2000). A possible link to liberalization is that the old administrative foreign trade links were disrupted before they could be substituted by new ones based on international market mechanisms. However, there are two problems with this line of argument. First, the effects appeared regardless of liberalization in a given country – it was sufficient that the neighbouring countries liberalized. And, secondly, a more important effect is not that the old coordinating mechanism was replaced by market structures. In fact, trade openness was associated with better trade and output performance, as exemplified by Estonia and several other CE countries. The problem was rather that the old coordinating mechanism was not replaced by international market arrangements but by new set of barriers and inefficient exchange rate mechanisms, in particular in the CIS countries (see Gros and Steinherr 2004). This is an example of partial reform issue, and should not be discussed as an impact of a (coherent) liberalization programme.

This leaves us with theories of 'transitional' recessions that may be grouped under two main headings, although they may be seen more as complementary than as alternatives:

(1) Shocks in relative prices,
(2) Disorganization.

We will discuss both in turn.

Shocks in relative prices

Shocks in relative prices are typically exemplified by two channels. The first relates to the elimination of the 'soft' budget constraint, i.e. introducing 'hard' credits and the reduction/elimination of budgetary subsidies to enterprises (see previous chapter), which results in a different set of producer prices (Blanchard 1997).

The second relates to the effect of price liberalization: the shift of prices of energy (and energy-intensive products) towards world prices (even if energy prices were not liberalized fully, prices were at least partially adjusted upwards) (McKinnon 1993).

There are two possible mechanisms linking a change in producer prices with recession. First, financial market imperfections may imply that firms with good projects have no resources to expand quickly, while firms with bad projects are immediately hit and reduce output. Recession follows (Calvo and Coricelli 1992). Secondly, firms hit by price shocks are unable to adjust their labour costs downwards. A reduction in both employment and production follows (Blanchard 1997).

Let us start with the latter. In Blanchard's (1997) version, the theoretical model (under the name of 'reallocation') relies on labour market mechanisms, not on financial sector imperfections. It makes a distinction between those firms which lost out from the shift in relative prices, and those which gained. In the first category we find firms that were subsidized under the old system, in the second those which had to pay the cost of it in terms of higher taxes. The losers (the 'old' sector) may be identified with the state sector, and the gainers with the new private sector or with firms restructured after privatization (the 'new' sector). Alternative categorizations are possible: the 'old-sector' label may be attributed to firms controlled by insiders (both 'old' state and privatized to insiders) and the 'new sector' label to firms where either outsiders or owners-managers (entrepreneurs in the case of small firms) are in control.

The key economic distinction relates to the fact that the 'new' sector is more productive – in Blanchard's model, the quality of a representative consumer good produced is higher. In contrast, the old equilibrium, where firms producing lower quality could carry on unhindered was supported by fiscal distortions (subsidies and taxes) and resulting price distortions.

Elimination of fiscal intervention makes the prices of the goods produced by both sectors equal, and the consumer demand shifts towards the 'new' sector due to the positive quality differential. If wages in the 'old' sector adjust downwards, there are no negative effects on employment and production, otherwise the transition leads to an initial increase in unemployment and a slump in production.

In Calvo and Coricelli's version (1992, 1993) companies face a shift in costs resulting either from the removal of subsidies or the higher prices of energy-related products. 'Bad' firms (those for which command economy distortions were favourable) are hit immediately and reduce production while good firms cannot adjust quickly, as they face credit constraints (and investment processes take time). A recession follows:

> Over time, firms can accumulate monetary balances and converge to the optimal level of output that would have been reached in the presence of perfect credit markets. Accordingly, the implied behaviour of output would follow a U-shaped pattern. An implication of this view is that output decline should be accompanied by a decline in productivity. Moreover, real wages would drop as well, as enterprises attempt to generate liquidity to purchase inputs. (Campos and Coricelli 2002: 820)

There is thus a direct link between credit market and labour market explanations, as from the finance perspective, lower wages can be seen as substituting for external credit. However, Blanchard's model imposes stronger labour market rigidity assumptions than Calvo and Coricelli's model. In the latter, not only wages can adjust downwards, but in fact this is to be expected along the lines quoted above: the credit constraint implies that it is in the interest not only of producers of 'bad' products, but also of 'good' producers to cut wages temporarily. However, wages can neither go down to zero nor become negative (so that firms could borrow from their employees). Workers are restricted by their access to credit and by their risk preference, and have some non-negative reservation wage. There are thus limits as to how far the internal finance can be generated by a drop in real wages.[3] That explains why firms producing 'good' products cannot accumulate the financial resources quickly enough to expand production. However, the recession also results from the fact that wages in firms producing 'bad' products cannot cut wages deeply enough to match the impact of the slump in product prices, and the latter effect is parallel to Blanchard's model.

With the benefit of hindsight, what can we say about the empirical explanatory power of these two 'transitional recession' models? The first issue to consider is wage flexibility. Contrary to some expectations, wages turned out to be flexible downwards, at least during the 'transitional recessions' (we will return to it when discussing labour markets). This is consistent with the model stressing financial constraints and inconsistent with the model stressing labour market rigidities.

However, additional theoretical insights may be gained from a reference to the labour-controlled model of enterprise, of which state firms at the onset of transition would be a clear example: with dismantling of the old command economy administration, state firms were left without effective control neither from above, nor from outside owners, that is with full insiders' control. A standard expected result here is that while employment is less flexible in insiders-controlled firms, wages may in fact be more flexible, including the recession period. Theoretical support for wage flexibility in insiders-controlled firms comes from several arguments.

First line of reasoning hinges on the impossibility of a complete inter-temporal contract between owners (or managers) and employees in private firms. In the latter, workers may be unwilling to accept wage cuts because they cannot be guaranteed to participate in future rents resulting from a successful restructuring. The problem may be easier to overcome in worker-owned companies.

Secondly, insider ownership may be seen as equivalent to the 'efficient contract' solution, where not only wages but also employment is taken into account in firms' optimization decisions and the employment effects of higher wages are taken into account, in contrast to no-coordination, 'right to manage' models.

The third argument, which highlights a counterbalancing negative effect, however, is that the worker may discount the future gains more than the private investor, and therefore may opt for higher wages now at the cost of future gains, as they are credit constrained. This, again, assumes imperfect financial markets, demonstrating how strong the link is between the finance and labour perspectives.

Wage flexibility turned out to be high in the initial period of transition, either due to financial reasons (as presented by Campos and Coricelli

2002), or due to the implications of effective employee control in the state sector.[4]

Additional empirical support for financial explanations of the 'transitional recession' comes from the well-documented fact that underdeveloped financial intermediation is one of the most characteristic features distinguishing the transition economies from others (Gros and Suhrcke 2000; Gros and Steinherr 2004). We shall discuss finance in more detail later on. Yet from this perspective again the theory discussed here is not necessary a theory of a (uniform) 'transitional recession'. Rather, this is a theory of partial reforms, that is, where liberalization is introduced without the financial sector reforms; the latter would lead to better targeted and more accessible finance.

Disorganization

The second model (disorganization) has been presented by Blanchard and Kremer (1997) and Blanchard (1997) in two related versions, describing either a representative production chain or a representative firm facing a number of suppliers. In both cases, previous to liberalization, coordination was imposed by the economic administration of the command economy system. Liberalization leads to outside opportunities being open to all parties involved. The possible inefficiency results from the fact that the suppliers and purchasers of intermediate products have to negotiate prices. Bargaining under informational asymmetries may lead to inefficient outcomes, where efficient links are broken, as the suppliers may chose alternative trade partners even if the real opportunity cost exceeds the benefit. The output fall is more likely in industries with a large number of rigid connections between producers of intermediate goods. This empirical prediction is confirmed by Blanchard and Kremer (1997).

The details of their model are as follows. A good is produced according to a Leontief technology (i.e. there is no substitution between factors) and requires n steps of production (or distribution). One unit of the primary good leads – after the n steps – to one unit of the final good. Along the production process, intermediate goods have a value of zero. The price of the final good is normalized to one.

With liberalization, the supplier of the primary good has now an alternative use for the input; value of this option is equal to c. Similarly, along the production chain, movement of the intermediate product is no longer decided by planning administration: the end of central planning leaves firms with n bargaining problems: there is bargaining at each step over price; we assume that this bargaining results in an equal division of the surplus from the match (a simplification, which is not essential for the results).

Solution of this new coordination problem is obtained by working backward from the last stage. The value of the surplus in the last bargaining problem, to be shared between the final producer and the next-to-last intermediate producer, is equal to 1 (by assumption, the partly-processed good is useless before the final stage, so the value jumps from 0 to 1). Without making any assumptions about a corresponding bargaining strength, we arrive at a simple Nash outcome, where the surplus is shared in equal proportion, which implies that the next-to-last intermediate producer receives 1/2. Solving recursively along the production chain with n producers, the first intermediate producer receives $(1/2)^n$. Thus, the surplus to be divided between the first intermediate producer and the supplier of the primary good is equal to $(1/2)^n - c$.

If $c < (1/2)^n$, the surplus is positive and production takes place along the chain. If instead $c > (1/2)^n$, the primary producer prefers to use the outside option. In this case, the decrease in total output resulting from the breakdown of the production chain may be as large as $1 - (1/2)^n$ (this maximum fall is for $c = (1/2)^n$ when the first supplier breaks the production chain). Moreover, the more complex the structure of production (the higher n), the smaller the private opportunities needed to trigger the collapse of the production chain.

Thus, the (temporary) collapse in output is due to the combination of two factors:

(1) the improvement in outside opportunities, and
(2) the loss of coercive power by the government.

The model is illustrated by Figure 6.1 below.

To assess the model, the first thing is to consider the empirical evidence provided by these authors. Based on input-output tables for nine tran-

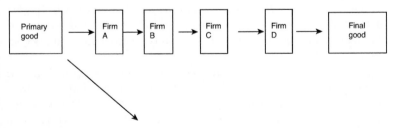

Figure 6.1 Blanchard-Kremer model

sition economies, Blanchard and Kremer construct an index of complexity of production structures and find that it correlates with recession, controlling for an appropriate set of other variables. However, the problem with the estimations provided by Blanchard and Kremer (1997) is that we are unable to distinguish between the effects of full liberalization and those of some partial reforms. In fact, their sample (Albania, Armenia, Azerbaijan, Belarus, Georgia, Kyrgyzstan, Macedonia, Moldova, Russia) relates to economies which were not in the group of 'fast reformers' at the time the data was collected.

Indeed, Blanchard and Kremer (1997) note the difference between the group of countries in the dataset used for econometric estimations and the CE economies. They present additional OECD data showing that shortages of materials were no longer the major constraint for producers in Central Europe (the Czech Republic, Hungary, Poland) in contrast to economies such as Bulgaria, or Russia which still experienced serious problems.

However, their provisional explanation is that the differences between the two groups of countries result from initial conditions, not from differences in economic policies and reforms. The two initial conditions they mention relate to the degree of centralization in industrial structures and enterprises (and therefore more specialization leading to the negative impact of disorganization) and to the further distance to the main EU markets and volume of trade, which decrease a possibility to alleviate the problems of specificity (1997: 1122).

The first argument (centralization) may be valid, the second (trade links) seems to be partly invalid, as will also be confirmed by the estimates reported in the next section: more open economies suffered more not less from recessions – initially, the negative effect of breaking the existing trade links was stronger than the positive effect of overcoming specificity. More importantly, however, it is not the difference in initial conditions but in the timing of the basic set of liberalization measures and stabilization that may be the key dimension explaining the post-communist recessions. From the SUR regression we will reported later, we may see that early introduction of full liberalization was linked to a shallower output slump (with the estimated difference being 13 per cent of the 1989 GDP value).

All this does not invalidate the Blanchard and Kremer (1997) model; it may suggest, however, that instead of being a general model of 'transitional recession' it may in fact be a more narrow model of disorganization under partial liberalization conditions. There are two possible lines of argument here.

First, one may note that liberalization accompanied by private sector growth has two dimensions. The first is that the set of available transactions for existing suppliers expands, which may lead to a breakdown of existing production chains and decrease in the old sector output and recession, along the lines discussed above. The second effect, however, is the creation of new suppliers, which is likely to work the other way round: the increase in the number of suppliers is likely to decrease specificity and hold-up problems, provide alternative opportunities for producers and thus increase output. In fact, Blanchard and Kremer (1997) note a major important channel that may operate in this way – i.e. the availability of external options provided by foreign trade. However, the issue links more to liberalization than to initial conditions. While initial trade dependence had a negative effect (the breaking down of old links), it is trade liberalization and openness which led to new connections being established in place of old ones. More generally, to the extent that the entry of new suppliers takes time, the first (negative) dimension could still dominate early in the transition; the second, however, may prevail later on (provided there is sufficient freedom of entry). From this perspective, the recovery is created not just by the efficient completion of the search and bargaining process aimed at the new equilibrium set of prices, but also – or even more importantly – by the entry of new suppliers.

A second argument which would link the model to incomplete liberalization is slightly different. Some prices along the production chain may be still controlled, while freedom of contract may be introduced early. That makes outside options more attractive – in other words, the disrupting effect of partial liberalization of prices may be more serious than that of full liberalization. For that reason, incomplete liberalization may lead to the outcomes that a combination of selective price controls and new outside options (including in the 'underground' economy) leads to long-lasting disruption. A good example of that may be the situation which developed in the CIS area with underpriced energy coupled with inadequate control over the sale decisions of enterprises, including illegal exports (see Gros and Steinherr 2004).

In general, it is likely that the disorganization mechanism was one of the sources of post-communist recessions, but its serious negative effects apply to the case of partial liberalizations and incomplete transitions.

Empirical results: Initial conditions, wars, stabilization, liberalization and the slump in output

The empirical literature

The lesson emerging from the empirical literature on economic growth in the region is that both transitional reform and stabilization was conducive to economic growth. At the same time, the reforms could result in J-curve short-term output paths, as did some (but not all) types of stabilization policies. At the same time, as already mentioned, J-curve result may be driven by ignoring the time-series dimension of the data (Rzońca and Ciżkowicz 2003; Mickiewicz 2005; Falcetti *et al.* 2006).

Econometric evidence on the output response to reforms can be found in seven published studies on economic growth in the region based on panel data: Loungani and Sheets (1997), Selowsky and Martin (1997), Christoffersen and Doyle (2000), De Melo *et al.* (2001), Falcetti, Raiser and Sanfey (2002), Havrylyshyn and van Rooden (2003) and Merlevede (2003). All these studies are consistent in finding that the overall impact of reform on economic growth (as measured by EBRD indicators) is positive.

The second set of results relates to the link between macroeconomic stabilization and output. In the studies quoted above, empirical results show that macroeconomic instability (measured as either high inflation or a low (negative) government budget balance) affects growth negatively. There is no indication of a short-term positive correlation between inflation and growth (and of a negative impact of disinflation on growth). Campos and Corricelli (2002) summarize the existing evidence in the light of theoretical insights, noting that:

> based on the experience of programmes implemented in developing market economies, stabilization *per se* should not have caused a sharp fall in output. (Campos and Coricelli 2002: 819)

All this evidence still does not exclude the possibility that some types of stabilization programmes could have had a negative impact on growth. As far as we know, the only published econometric evidence on the impact of stabilization programmes which distinguishes between different types and is based on a cross-country panel of transition economies comes from Christoffersen and Doyle (2000). They did not find any systematic, general impact of stabilization on output (other than a positive one via disinflation). This can be easily corroborated by the evidence provided in Table 6.1 above. The only two countries where the beginning of recession coincided with stabilization were again Hungary and Poland. However, Christoffersen and Doyle (2000) found one significant effect: where sharp disinflation (inflation more than halved in one year) was implemented under the presence of a pegged exchange rate regime, the policy had a negative effect on growth. Even in this case, however, the longer-run impact of these programmes should be positive, as short-term negative effects may be counterbalanced by the subsequent positive effect of macroeconomic stabilization on growth.

While panel estimations offer powerful econometric tools, there are less suited to capture the longer-term impact of institutional change. In this respect, it may be useful to follow the empirical tradition established by studies on economic growth based on non-transition samples, where initial institutions and policies are used to explain a subsequent average growth rates taken over a longer period of time (Sala-i-Martin *et al.* 2004). The results we report below are based on similar design.

Explaining recessions: Empirical results

We intend to look for a possible set of factors that can explain the recessions experienced by the post-communist economies during the 1990s. There is more than one way of measuring the economic cost of recession. Moreover, the presence of serious measurement errors (Åslund 2001) calls for the use of a battery of alternative indicators to check the robustness of results. We propose to focus on four alternative measures:

- The first is the depth of the recession, as measured by the ratio of the lowest value of output to its 1989 value. For most countries, the indicator was provided directly by the EBRD (1999, Table 3.1: 63); however, here it was verified for the two countries which were still in recession in 1999 (Ukraine and Moldova) and supplemented for the missing countries (Bosnia and Hercegovina, Serbia and Montenegro) using EBRD and World Bank statistics. The indicator shows that the recession had been most shallow in the Czech Republic and the most dramatic in war-torn Bosnia and Hercegovina.
- The second relates to the length of recession. Here, the range of outcomes varies between two years for Poland and ten years for neighbouring Ukraine and also Moldova.
- The third is a close correlate. Instead of length, it measures the time span between 1989 and the exit from recession. Thus, while the former measure shows lower values for countries that entered recession later, the latter is defined by the timing of the final entry on the

post-communist positive growth path. The indicator can be easily computed from the fifth column of Table 6.1 above. It has some advantage over the previous one, if we take into account that the early output statistics may be more problematic for some of the transition economies while in contrast there is little measurement error related to timing of exit from recession.

- Finally, the fourth is a crude proxy for the overall *cost of the recession*, as measured by a combination of both depth and length. It is calculated as a product of the depth of output slump at the lowest point and the length of the recession.[5]

The set of explanatory variables used is based on information provided in Tables 6.1 and 6.2 (below).

We follow the existing research tradition, where the timing of the beginning of a transition is interpreted as equivalent to the introduction of some basic set of liberalization measures. This approach is used in De Melo *et al.* (2001), Falcetti, Raiser and Sanfey (2002) and Merlevede (2003), where the time dimension is adjusted taking the starting point to be when the basic set of liberalization measures was implemented. A similar approach is presented by Blanchard (1997). The most explicit discussion of measurement and empirical applications of the threshold level of reforms can be found in earlier work by De Melo and Gelb (1997). We follow this tradition, additionally motivated by our own results in Chapter 3, where PCA resulted in reforms split along two latent dimensions: liberalization and second stage institutional reforms. However, for the sake of comparability, instead of a latent variable we opt for a measure used in the empirical studies discussed above and based on the same set of indicators; namely on a simple average of the three EBRD indicators, measuring (1) Internal price liberalization, (2) External liberalization and (3) Small-scale privatization and freedom of entry. The 'liberalization threshold' is defined as the time when this average reaches 3 (which is equivalent to the Polish score in 1990). The data comes from Falcetti, Raiser and Sanfey (2002) and EBRD (1994–2005), taking into account the fact that the price liberalization indicator was re-defined by the EBRD from 2003 onwards, with new value of 4 being equivalent to the old value of 3 (we rely on the old definition). One may note that, using this criterion, at the time of writing there is no liberalization in Belarus, Turkmenistan and Uzbekistan. The EBRD indicators cover second stage institutional reforms as well. However, unlike liberalization, these were spread over a longer period of time. Moreover, the theoretical arguments linking output slumps with reforms discussed above relate to components of liberalization.

Table 6.2 Recession: More explanatory variables

Country	War	Years under commun- ism	Rich resource base	Repressed inflation 1987– 1989	Black market exchange rate premium 1990 (%)	Trade depend- ence 1990 (%)	Formerly part of federa- tion (USSR, Yugo- slavia, CSSR)
Central Europe and South Eastern Europe							
Albania	0	45	0	4.3	434	6.6	0
Bosnia	1	44	0	12	27	6	0
Bulgaria	0	43	0	18	981	16.1	0
Croatia	1	44	0	12	27	6	1
Czech Republic	0	43	0	–7.1	185	6	1
Estonia	0	51	0	25.7	1828	30.2	1
FYR Macedonia	0	44	0	12	27	6	1
Hungary	0	41	0	–7.7	46.7	13.7	0
Latvia	0	51	0	25.7	1828	36.7	1
Lithuania	0	51	0	25.7	1828	40.9	1
Poland	0	42	1	13.6	277	8.4	0
Romania	0	43	1	16.8	728	3.7	0
Serbia	1	44	0	12	27	6	1
Slovakia	0	43	0	–7.1	185	6	1
Slovenia	0	44	0	12	27	4	1
Commonwealth of Independent States							
Armenia	1	74	0	25.7	1828	25.6	1
Azerbaijan	1	75	2	25.7	1828	29.8	1
Belarus	0	75	0	25.7	1828	41	1
Georgia	1	70	0	25.7	1828	24.8	1
Kazakhstan	0	75	2	25.7	1828	20.8	1
Kyrgyzstan	0	75	0	25.7	1828	27.7	1
Moldova	1	52	0	25.7	1828	28.9	1
Russia	1	74	2	25.7	1828	11.1	1
Tajikistan	1	75	0	25.7	1828	31	1
Turkmenistan	0	75	2	25.7	1828	33	1
Ukraine	0	75	1	25.7	1828	23.8	1
Uzbekistan	0	75	1	25.7	1828	25.5	1

Notes:
(i)   War: a military conflict, either internal or with neighbouring countries (based on author's assessment)
(ii) Number of years a country spent under communism and indicator of rich resource base: both based on Fisher and Sahay (2000).
(iii) Black market exchange rate premium and trade dependence, both based on De Melo *et al.* (1997).
(iv) Trade dependence defined as average of exports and imports divided by GDP.
(v)   CSSR – Czechoslovak Socialist Republic.

Stabilization dates are taken from EBRD (1999). However in a few cases, where repeated attempts at stabilizations were undertaken (i.e. the first programme was unsuccessful), the date of the latest programme is used.

The timing of both liberalization and stabilization programmes is measured in the following way. In both cases, we divided the observations roughly into two halves, creating dummy variables which represent 'early' and 'late' implementation of the liberalization and stabilization programmes, respectively. The resulting cut-off point divides stabilization programmes into those introduced in 1992 or earlier and those implemented after 1992. For liberalization, the corresponding year is 1994. Our motivation in constructing the variables this way is to minimize the problem of endogeneity of reforms. We intend to explore how the early implementation of liberalization and stabilization measures affected recessions over the long term. In contrast, any measure based on subsequent paths of reform may be endogenous – i.e. affected by economic growth.

Next, we have a set of variables corresponding to the initial conditions.[6] First, we have 'War' indicator, which relates either to internal or external conflict in the initial period of transition. 'Years under communism' is an indicator based on the assumption that the longer the time span under the old regime, the more distortions were introduced and the more difficult would be the return to a market economy. With this measure, some degree of arbitrariness is unavoidable; for consistency, we follow figures by Fischer and Sahay (2000), being fully aware that there may be reason to modify some of their entries. The next measure – an indicator of the rich (natural) resource base – is also based on the same source, but measurement appears less problematic. The next three indicators of initial conditions are based on De Melo *et al.* (1997). The first two are measures of repressed inflation and the 'black market' exchange premium at the onset of reforms. Unfortunately, these cannot distinguish between half of the observations in our sample – i.e. the reported value is exactly the same for the 15 countries emerging from the FSU. For this reason, both measures may be strongly correlated with some other omitted variables and therefore remain problematic. The third indicator – a measure of trade dependence on other command economies – is better in this respect, as it distinguishes between the former Soviet republics based on data on intra-Soviet trade.

Finally, we wish to explore if formerly being in a federation counts; the corresponding indicator takes a value of one for countries emerging from Czechoslovakia, the Soviet Union and Yugoslavia, and zero otherwise. We also investigate if the narrower dummy, for the CIS only, captures any specific influences.

Results

Most of the indicators correlate with recession measures with the expected sign. The strongest effect links war with the depth of recession (correlation between the war dummy and the lowest/1989 output ratio is –67 per cent).[7] Similarly, both time spent under communism and inherited disequilibrium (repressed inflation, 'black market' exchange rate premium) correlate well with recession. Initial trade dependency made things worse, as more open economies were more exposed to the initial disruptions in trade. Being in a federation does not have such a clear impact on recessions, due to the fact that the indicator includes three successful economies: the Czech Republic, Slovakia and Slovenia. Being a CIS country, on the other hand, is significantly linked with recession. Possibly the most interesting results relate to the timing of liberalization and stabilization programmes. First, the time discrepancy between stabilization and liberalization correlates with the recession indicators. When we take the absolute value of the time difference between the stabilization and liberalization programmes, and correlate it with the lowest/1989 ratio of output, the correlation coefficient is –29 per cent. However, the effect is dominated by simple measures of the timing of both programmes. The correlation coefficient between early stabilization (as defined above) and the lowest/1989 ratio of output is a hefty 54 per cent; for early liberalization it is almost the same, at 53 per cent. The unambiguous result is that the early introduction of both liberalization and stabilization programmes correlates with less serious recession.

Things become more challenging, however, as soon as we move from bivariate correlations to multivariate regression models. The sample is small, and does not allow for models with a larger number of variables. Moreover, results are sensitive to specification due to multicollinearity. What emerges from the regression analysis is that war remains a single variable with a clear and robust impact on the depth of recession and therefore on the overall cost of recession, but not on the length of recession. Next in the ranking come three factors: timing of stabilization, timing of liberalization and initial trade dependence. However, here multicollinearity between liberalization and stabilization measures becomes a problem. While, when measured by simple correlation, the link between the timing of liberalization and recession was almost as strong as the link between the timing of stabilization and recession, as soon as we move to the multivariate regression settings the effect of early liberalization becomes dominated by early stabilization.

Why is the positive impact of early stabilization so strong? Delay in successful stabilization programmes was typically itself an indicator of the more fundamental problems with the fiscal side – i.e. problems with tax collection, tax structure and control over public expenditures. All these reflect the most important aspects of inadequate institutional reforms, an issue to which we shall return in more detail when discussing public finance. One may also note that those issues are not captured by the EBRD indicators of institutional reforms, as those do not cover fiscal issues (apart from one important dimension, we already discussed i.e. the 'soft' budget constraints for firms). Our result on importance of macro-economic stabilization is in line with Rodrik (1996) who strongly argues that fiscal imbalances (and exchange rate distortions) are key dimensions affecting long-term economic performance. At time of writing, the importance of this dimension is confirmed again in the context of global financial crisis.

Table 6.3 below presents regression results. The reported models are only those corresponding to the set of explanatory variables which prove most significant and robust to specification. As mentioned, the effect of timing of liberalization tends to be dominated by other variables for the depth of recession, where the impact of war and initial conditions (initial trade dependence on other command economies) is most critical.

However, as one would expect, initial conditions have a smaller impact on the length of recession, which is clearly dominated by stabilization ((3) and (5) in Table 6.3) and less clearly by liberalization ((4) in Table 6.3). The impact of initial conflicts (war) on the length of recession is highly insignificant (in contrast to its impact on the depth of recession) and the corresponding variable is not included in the reported specifications. Once we combine both dimensions into one proxy of the cost of recession, the timing of both stabilization and liberalization seems to dominate the impact of initial conditions, with the negative impact of war remaining significant.

Generally, early stabilization comes across as the significant predictor associated negatively with both the length and the depth of recession. We did additional checks, constructing a continuous variable representing the exact timing of stabilization, and it worked equally well. Early liberalization also has a positive impact in making a recession shorter, but does not come across as a significant predictor of the depth of recession. In contrast, initial conditions count for the depth of recession, and far

Table 6.3   Determinants of post-communist recessions

Dependent variable / Explanatory variables	Depth of recession: Lowest value of output/1989 value of output		Length of recession in years		Time recession ended relative to 1989 (year of lowest output + 1 − 1989)		Cost of recession; a proxy calculated as: [1 − (lowest output / 1989 output)]* (length of recession)	
	(1)	(2)	(3)	(4)	(5)	(6)	(7)	(8)
Stabilization before 1993 (dummy variable)	.088 (.063)		−2.536*** (.673)		−2.143** (.674)		−1.456* (.623)	
Liberalization before 1995 (dummy variable)		.100 (.065)		−1.576† (.809)		−1.039 (.797)		−1.265† (.672)
Initial trade dependence (def. as in Table 3A.2)	−.005* (.002)	−.004 (.002)	.054* (.026)	.042 (.033)	.072* (.026)	.066† (.032)	.049* (.021)	.036 (.024)
War dummy (def. as in Table 3A.2)	−.236*** (.062)	−.229** (.062)					1.350* (.618)	1.437* (.649)
Constant	.699*** (.063)	.648*** (.084)	5.618*** (.655)	5.891*** (.98)	5.819*** (.656)	5.796*** (.97)	1.907** (.632)	2.346* (.877)
Number of observations	27	27	27	27	27	27	27	27
F statistics	12.02***	12.37***	10.51***	4.37*	10.16***	4.70*	9.35***	8.21***
R-squared	.611	.617	.467	.267	.459	.282	.550	.517
Adjusted R-squared	.560	.567	.422	.206	.414	.222	.491	.454

Notes:
(i)   estimator: ordinary least squares
(ii) standard errors in parentheses
(iii) significance levels: *** .001; ** .01; * .05; † 0.1.

less for the length of recession. Specifically, the more open a given economy was to its communist trade partners, the more serious was the effect of initial disruption in the trade patterns and contamination coming from neighbouring economies facing their own crises. This effect was particularly serious for smaller post-Soviet Union republics affected by the initial slump in Russia, as demonstrated by Christoffersen and Doyle (2000). Again, the effect of initial trade patterns on the depth of recession is robust and significant. Finally, the last dimension that emerges as a very robust predictor of the depth of recession is the war indicator. It also has a significant impact on the aggregate measure of the cost of recession.

Finally, in Table 6.4 (below), we present an alternative approach, where direct interdependence between the depth and length of recession is taken into account in a seemingly unrelated regression model. In this context, we return to the liberalization indicator, whose significance was slashed due to multicollinearity in the OLS regression models. The specification presented includes indicators of early stabilization, early liberalization and the war dummy. Here, early stabilization seems to

Table 6.4 Determinants of Post-Communist recessions: Seemingly unrelated regression model

Dependent variables / Explanatory variables	Depth of recession: Lowest value of output/1989 value of output	Length of recession in years
Stabilization before 1993 (dummy variable)	.040 (.075)	−2.418* (.989)
Liberalization before 1995 (dummy variable)	.131† (.070)	−.647 (.923)
War dummy (def. as in Table 3A.2)	−.191** (.066)	−.255 (.870)
Constant	.530*** (.055)	7.065*** (.725)
Number of observations	27	27
F statistics	10.42***	4.78**
R-squared	.576	.384

Notes:
(i)   estimator: Zellner's seemingly unrelated regression model
(ii) covariance matrix for the residuals computed with a small sample adjustment
(iii) standard errors in parentheses
(iv) significance levels (for coefficients, based on t-statistics): *** .001; ** .01; * .05; † 0.1
(v) correlation of residuals from the two equations: −.367; $\chi^2(1) = 3.629$†.

make the recession shorter by 2.4 years, and the effect is significant. It has no significant effect on the depth of recession. On the other hand, early liberalization reduces the depth of the slump in output by 13 per cent on average, but has no significant impact on the length of recession. Again, war leads to a more serious slump, but its impact on the length of recession is highly insignificant (with the wrong sign).

To conclude: economies which introduced effective stabilization and liberalization programmes early suffered less from the post-communist recessions. However, the initial conditions were also important. More open, smaller economies suffered more initially, as they were more affected by the initial disruption in trade patterns after the Soviet bloc disintegrated.

And, finally, war is not good for growth. Czechs and Slovaks, who decided to separate without a single shot being fired, did much better than the former Yugoslavia republics (apart from Slovenia) and some of the former Soviet republics.

7
Unemployment

This chapter focuses on unemployment. The first section will discuss unemployment in the transition economies, looking into flows between alternative labour market states. Subsequently, we shall use this approach to summarize the main factors that are likely to affect unemployment levels in the transition economies. Finally, we shall offer a brief overview of the empirical econometric results on the main labour market characteristics of the more narrow group of 'new' EU member states.

The Central and Eastern European (CEE) labour markets have been subject to far-reaching transformation since 1989. The introduction of market principles to the allocation of labour has had positive results, accompanied by negative side-effects, of which unemployment is the most important. The repercussions for the labour markets of the region were initially serious. Dealing with unemployment, poverty and social exclusion for some vulnerable social groups has been one of the most important challenges that emerged after the transition. However, the transition policy-makers were not always able to find a satisfactory solution to all these problems and then to implement them. As a consequence, the majority of the countries of the region were confronted by serious labour market problems reflected in high unemployment figures. In turn, those led to popular dissatisfaction and affected political choices, as voters punished the incumbent governments in elections (Bell, 2001). While unemployment is no longer a serious problem in some of the transition countries, it remains very high in few others (Figure 7.1).

What is striking in Figure 7.1 is that there is no clear-cut association between the degree to which market reforms were implemented and the unemployment level. Two countries which retained many elements of the command economy system (i.e. introduced very limited reforms, see Chapter 3), Uzbekistan and Belarus are characterized by exceptionally

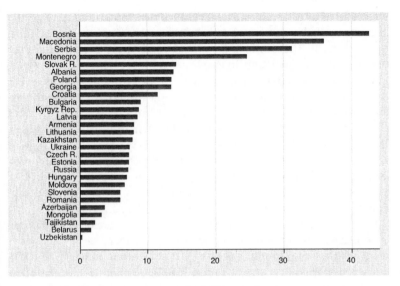

Figure 7.1   Unemployment rates, 2003–2009 averages

Source: EBRD.

low unemployment. However, three Balkan economies where reforms remained very partial, score highest. One could argue that the pattern of unemployment – reform link is non-linear. Lack of reforms is associated with no unemployment (as similarly, there is no unemployment under command economy). In turn, partial, limited reforms produce worst possible outcomes. And finally, under full reforms unemployment goes down. This interpretation would be parallel to our argument in Chapter 6: it was not liberalization but partial liberalization that produced worst results.

However, to understand unemployment we need to look beyond liberalization indicators and investigate also factors, which are more specific to labour markets. This is what we intend to do in this chapter. We will start with the dynamics of unemployment during transition and move to a recent assessment.

'Transitional unemployment' and the flows between labour market states

Unemployment was not easy to avoid and an optimum policy response was difficult to design. The transition/liberalization programmes in the region were introduced as a response to the economic crisis and the meltdown of the command economy system. Reforms led to enormous shifts in the production structures of these countries and to corresponding adjustments in employment.

Moreover, the systemic features of all these economies implied that at the initial starting point (typically taken as 1989), they were characterized by a significant level of 'labour hoarding' (i.e. employment above the technically efficient level) in their industrial enterprises. Existing estimates of 'labour hoarding' suggested levels in a range of 15–20 per cent for the USSR, 18 per cent for Czechoslovakia and between 20–25 per cent for Poland (see Porket 1984; Brada 1989; Rutkowski 1990, 1995, respectively). Both labour reallocation and 'labour shedding' implied the emergence of high unemployment levels.

Indeed, the countries that implemented a coherent reform programme experienced a faster and more dramatic initial increase in unemployment. With some simplification, this may be exemplified by the difference between the pattern typical for CE economies (i.e. the eight countries from the region which joined the EU in 2004) and that which characterizes the CIS economies. Two South East European (SEE) economies – Bulgaria and Romania – lie in between, as they were characterized by an erratic path of 'stop-go' reforms. The Czech Republic – with a combination of advanced reforms and low unemployment for most of the 1990 – has been an interesting exception, which we will discuss below.

The differences in unemployment correspond to differences in production paths. In the CE economies, implementation of coherent reform programmes led to both a rapid emergence of unemployment and to quicker end of recessions that already started under the communist regimes. Yet, in those countries, the period of recession was relatively short and, following recovery, growth was relatively strong (see previous chapter). In the CIS countries, the recession was more protracted and while the initial increase in unemployment was slower, it rose to levels similar to those observed in CE economies. There is thus no empirical evidence of any sustainable social gains from delaying the reforms.

One should also note that – where implemented – the coherent reform packages not only introduced market liberalization measures but also relatively well-functioning welfare systems. Paradoxically, under the old command economy regimes social welfare systems were underdeveloped, as social benefits were typically associated with employment status, and enterprises performed strong social functions (on this see, for instance, Rein, Friedman and Wörgötter 1997).

Another way of interpreting the slower emergence of unemployment in the CIS countries is to note that where the level of social welfare protection remains inadequate workers may stick to their jobs in spite of dramatic wage decreases and wage arrears. Open unemployment may still therefore be a socially better outcome (Mickiewicz and Bell 2000).

This leads us to a more general question. Given the initial level of labour hoarding (in the region of 20 per cent), why did unemployment not reach that level in transition countries? The mean/median values of unemployment rates in the transition countries remained far closer to 10 per cent than to 20 per cent.

To answer this question it is useful to look at unemployment issues directly from a flow perspective. In accordance with the transition economic literature (Blanchard 1997; Roland 2000), the basic framework splits employment into two categories: the 'old' and the 'new' sector. This distinction may be given more than one empirical interpretation. It may relate to the ownership dimension, where 'old' means state and 'new' means private. Yet in this case a more relevant distinction may relate to the contrast between:

(1) the firms controlled by insiders (including typically state firms at the starting point of transition and also 'insider privatizations') and
(2) those where corporate control was transferred to outsiders (either as a result of privatization or in new companies).

In both cases, the 'new' sector is the one where economic restructuring and adjustment in firms' objectives consistent with a new market environment took place. Apart from ownership, 'new' and 'old' sectors may also be identified in purely structural terms. 'New' (i.e. expanding) sectors are in services and in consumer products while 'old' (shrinking) sectors relate to heavy industry and mining. The distinction is highly correlated with the ownership cross-section: from the very beginning of the transition, the service sector was dominated by private firms, as a result of rapidly implemented 'small privatization' programmes and new start-ups and, on the other hand, the privatization process was slowest in heavy industry and mining so those sectors remained dominated by state companies.

Taking these distinctions into account, the underlying idea of labour market flows during the transition is illustrated by Figure 7.2, where the thickness of the arrows representing flows corresponds to the empirical data on transition countries.

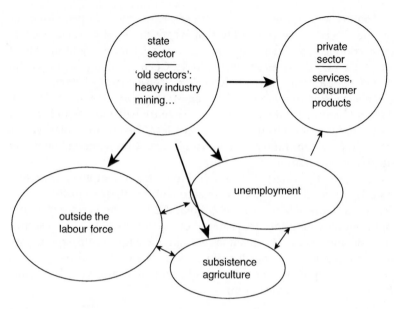

Figure 7.2 Labour market flows during the economic transition

The first explanation of the unemployment rates observed during transition may relate to the speed of inflows into unemployment. In particular, as already mentioned, in slow-reform countries inadequate provision of social welfare-created disincentives to enter unemployment. Workers in the CIS countries preferred to accept a dramatic decrease in wages and face wage arrears rather than quit their jobs. Parallel to that, in slow-reform countries some sections of industry were still operating under 'soft' budget constraints: various fiscal and financial channels were used to support employment in the 'old' (unrestructured) sectors. In the longer run, this policy of postponed restructuring turned out to be self-defeating as the prolonged recession associated with a lack of efficient restructuring and crises in public finance made high employment levels unsustainable (Mickiewicz and Bell 2000).

A parallel explanation relates to the differences in privatization programmes. Unlike Central Europe, the dominant privatization methods applied in the CIS countries, and in Russia in particular, were equivalent to an 'insider privatization'. As is well documented in the employee ownership literature, this form of ownership is typically associated with higher wage flexibility and lower employment flexibility (both downwards and upwards; see also previous chapter). It follows that expected inflows to unemployment are lower.

Another explanation relates to the outflows from employment outside the labour force instead of to unemployment. Some of those flows represent positive social phenomena resulting from adjustment to the new market conditions, but some follow from misguided policies.

In particular, one factor decreasing activity rate, among younger people in particular, relates to inflows into higher education. Under the command system returns to education were low, and so were incentives to study. Liberalization of wage systems led to an increase in relative returns to education and following that, to a significant increase in the number of students. The inflow to education was also partly responding to a mismatch of skills resulting from a change in the economic environment. Programmes in business studies (finance, marketing, management), economics and information technology (IT) experienced the largest increases, responding to a change in the structure of labour demand.

Arguably, a parallel and more general development reflected a 'natural' adjustment in activity rate consistent with preferences, following the dismantling of the command economy system. The argument relies on the fact that the activity rates in Central Europe at the beginning of the transition process were much higher than those in the economies with a similar level of income *per capita* in different parts of the world. The command economy operated in a way which, on the one hand, guaranteed employment but on the other had built-in penalties for those not working. Thus, employment was both a right and an obligation. As mentioned earlier, without employment, access to social benefits was difficult. Moreover, people not in employment could find themselves directly persecuted as social parasites, albeit the official policy became relatively more relaxed in this respect in most countries in the late communist period. Employment and labour was strongly promoted as a key social virtue by official propaganda. Thus, after liberalization, some downward adjustment in activity rate was to be expected: in middle-income countries, the value-added from households' occupations outside formal employment might in some cases be higher as compared with wage earning. Thus, when people became free to choose their lifestyle, some adjustment followed.

Some other outflows into inactivity resulted from questionable policies. A visible decrease in child care provision pushed many women with children outside employment. Yet, generally, women's participation rates remained high in CE countries, thanks to two counterbalancing factors: new employment creation was in services, where female employment is typically higher and last but not least – because of the fact that the women in the region scored highly in terms of educational endowment, quite different to the position in comparator middle-income countries outside Central Europe.

Another channel of outflow into inactivity resulted from a policy which substituted open unemployment with early retirement programmes. The problem with this approach results from rather naïve view of employment as a zero-sum game, where the removal of older people from employment releases jobs for younger people. In fact, the resulting pattern may be a mismatch between the supply of released jobs and the skill and experience characteristics of the labour supply. Arguably, the departure of some skilled older workers might have an overall negative effect on average productivity, creating negative results for employment.

Looking more closely into CE statistics, one can see easily that Slovenia has a very low activity rate in the two oldest working age groups – 55–59 and 60–64 (Figure 7.3). This corresponds to over-reliance on early retirement programmes. Similarly, Hungary is an example of a country where unemployment rates also remains low, but at the cost of a significant decrease in the activity rate and a low employment rate in the oldest age groups. Poland is in even worse position, combining both higher

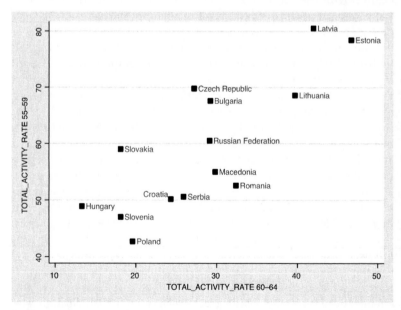

Figure 7.3   Activity rates in the two oldest age groups of the working age population, 2008

Source: International Labour Office.

unemployment rate (Figure 7.1) and low activity rates in oldest age groups (Figure 7.3). We find the three Baltic republics at the other end of the spectrum.

The third explanation of observed unemployment levels below these expected initially relates to inflows into new employment. Job creation in new sectors remained a most efficient channel of suppressing unemployment.

In the sectoral perspective, restructuring by job creation may be defined as job creation consistent with a structural change converging towards the employment structure in high-income EU economies. In this respect, in the second half of the 1990s, Poland was the best performer in Central Europe, followed by Slovenia. Interestingly, fast structural change in that period was also observed in some EU economies. Spain, in particular, scored as highly as Poland on this measure of restructuring by new job creation, in contrast to both Portugal and Greece (for computational details, see Mickiewicz 2003).

The process of job creation was parallel to the rate of creation of new enterprises, where Poland again scored high during the 1990s among other transition countries. The process could be partly fuelled by social attitudes: a cross-country study by Blanchflower, Oswald and Stutzer (2001) found that the willingness to become self-employed in Poland was matched only by Italian respondents (with East Germany and Russia located at the opposite end of the spectrum). Nevertheless, the combination of tax policies, an increase in bureaucratic barriers and the possible impact of macro policies resulted in a considerable slow-down in the dynamics of the Polish entrepreneurship sector around 2000, matched by a considerable increase in unemployment.

The share of self-employment in total employment can be taken as a proxy for the size of the entrepreneurial sector. However, when using this measure we have to control for the size of the agricultural sector, as the two dimensions are closely correlated. It therefore makes sense to compare economies with a similar size of agricultural sector. Both Czech Republic and Slovak Republic have a much larger entrepreneurial sector than Hungary, even if the three economies are characterized by a similar size of agricultural sector. Similarly, Croatia (and to smaller extent Poland) actual size of the entrepreneurial sector may be favourably compared with the expected size entrepreneurial sector based on the size of their agricultural sectors (Figure 7.4).

While discussing inflows into employment, it is important to distinguish between job creation in the new and in the old sectors. The latter relates primarily to (subsistence) agriculture. Jobs created in this sector are

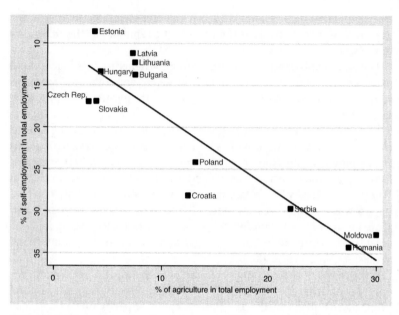

Figure 7.4   The share of self-employment (%) compared with the share of agriculture in employment (%), 2008

Note: The share of self-employment (vertical axis) is interpreted as 100% – share of employees; therefore it consists of employers, own-account workers, members of cooperatives and contributing family workers.

Source: International Labour Office.

only a temporary buffer for unemployment and represent low value-added, and the corresponding structural change is inefficient in the sense that sooner or later it has to be reversed, if the productivity and income levels are going to increase. Again, open unemployment may be socially superior as it may be a temporary stage followed by some labour market participants finding jobs in new sectors. On the other hand, subsistence agriculture may be associated with a fast erosion of skills or their replacement with skills which are not consistent with the new economic system. Both Romania and Moldova are economies which exemplify the case of relatively low unemployment matched with a continued very large share of agriculture in employment and poor performance in terms of aggregate productivity and income dynamics (compare Figures 7.1 and 7.4).

Finally, the outflows from unemployment into employment may be enhanced thanks to active labour market policies (ALMP). In this context, the Czech Republic is a very interesting case. Until mid-1997 (the Koruna exchange rate crisis), the unemployment levels were exceptionally low, despite the fact that the country had been regarded as one of the leading reformers. At the same time, spending on labour market policies was high and existing evidence showed that the programmes had made some difference. One of the most telling indicators was the number of registered unemployed per staff member. In the early transition period (1993) it was 675 persons per staff member in Romania, 270 in Bulgaria, 235 in Poland, 162 in Hungary, 123 in the Slovak Republic and only 30 in the Czech Republic. The Czech ratio was even lower than in the Scandinavian countries, where ALMP traditionally play a significant role (data from Boeri 1997).

Unfortunately, ALMP alone can never solve the unemployment problem and in this respect, without other complementary policies, may even be ineffective in the longer run. The Czech case exemplifies that. The main problem was that in the Czech case, despite some formal institutions of tripartite wage bargaining, the wage-setting mechanisms did not result in sustainable labour market equilibria for both low unemployment and wage dynamics consistent with changes in labour productivity. In the period of low unemployment – i.e. between 1991 and 1997 – Czech wages (as measured in US dollars) increased dramatically from the lowest level in the Visegrad Group (which includes the Czech Republic, Hungary, Poland and the Slovak Republic) to the highest among those four economies. That alone would not have had serious implications, had it not been for the insufficient increase in labour productivity, which might be linked to the chosen privatization methods (the mass privatization programme and a correspondingly low initial inflow of foreign capital). As a result, the combination of a strong increase in labour costs, inadequate pace of industrial restructuring and productivity enhancement, the fixed exchange rate regime and lack of adjustment in fiscal policy triggered an exchange rate crisis in mid-1997. Unemployment started to grow, with spending on passive labour market policy crowding-out spending on ALMP. The ratio of ALMP spending per unemployed person decreased quickly and the Czech labour market moved from a 'good' labour market equilibrium to a 'bad' one, no longer dissimilar from neighbouring economies. The Czech Republic is still characterized by one of the more efficient labour markets in Europe (see Figures 7.1, 7.3, 7.4), but is no longer the outlier it used to be in the early 1990s. Again, the basic lesson is that ALMP alone are not capable of guaranteeing 'good' equilibrium in longer term if wage-setting produces inefficient outcomes (Mickiewicz and Bell 2000).

This stylized account of labour market development in the Czech Republic is not intended to question the importance of ALMP. They may have an important role to play in particular in combating long-term unemployment. Decreasing long-term unemployment rates and rising labour turnover are improving the performance of the labour market, regardless of its impact on the aggregate unemployment level. Active measures in the labour market are designed to introduce an early identification of the needs of unemployed persons and to promote programmes leading to the improvement of human resources quality (training courses, practical vocational training, subsidized employment) (Sztanderska and Piotrowski 1999).

Yet CE countries continue to devote scarce amounts of budgetary resources to this aim. EU average resources destined for labour market policies are 3 per cent of GDP, while in the CE countries they are less than 1 per cent. In Poland, for example, expenditure on passive labour market policies such as unemployment benefits in the 1990s constituted around 2 per cent of GDP and were approximately three times larger than the expenditure on ALMP (Sztanderska and Piotrowski 1999).

Post-transition labour market equilibria?

We may now summarize the factors affecting unemployment rates in the (post-) transition countries.

First, the inflows from employment into unemployment resulted from the elimination of the initial 'labour hoarding' and the unprecedented scale of restructuring. While there is some microeconomic evidence that 'labour hoarding' is now over (Mickiewicz, Gerry and Bishop 2005), the restructuring process is still far from complete, and will continue to affect the labour market.

Second, the outflow from unemployment into jobs, in particular to jobs in the 'new' sectors (see pp. 88–90), remains a key factor. This outflow may be negatively affected by a range of factors. Wages may not be flexible and wage growth may be too strong in relation to changes in productivity, due to inadequate wage-setting/wage-bargaining mechanisms. The taxes on wages may be too large, as the structure of taxes relies too much on labour taxation in these countries. The financial system and legal protection for the providers of finance may be inadequate, slowing down investment related to new job creation. General uncertainty in the business environment may not create the incentives for growth. Bureaucratic barriers and corruption may severely diminish the benefits from the creation and expansion of new enterprises (Aidis and Mickiewicz 2006).

These last two factors may play a more serious role in SEE (such as Romania) and CIS countries (especially Ukraine) than in Central Europe. For the CE economies, the tax burden on labour may play a significant negative role hampering employment. The European Commission (2003) reports the heavy burden of labour taxation for low-wage earners (below 67 per cent of the average wage), a group which is particularly vulnerable in terms of unemployment. When measured as a share of the total tax cost (income tax on gross wage earnings plus employer and employee social insurance contributions) in labour costs, the CE percentage (38 per cent) is higher than the EU average, apart from Estonia, which is at the EU average level.

On the other hand, there is no strong evidence that labour market outcomes can be linked to the role of CE trade unions. When the position of trade unions is approximated by union density, CE economies score between 15 per cent for Estonia and Poland and 41 per cent for Slovenia, which corresponds to the lower part of the EU spectrum (European Commission 2003). CE Union density levels decreased significantly over the 1990s (compare European Commission 2003 with Riboud, Sanchez-Paramo and Silva-Jauregui (2002), who present data on an earlier period). If there are problems resulting from inadequate patterns of industrial relations, they tend to be restricted to few sectors in some countries only. The mining sector in Bulgaria, Poland and Romania may be one of those cases. Miners in these three countries enjoy large wage premium, much higher than in any other EU country apart from the Netherlands (59 per cent of the country average wage for Bulgaria, 68 per cent for Poland and 65 per cent for Romania, as of 2000 – see European Commission 2003). Meanwhile ineffective restructuring programmes in the mining sector and the cost of implicit subsidies affect public finance and indirectly other sectors (see Driffill and Mickiewicz 2003 and also Chapter 7).

Outflows from unemployment may be hampered by the mismatch between the structure of the labour supply and that of job offers. That is, the Beveridge curve (unemployment-vacancies) may be positioned unfavourably high. This mismatch has several dimensions. One is that occupational mobility is negatively affected by the major mismatch in skills, as the 'old' structure of skills is not consistent with a market environment and this heritage has not yet been overcome. Another relates to low spatial mobility, which is – among other things – related to badly functioning housing markets. The resulting problems would be less serious if the quality and density of transport infrastructure were high. But it is not. The role of migration in adjusting the labour market mechanism has been small until the time of EU accession (as confirmed by Gacs and Huber 2003a), but for the new EU countries its role increased considerably later on (see next chapter). Finally, a careful reader may notice that three factors are missing from our analysis.

First, so far we have not mentioned the level of unemployment benefits and social welfare provision as a factor affecting unemployment rates in these countries. The first reason is that there is no evidence that the replacement rates in those countries are particularly high. And, more importantly, we need to assess the unemployment problem in the wider context of economic efficiency. As we have argued, from that point of view while adequate provision of benefits may increase unemployment in the short term, in the longer term it may facilitate job quits and subsequent matching with new jobs, therefore leading to reduced unemployment later. The dynamic perspective may thus lead to different conclusions than the static one and suggest that an adequate level of unemployment benefits may be advantageous.

Second, the level of the minimum wage is unlikely to have much impact in Central Europe. It is in the range of 25–40 per cent of the average wage for the accession countries, similar to the three south European 'old' EU members: Greece, Portugal and Spain, and lower than other EU countries, which are in the range of 40–60 per cent.

Third, CE employment protection indicators and more generally indices of labour market vary significantly between the transition economies as compared with the 'old' EU member states. We postpone the discussion of labour market institutions to the next chapter.

'New' and 'old' Europe: Some stylized facts

In an assessment of the unemployment rates across the CEE regions and the 'old' EU member states, Gacs and Huber (2003b) found three key characteristics of CE labour markets, using standard econometric tests. CE labour markets are characterized by the following significant differences, as compared with the 'old' EU member states:

(1) Unemployment rates are higher than in the 'old' EU member states; 78 per cent of the 'new' member states' population live in regions with unemployment rates in excess of 10 per cent, the corresponding figure for the 'old' EU regions is only 34 per cent.

(2) Both long-term unemployment and youth unemployment is higher. This is consistent with (1), as both long-term and youth unemployment typically respond more than proportionately to

the increase in the base unemployment rate. Here, Gacs and Huber's (2003b) results may be supplemented by those of Góra and Schmidt (1998) and Lehmann (1998): those who dominate long-term unemployment are 'individuals with unfavourable demographic and skill characteristics, i.e. workers who are old and have obsolete skills'.

(3) The 'new' member states are characterized by significantly lower gender-based differences along the labour market dimension, including unemployment rates, than the 'old' member states.

(4) There is more polarization among the regions of the 'new' EU states than in the 'old' members' group. This relates to both unemployment rates and participation rates. An obvious implication is that the new members create a serious challenge for EU regional policies.

(5) In Central Europe, factors on a national level affect unemployment relatively more than factors on a regional level, as compared with the relative importance of these factors in the 'old' EU member states.

(6) Industrial patterns are more important in explaining unemployment in the CE than in the 'old' member states.

Point (6) relates closely to the issue of transition-related restructuring shocks, as discussed above. Gacs and Huber's (2003b) results corroborate findings by Newell and Pastore (2000), who demonstrated that regions with higher unemployment were those experiencing greater change in industrial structure. A corollary is that high-unemployment regions are those with higher inflow rates to unemployment.

At the outset of the transition, big and typically inefficient SOEs dominated not only in industry but also in agriculture, which was particularly resistant to the command economy method of coordination. Apart from Poland, the private sector in agriculture was practically non-existent, or played only a limited role. A decrease in agricultural employment was one of the main dimensions of structural change. The restructuring of the agriculture sector caused a situation where the highest unemployment was reported in rural, economically backward, mainly agricultural areas (see Gacs and Huber 2003b for evidence). Because of ownership transformations a great number of former state-owned farms' employees became unemployed. These were mostly people with low skills, for whom the opportunities of finding jobs, both within and outside their area of residence, were particularly limited. Mickiewicz and Bell (2000) show that the initial percentage of state-owned farms in agricultural land was a significant predictor of decrease in both employment and participation rates across the Polish regions. In contrast with agriculture, services remained the sector, which was mostly associated with job creation. Rutkowski and Przybyła (2002) found a strong correlation between regional specialization in services (a high percentage share of services in total employment) and the hiring rate.

Conclusion

If the analysis of the economic transition in Central and Eastern Europe has contributed to our general understanding of labour market processes, it is largely due to a renewed interest in the link between structural change and labour market outcomes. A low level of unemployment is not desirable when it comes at the cost of a large agricultural sector with subsistence farming being a substitute for social welfare. Similarly, jobs in the 'old' industrial sectors may be preserved by a combination of inadequate social welfare provision and industrial subsidies, typically of an implicit nature. That route turned out to be self-defeating, and is more typical of those East European countries which were not able to gain a place in the first (2004) round of EU enlargement. The distinction between 'old' and 'new' sectors is thus important. Sustainable jobs are created in services and 'modern' branches of industry, which is why the unemployment problem is related to structural change.

Focus on structural change is connected to the analytical approach which stresses flows and dynamics. The key labour market questions relate to factors affecting inflows and outflows from unemployment. The lesson from Central and Eastern Europe is that policies to slow down the inflow into unemployment turned out to be inefficient. The main challenge is thus how to remove the constraints which hamper outflow to employment. Our one preferred recommendation for Central Europe would be to look closer into the issue of tax structure, and the level of labour taxation in particular. However, a full list of policy recommendations is longer, and not uniform across the region. High unemployment levels and the continued process of structural change remain a challenge, one becoming more and more similar to that faced by the 'old' EU members.

8
Labour Market Institutions

While the previous chapter focused primarily on labour market dynamics along the process of economic transition, in this chapter we discuss labour market institutions and performance of the transition economies in wider comparative, cross-country perspective, using worldwide sample. The motivation for this is that to understand the transition countries better, we need not just to compare those between themselves but also to understand if and how they differ from other countries around the world.

The first part of the chapter is more general in nature. We focus on correlations between the institutional characteristics and the equilibrium rate of unemployment and find the latter positively correlated with both the rigidity of employment regulations and with regulatory barriers to entrepreneurial entry. In addition, the regulation of industrial relations is correlated with unemployment in a non-monotonic way, with medium level of regulation intensity being associated with the highest level of unemployment.

In the second part of the paper we use the cross-country data in a slightly different way. We aim to identify the country clusters representing patterns in labour market institutions, structures and outcomes. We find that economies of English legal origin are associated with a lower degree of regulation, but not with lower generosity of the social security system. In addition, there is a considerable degree of heterogeneity within both the EU and the transition economies. The latter split between several types of labour market institutional set-up and performance.

Labour market institutions and the significance of entrepreneurial entry

As discussed already in Chapter 3, an institution may be seen as any form of norms (constraints) that are introduced by people to shape their interactions (North 1990). Those norms (constraints) make expectations of those involved in human interactions converging and therefore may lower transaction costs. Formal institutions are visible, codified rules that come with explicit sanctions (Crawford and Ostrom 1995) including property rights, government regulation and legal systems. Informal institutions relate to accepted patterns in behaviour represented by values, norms and codes of conduct that form part of the prevailing culture. While not legally enforced, the informal institutions are key determinants of human behaviour.

Institutional evolution is a slow process. When formal institutions are modified, the effectiveness of the change is limited without the corresponding change in informal institutions and those evolve even slower than the formal ones. Informal institutions survive for long and they provide a sense of stability. As we discussed in Chapter 3, this kind of inertia has been documented for the post-Soviet societies, where attitudes inherited from the command economy period persist.

The path dependence in institutional evolution implies that institutions may survive even if they are no longer efficient (DiMaggio and Powell 1983; North 1990). Support for maintaining the institutions, which are inefficient when seen from the general welfare perspective, may come either from special interest groups in democracies (Tullock 1967) or from embedded political elites in autocracies (Acemoglu 2006).

Theoretical interest in institutional inertia is closely related to the concept of 'legal origin', which was developed in the context of empirical research and introduced by La Porta *et al.* (1998, 1999). The authors distinguish between common-law (English) legal origin on the one hand and civil law systems on the other and distinguish further within the latter group between French, German and Scandinavian legal origin. In addition they introduce the category of 'socialist legal origin' to capture the influence of the command economy (communist) period. These categories, which can been seen as exogenous with relation to current law and current economic performance demonstrate high explanatory power. In general, common-law countries are characterized by more limited scope of government regulation.

Botero *et al.* (2004) provide a key recent contribution on the labour market institutions that directly follows the research themes and methodology developed by the 'legal origin' school. The authors develop a set of cross-country labour market indicators that cover employment laws, industrial (collective) relations laws and social security indicators. They demonstrate that the common-law origin countries implement lighter regulation of labour markets. In addition, they show that rigid employment regulation is associated with higher equilibrium unemployment and also with youth unemployment in particular.

Their findings give support to one of the key modern theories of unemployment, that is to the insider-outsider theory of unemployment developed by Lindbeck and Snower (1988). Consistent with this approach, high labour turnover cost increases the market power of the incumbent workers ('insiders') who do not take into account the interests of the unemployed ('outsiders') in the wage setting process.

It seems to us however, that the main omission in the Botero *et al.* (2004) discussion relates to the barriers to entrepreneurial entry. Exit from unemployment may happen either through employment or through self-employment. If regulatory barriers to employment creation and employment flexibility bite and lead to higher unemployment, the same should relate to the barriers to self-employment. Indeed, as documented in recent work by Audretsch *et al.* (2006), high unemployment in OECD countries leads to intensified exit via self-employment, which in turn may lead to the subsequent reduction in unemployment, both as a direct effect of self-employment and as an effect of further employment creation by some of the new entrepreneurial entrants.

However, this mechanism may not be possible in countries, where entrepreneurial entry is costly and difficult. Nicoletti and Scarpetta (2005) compiled a detailed set of institutional indicators for the OECD countries and demonstrated that barriers to entry have detrimental effects on employment creation, while creating insiders' rents for existing producers and employees. However, while a considerable amount of heterogeneity exists within the OECD group, it went through a period of liberalization in the 1990s, in the EU in particular (see discussion in Blanchard and Philippon 2003). More generally, to better capture the impact of institutions on unemployment, one needs to reach beyond the OECD group and expand the sample coverage.

In this chapter we intend to build directly on both Botero *et al.* (2004) and on the literature linking labour market outcomes with barriers to entrepreneurship, but expand it in two ways.

Firstly, we build on Botero *et al.* (2004), exploring whether their revealed correlations pertaining to unemployment hold once we extend both the sample and the number of explanatory variables.

Second, results of this exploratory analysis are used to choose the variables that are most strongly associated with labour market performance; using those variables we apply cluster analysis to produce a worldwide institutional pattern of labour market institutions.

Unemployment and institutional variables

Choice of variables and data

Institutions change slowly and estimation strategies based on 'within' variation across time is risky, not least because this type of variation may be spurious, resulting from definitional changes and reassessment of previous indicators in light of new data, as corrections are not always applied retrospectively producing inconsistencies in time series on institutional indicators (Knack 2006). For this reason we follow a very simple but robust methodological design, standard in the literature on the link between economic performance and institutional indicators. That is, we regress long-run averages of dependent variables (in our case: unemployment) on institutional indicators and on other potentially important controls.

We take three institutional measures used by Botero *et al.* (2004). They are:

- the social security index, and
- the industrial (collective) relations index,
- employment regulations index.

Consistent with the literature, we also allow for non-linearity in the index of coordination of industrial relations. The argument for non-linearity is that the worst labour market outcomes may be associated with a medium level of coordination (typically, at the sectoral level). In contrast, both fully decentralized labour markets (like the US) and labour markets that rely on centralized bargaining are more efficient (as in some smaller economies, esp. in Scandinavia; see Calmfors and Driffill 1988). According to this argument, in the case of decentralized labour markets the insiders exert little market power, while in the case of fully centralized labour market bargaining, the insiders internalize the interests of outsiders in the wage setting process. In both cases good market performance may be achieved.

The first two measures are taken directly from Botero *et al.* (2004). The third measure used by Botero *et al.* (2004) was aggregated from employment regulations indicators. By now, based directly on their methodology, the corresponding indices became a part of Doing Business World Bank database, which offers more extensive coverage, and this is the source we use.

From the same source comes our measure of barriers to entrepreneurial entry; it was not included in Botero *et al.* (2004), but as argued above, it is of potentially critical relevance for exit from unemployment.

The next group of factors we look at relates to fiscal, financial and monetary policy parameters or outcomes. We take the share of non-wage labour cost in salary, which captures mainly the compulsory insurance components and can be taken as a proxy for labour tax wedge. A similar interpretation relates to social contributions (direct labour taxation) as a percentage of government revenue. Additionally, we include several measures of both marginal tax rates and overall size of taxation, to investigate if they are associated with unemployment via their potential detrimental effects on employment creation by businesses. In addition we look at the average inflation rate and two financial measures: average real interest rate and the interest rate spread between lending and deposit rates. The latter may capture some impact of potential constraints in financial sector, which may impede job creation. The former (real interest rate) features strongly in some theoretical macroeconomic models of unemployment (in particular, see Phelps 1994) while less strongly in other (Pissarides 2000).

The expected correlation between economic growth and unemployment should normally be taken as positive, albeit it is complicated by the possibility that in addition to the 'capitalization effect' (an increase in growth raises the capitalized returns from creating jobs) we may also have the 'creative destruction effect' (the duration of the job match may be reduced) (Aghion and Howitt 1994). Of equal interest is the link between the openness of the economy, exporting in particular and unemployment, especially in the context of the current debates on the impact of globalization. The economic openness may be associated with unemployment via increased competition. This is in line with Nicoletti and Scarpetta (2005) as discussed above.

Amongst the macroeconomic performance indicators, we also include two measures of productivity: GDP *per capita* and value added per worker in agriculture. Again, higher productivity (other things equal) may be associated with higher returns from job creation.

Next group of variables relate to the structural characteristics of production. We take into account the sectoral structure of production (agriculture, industry, services; additionally: manufacturing) and, more importantly, the size of small- and medium-size firms share in overall employment. The limitation here is that there may be simultaneity between the sectoral composition of employment and unemployment. In particular, low level of economic activity may be associated with both higher unemployment and with loss of employment in manufacturing. A corollary to this is that both subsistence agriculture (see previous chapter) and low-paid services employment may be part of the same structural response as unemployment (Mickiewicz and Zalewska 2006).[1]

In addition, as argued by Audretsch *et al.* (2006) there may be two-way causation between the size of the small business sector and unemployment. While high unemployment may lead to exit via self-employment and small firms creation (generating a positive correlation), the larger small firms sector may next be associated with reduction in unemployment (a correlation with negative sign).

Similar simultaneity problem relates to migration. Larger unemployment may result in higher level of migration, however, in turn, migration may significantly alleviate the unemployment problem.

With respect to other demographic variables, high rate of increase in labour supply (as captured by working-age population dynamics) may potentially result in higher unemployment. In addition, high dependency ratio (dependents, i.e. old age and children, to working age) may create detrimental effects on employment, reducing the value of new jobs because of higher taxation associated with corresponding social transfers. On the other hand however, incentives for work for those in the working-age group may increase, provided that the family links and responsibilities are strong enough, which may be culturally determined.[2]

Last but not least, higher educational level may be associated with higher value of job matches (via increased productivity) leading to higher employment. In addition, higher enrolment rate may imply a direct effect alleviating unemployment in the corresponding age group.

Last but not least, we are interested in transition countries. As discussed in the previous chapter, the transition from the command to market economy is associated with a high level of job reallocation and adjustment following initial labour hoarding, resulting in a relatively high level of unemployment. It is interesting to investigate the correlation between being located in the transition region and unemployment rate in the context of the worldwide sample of countries. In addition, it is also interesting to verify if (old) European Union is still a high-unemployment region, given that some labour market reforms were introduced in 1990s (Blanchard and Philippon 2003). And last but not least, given the significance of the legal origin dimension for labour market regulations, there could be a direct link between the common law legal system and labour market performance.

Bivariate correlations

Similar to Botero *et al.* (2004) we focus first on bivariate regressions of unemployment on the variables discussed above. The key motivation

Table 8.1   Results of bivariate regression models, with mean unemployment rate in 2000–2004 as dependent, for the worldwide sample of countries

Independent variable definition	Coefficient	No of observation
regulation indicators:		
start-up procedures (number)	0.38*	101
	(0.18)	
average time required to deal with start-up procedures (days)	0.04†	103
	(0.02)	
cost of start-up procedures (% of income per capita)	–0.01	101
	(0.01)	
minimum capital required legally for a start-up (% of income p.c.)	–0.001	98
	(0.003)	
difficulty of hiring Index	0.05*	103
	(0.03)	
rigidity of hours Index	0.06**	103
	(0.02)	
difficulty of firing Index	0.04*	103
	(0.03)	
rigidity of employment Index	0.10***	103
	(0.029)	
social security Index	0.79	74
	(0.67)	
industrial (collective) relations index	7.48*	74
	(3.68)	
industrial (collective) relations index squared	–2.26	74
	(1.39)	
fiscal, monetary and financial indicators:		
non-wage labour cost (% of salary)	0.04	105
	(0.06)	
social contributions (% of government revenue)	–0.03	70
	(0.05)	
total tax payable by businesses (% of gross profit)	0.48	103
	(0.35)	
highest marginal tax rate, individual rate (%)	0.02	93
	(0.03)	
taxes on income, profits and capital gains (% of total taxes)	0.02	85
	(0.70)	
tax revenue (% of GDP)	0.11	86
	(0.12)	
inflation, consumer prices (annual %)	0.03	109
	(0.03)	

Table 8.1 Results of bivariate regression models, with mean unemployment rate in 2000–2004 as dependent, for the worldwide sample of countries – *continued*

Independent variable definition	Coefficient	No of observation
real interest rate (%)	0.06 (0.05)	98
interest rate spread (lending rate minus deposit rate)	0.03 (0.05)	97
macroeconomic performance indicators:		
GDP growth (annual %)	–0.49† (0.26)	114
exports of goods and services (% of GDP)	–0.03* (0.02)	108
GDP per capita, PPP (constant 2000 international $)	–0.0002*** (0.0)	107
agriculture value added per worker (constant 2000 US$)	–0.0002*** (0.0)	100
structure of production:		
employment in small & medium size enterprises (% of total employment)	–0.07* (0.03)	57
manufacturing, value added (% of GDP)	–0.23* (0.10)	105
services, value added (% of GDP)	–0.02 (0.07)	107
industry, value added (% of GDP)	0.09 (0.09)	107
agriculture, value added (% of GDP)	–0.59 (0.05)	106
demographic characteristics:		
migration rate	–55.54*** (9.85)	114
population, working age, log difference	–45.23 (32.52)	114
age dependency ratio (dependents to working-age population)	2.10 (5.09)	114
school enrolment, tertiary (% gross)	–0.03 (0.03)	107
literacy rate, adult total (% of people ages 15 and above)	0.06 (0.06)	73

Table 8.1 Results of bivariate regression models, with mean unemployment rate in 2000–2004 as dependent, for the worldwide sample of countries – *continued*

Independent variable definition	Coefficient	No of observation
country groupings (dummy variables):		
transition economy in Europe & former Soviet Union & Mongolia	(1.47) 4.39**	117
EU member states before 2004	−3.91*** (0.94)	117
common law (English) legal origin	−1.68 (1.34)	116

Notes:
(i)   robust standard errors in brackets
(ii) significance levels: *** 0.001, ** 0.01, * 0.05, † 0.01
(iii) sources of data: regulation indicators – World Bank, Doing Business database, 2005, apart from social security and industrial relations regulation, which is taken from Botero *et al.* (2004); fiscal and financial indicators – the first two (none wage cost share and taxes on profits) taken from Doing Business 2005 database; all other variables are taken from World Bank, World Development Indicators (WDI) and represent 2000–2004 averages over all available data points; macroeconomic, structural and demographic indicators – 2004–2005 averages based on WDI; country groupings – the first two constructed by the author, the English legal origin taken from La Porta *et al.* (1999).

behind the adoption of this simple approach is that given the large number of potential exploratory variables, there is a degree of arbitrariness in the choice of any specific model, and with any larger number of variables, multicollinearity may become a serious obstacle, masking existing correlations. The results are reported in Table 8.1 below. Unemployment figures relate to the 2000–2004 averages, and the sources of data and description of variables is also presented in Table 8.1.

The key findings relate to the strong correlation between regulation and unemployment rates. Consistent with both the Lindbeck and Snower (1988) theory and with the Botero *et al.* (2004) empirical results, we find that the rigidity of employment is clearly associated with higher unemployment rates. Moreover, going beyond Botero *et al.* (2004) we also confirm that all three components of the employment rigidity index (difficulty of hiring, difficulty of firing and rigidity of working hours) matter. The first of these has obvious direct impact. The second affects unemployment, because employers anticipating future costs of firing, do not increase employment either when they require a temporary increase or are uncertain about future prospects. In both cases they match the gains from increased production and employment against the future adjustment costs. Similarly, flexibility of decision on working hours is important. It affects both demand and supply of labour. From the demand side, constraints on working time imply that some jobs will not be worth offering. On the supply side, less variation in time structure of employment makes entry into employment less attractive to some categories of potential workers. Essentially, all these types of employment regulation narrow down the feasible set of efficient matches.

The highest levels of employment rigidity may be found in Venezuela and a large number of sub-Saharan African economies (Angola, Burkina Faso, Central African Republic, Chad, Congo, Niger, Tanzania; but with notable exception of Uganda). At the other end of the spectrum we find Hong Kong and Singapore, Australia, Canada, New Zealand, United States, Saudi Arabia and Kuwait. In Europe, UK and Denmark are characterized by low employment rigidity. The transition economies cover the whole spectrum. Their position on employment regulation indices do not always coincide with their position on other reform indicators. There seems to be almost no constraints on employment decisions in Georgia, which is consistent with general pattern of liberalization, but surprisingly, Belarus seems very similar, even if it is lagging in other reforms. However, with widespread state ownership, employment may be rigid in Belarussian firms without any need for explicit regulation. Interestingly, on the other end of the spectrum, we find Estonia and Slovakia, with rigid employment regulation, even if they are very liberal along some other aspects of reforms.

Similar to Botero *et al.* (2004) we do not find increased social security coverage (health, disability, old age and unemployment benefits) to be significantly correlated with unemployment. Indeed, social security may have ambiguous effects on unemployment. On the one hand, availability of sufficient benefits may facilitate job search of unemployed and lead to faster and more efficient job market matches. On the other hand, higher benefits may encourage employees to bargain higher wages (cutting employment opportunities for other) and discourage individuals to accept low-wage job offers (i.e. increase their reservation wage). Consistent with this, generous social security benefits may create incentives to many potential job market participants to remain economically inactive, especially, if incapacity benefit award system is lax or when early retirement is offered as alternative to unemployment. Both of these policies have detrimental effects for the overall economic efficiency, given that the benefits have to be financed by higher taxes on employees. Nevertheless they may result in lower rates of open unemployment, if the direct effect of shifting people from unemployment to other forms of welfare outside the labour market prevails over the indirect effect of decreasing the value of new jobs via higher taxes and therefore lower job creation.

Next, again consistent with Botero *et al.* (2004), we found the linear effect of the index of coordination of industrial relations on unemployment marginally insignificant. However, in this case we suspect it to result from misspecification. Indeed, when we augment the linear term with a quadratic one, both become jointly significant. The increase in the industrial relations coordination index is first associated with higher unemployment rate, and next with lower rate, consistent with the pattern first established by Calmfors and Driffill (1998). Thus, both countries with highly decentralized industrial relations (Canada, United States, New Zealand, Malaysia) and with highly centralized industrial relations (Norway, Portugal, Italy, France) may experience less unemployment. Note however, that in multivariate analysis, the impact of this factor may be counterbalanced by other institutional characteristics, starting with employment rigidity as discussed above, as is clearly the case for some of the countries in the second group.

As argued above, we should expect entry barriers to be as important for unemployment as employment rigidity. This is indeed what we found, albeit a closer look into entry regulations reveals that while both the number of start-up procedures and time required to deal with those is associated with higher unemployment, the financial cost of the start-up (esp. minimum capital requirement) is not.[3] The smallest number of start-up procedures can be found in Australia, Canada and New Zealand. Interestingly however, also Scandinavian countries (Denmark, Finland, Norway, Sweden) are characterized by low entrepreneurial barriers, and the same applies to Belgium and Ireland. At the other end of the spectrum, we find a significant number of Latin American countries (Argentina, Bolivia, Brazil, Venezuela), few African countries (Chad, Uganda) and Greece. Within the transition group, some CIS countries have been characterized by particularly high formal entry barriers (especially Azerbaijan, Belarus and Ukraine). In the latter case, there is evidence that the phenomenon of entry barriers links with strong position of 'insiders' (i.e. existing business owners/managers) in the small firm sector (see Aidis *et al.* 2008).

Consistent with this, we also found the higher share of small- and medium-size enterprises in the economy correlated with lower unemployment (see also discussion of self employment in the previous chapter).

Interestingly, we found no support for the links between either fiscal parameters or financial parameters and unemployment. While signs are consistent with our expectations, the linkages are insignificant. Notably, we found no support for theories that link high real interest rates to unemployment (like Phelps 1994). We also found no indication for any potential inflation-unemployment trade-offs as seen in longer-term perspective.

More can be said however about the macroeconomic performance indicators. Stronger rates of GDP growth are significantly associated with lower levels of unemployment. In addition, more open economy, proxied by higher share of exports in GDP are also experiencing significantly lower unemployment level. While bivariate results should be taken with caution, this latter finding is interesting in the context of the discussion of the impact of globalization on labour markets. Export opportunities and competition enhanced by the process of international integration are associated with better labour market performance. In addition, we found that the overall level of productivity as captured by both GDP *per capita* and by labour productivity in agriculture is associated with lower level of unemployment. However, the relationship with agricultural productivity may be particularly difficult to interpret: in some economies, higher unemployment leads to additional inflows into subsistence agriculture, which leads to lower productivity (see previous chapter).

In general, the share of manufacturing in employment seems to be associated with lower unemployment. One may note however, that higher share of manufacturing is typically associated with openness and higher share of exports in GDP, so may mask the impact of the latter.

In the context of demographic variables, we found strong evidence that migration is associated with lower levels of unemployment. This is consistent with the experience of some of the new EU member states after the accession, when large migration outflows were associated with significant downwards adjustment in unemployment rates, especially in Poland (after 2004). This does not necessarily imply that the unemployed are most likely to migrate; the labour market effects of migration may be more indirect.

Last but not least, we found that the transition economies experience significantly higher levels of unemployment than the rest of the world. This is consistent with the previous chapter.

Interestingly, the 'old' (i.e. pre-2004) EU had lower level of unemployment than the rest of the world. This in turn may be coherent with the fact, that in 1980s and 1990s some EU countries went through the process of considerable labour market reforms as argued by Blanchard and

Philippon (2003). We also checked if the latter result was not driven by the difference between the old EU and the transition economies. Indeed, when we test the difference between these two groups only, the estimated mean difference in unemployment rate increases from 3.9 per cent (as reported in Table 8.1) to rather dramatic 6.9 per cent. However, we also found that the level of unemployment in the old EU is significantly lower than in all other countries excluding transition economies, albeit the mean difference decreases to 3.1 per cent and is significant at 0.1 only (as compared with 0.001 in the previous case).

We also did not find any direct link between the English (common-law) legal system and unemployment. While common-law countries are characterized by lower level of regulation, which should be already clear from both examples given above and from Botero *et al.* (2004), we detected no direct link with unemployment level.

Multivariate analysis

To see to which extent the bivariate results are sensitive to specification, we apply a multivariate regression model. We take into account the two key institutional dimensions we found significant in bivariate settings, namely, the rigidity of employment and the administrative barriers to starting new businesses. We also include a dummy representing the transition economies (EBRD definition) for the reasons already argued. As a control, we include the dynamics of GDP. This is important as we are interested in the direct impact of institutions on unemployment, not in its indirect impact, which may work via GDP growth.

In addition to regressing the unemployment rate on these variables, we also regress youth unemployment rate, as the latter is both important from the social point of view and may interact with institutional settings in a slightly different way (see also Botero *et al.* 2004). In particular, there is an interesting, if not unambiguous pattern, linking age with entrepreneurial entry. While young age is typically associated with higher motivation to entry, it is also characterized by more limited access to resources needed for a successful start-up. Thus the negative impact of the second effect counterbalances the positive impact of the first to some degree (see Parker 2004). In general we expect the formal barriers to entrepreneurial entry to have stronger negative impact on youth unemployment. The results of the multivariate estimations are presented in Table 8.2 below.

With respect to unemployment rate, we confirm that the two institutional variables of interest (employment rigidity and start-up barriers) have significant impact on unemployment rate even when we include

Table 8.2 Determinants of mean unemployment (2000–2004). Results of multivariate regressions

Dependent variable	Unemployment rate	Youth unemployment rate
Independent variables		
Rigidity of employment index	0.06†	0.78
	(0.03)	(0.61)
Start-up procedures (number)	0.30*	0.56†
	(0.15)	(0.29)
Transition economy dummy	5.50***	10.83***
	(1.64)	(3.28)
Annual percentage rate of GDP growth	−0.77**	−1.38***
	(0.25)	(0.38)
Constant	6.53***	13.79***
	(1.43)	(2.45)
F statistics	6.62	7.10
R-squared	.22	.26
Number of observations	103	85

Notes:
(i) Robust standard errors in brackets
(ii) Significance levels: *** 0.001, ** 0.01, * 0.05, † 0.01
(iii) Sources of data as in Table 8.1. Youth unemployment rate relates to the ratio of unemployed to all economically active in the 15–24 age group; it comes from World Bank WDI Indicators, 2006.

other controls. In addition, transition comes still as a significant factor associated with higher unemployment. On the other hand, good macro-economic performance as captured by GDP growth leads to better labour market performance. However, this last result should be taken with some caution. In this context, GDP growth may be representing an impact of some other factors of growth absent from the model. The main motivation to include it in the model is to have factors affecting unemployment net of their impact via macroeconomic performance; that is we focus on channels of influence specific to unemployment (as for instance, regulatory variables could have additional impact on unemployment via their effect on growth).

We next take the same set of variables as determinants of youth unemployment. Here, we need to emphasize that due to data limitations, our sample is reduced by almost 20 per cent, and that should naturally result in lower significance levels, which are therefore no longer directly comparable with the estimation of the general rate of unemployment.

Even with this limitation however, we found that start-up costs have significant impact on youth unemployment rate and the magnitude of the corresponding coefficient is always twice as large as in the case of general unemployment rate. It is clear, that barriers to entrepreneurship work against young people far more than against those who are already well established.

Extensions: Correlations structure between institutions and labour market performance

In addition to the direct links between regulation and unemployment, we also explored the second layer of correlations, i.e. those leading from the more fundamental factors, like legal origin and political frameworks, to regulation. The optimum set-up for this kind of analysis would be to introduce a multi-equation model, say two- or three-stage type of regression analysis. However, we are seriously constrained by the size of the sample. While for the regressions reported in Table 8.2, we had between 85 and 103 observations for our disposal, for some other key variables the available numbers go down considerably (see Table 8.1). To make matters worse, a pattern of missingness is such that for more ambitious multi-equation models the cumulative (multiplicative) effect implies very small samples. Thus, in our case it may be more practical again to look directly at the bivariate correlation structure between the variables. Accordingly, the Figure 8.1 below draws from the results reported in Table 8.1 and additional calculations of correlation coefficients between the institutional variables.

The logic of Figure 8.1 is the following. Only those correlations which are significant at least on the level of 10 per cent are represented by the arrows, and the positive/negative sign implies that an increase in one variable is associated with increase/decrease in another. The assumed direction reflects our prior knowledge, as discussed above. To avoid complicating the presentation unnecessarily, we do not include macroeconomic indicators, as bivariate correlations with those are not of primary interest here.

The correlations presented on the left hand side of the graph relate to the determinants of unemployment and were already discussed above. Our interest here is in the determinants of regulation, as illustrated by links in the upper right section of Figure 8.1.

Firstly, consistent with Djankov *et al.* (2002) we found political freedom being associated with lower level of regulation of entry (significant at 0.001) and, extending the results obtained by Botero *et al.* (2004), we found political freedom associated with lower level of employment

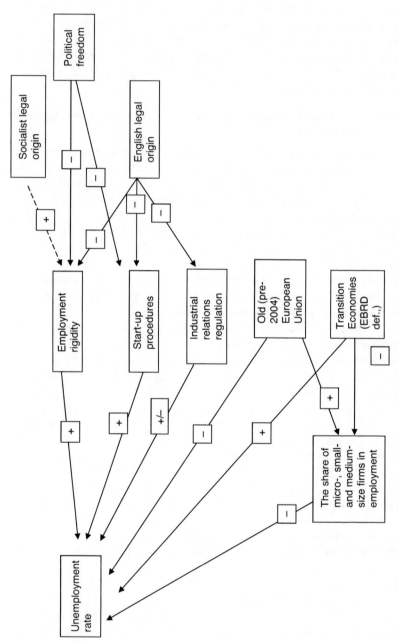

Figure 8.1 The structure of correlations between labour market performance and institutions

regulation (significant at 0.1). Our measure of political freedom is derived as an average of political rights and civil liberties index as reported by Freedom House. Similar measure was applied by Persson and Tabellini (2003). This is also consistent with the results discussed in Chapter 4 (see also: Mickiewicz 2005): economic liberalization goes hand-in-hand with political liberalization.

In addition, we found that while English legal origin is not significantly linked to the level of unemployment in any direct way, it is a strong predictor for all aspects of regulation we discussed so far. Namely, English legal origin is associated with lower employment rigidity, more decentralized and less regulated industrial relations and lower number of barriers to entrepreneurial entry. All these correlations are highly significant, at 0.001 level and consistent with the results obtained by Botero *et al.* (2004) and Djankov *et al.* (2002). In addition, again consistent with Botero *et al.* (2004), we found a link between Socialist legal origin and employment rigidity. While the correlation with the overall index is marginally insignificant, the Socialist legal origin is significantly associated (at 5 per cent level) with regulations restricting firing of employees. It is worth emphasizing that the Socialist legal origin variable is a wider category than the transition economies indicator, as the former encompasses both the countries that left the command economy system as well as those, which continue to apply it (see La Porta *et al.* 1999).

Given the significance of entry barriers for labour market outcomes, as confirmed by our results discussed above, we also took a closer look at the cluster of correlations around the size of the micro-, small- and medium-size enterprise (MSME) sector in the economy. Interestingly, we found no significant correlation between barriers to entry and the MSME sector. This is consistent with the argument developed in Aidis *et al.* (2008): in some countries one may observe a phenomenon of 'insiders' entrepreneurship', that is a situation where low entry is advantageous to the existing business owners/managers, who enjoy rents resulting from some degree of protection against competition analogous to large firms. Essentially, it is the inflow of new firms not the existing number of enterprises that may be the most important indicator of entrepreneurship, albeit it is more difficult to measure.

This argument does not contradict the fact, that the MSME sector *per se* may still be beneficial for the alleviation of unemployment as found above. In all likelihood, both the inflow and the volume of MSMEs matter for unemployment, but unfortunately we have no source which would cover the former wide enough. The Global Enterprise monitor, which is possibly the best available source on new entry covers about 40 countries only (see Minnitti *et al.* 2005).

Concentrating on the stock of small firms, instead of flows, we find that the MSME sector is significantly smaller in the transition economies. This implies that the impact of the old command economy is still noticeable. Some of this may be attributed to inherited norms, values and resulting attitudes. Those norms and values affect entrepreneurship directly via lower propensity to start new businesses, based on lower perceived self-efficacy and higher risk aversion, but also indirectly – norms and values shape political choices that result in institutional reform and affect the functioning of formal institutions. An optimistic feature is that – as found by Estrin and Mickiewicz (2010) – there seems to be a generational change under way in the transition economies: it is the older generation in which the old values are embedded most strongly.

Contrary to stereotypes, the old EU is on average characterized by larger MSME sectors than elsewhere. However, these observations mask important differences both within the transition group and within the old EU. At which we now take a closer look.

Labour market performance, structures and institutions: Cross-country cluster analysis

This section is based on cluster analysis. We use the institutional indicators just discussed to produce a pattern identifying economies that are similar. However, in addition to the institutional dimension, we also created clusters of countries based on labour market performance, demographics and structural indicators. We discuss those new dimensions first, and turn back to the institutional indicators subsequently.

Labour market performance and demographic indicators

We start with four basic labour market characteristics: unemployment rate, rate of growth in working-age population (approximated by logarithmic difference), dependency ratio and migration ratio. As before, all variables are taken as five-year averages, 2000–2004. Applying standard cluster models based on minimum Euclidean distance and applying a cut-off point to produce four clusters we arrive at the groupings as reported by Table 8.3, which also presents the mean values for the underlying variables obtained for each clusters.

The first cluster relates to countries which are characterized by poor labour market performance. It is characterized by both high rate of unemployment (average: 16.6 per cent) and the highest outwards migration

Table 8.3 Labour market performance and demographic indicators

Clusters	1	2	3	4
Cluster averages:				
Unemployment rate	16.6	4.1	9.8	29.3
Net migration rate	–0.017	0.015	–0.009	0.003
Logarithmic change in working age population	0.011	0.019	0.013	0.024
Dependency ratio	0.55	0.57	0.57	0.69
Countries:	Albania	Australia	Bahamas, The	Algeria
	Argentina	Austria	Barbados	Macedonia
	Botswana	Bangladesh	Belgium	Namibia
	Bulgaria	Bolivia	Belize	South Africa
	Colombia	Cambodia	Brazil	West Bank
	Croatia	China	Cameroon	
	Dominican	Costa Rica	Canada	
	Republic	Cuba	Chile	
	Lithuania	Cyprus	Czech Republic	
	Mongolia	Denmark	Ecuador	
	Poland	Guatemala	Egypt	
	Slovak Republic	Honduras	El Salvador	
	St. Lucia	Hong Kong,	Estonia	
	Tunisia	China	Finland	
	Uruguay	Hungary	France	
	Venezuela	Iceland	Georgia	
		India	Germany	
		Ireland	Ghana	
		Japan	Greece	
		Korea, Republic	Guyana	
		Luxembourg	Indonesia	
		Macao, China	Iran	
		Madagascar	Israel	
		Malaysia	Italy	
		Maldives	Jamaica	
		Mexico	Jordan	
		Netherlands	Kazakhstan	
		New Zealand	Kyrgyzstan	
		Norway	Latvia	
		Papua	Malta	
		New Guinea	Mauritius	
		Portugal	Moldova	
		Qatar	Morocco	
		Saudi Arabia	Netherland	
		Singapore	Antilles	
		Slovenia	Nicaragua	
		Sweden	Pakistan	
		Switzerland	Panama	
		Tanzania	Paraguay	
		Thailand	Peru	
		Uganda	Philippines	
		UAE	Puerto Rico	
		UK	Romania	

Table 8.3   Labour market performance and demographic indicators – *continued*

Clusters	1	2	3	4
		US	Russian	
		Vietnam	Federation	
			Serbia	
			Spain	
			Sri Lanka	
			Syria	
			Trinidad &	
			Tobago	
			Turkey	
			Ukraine	
			Zimbabwe	

rate. In turn pace of increase in working-age population is average and so is the dependency ratio. We find no old-EU country in this group, yet a number of transition economies is located here (Albania, Bulgaria, Croatia, Lithuania, Mongolia, Poland and Slovakia).

In contrast, the second cluster represents the best labour market performance indicators. Unemployment is low (average: 4.1 per cent), working-age population dynamics is high, inflow of migrants is high and age dependency is average. We find the United States and Japan in this group. Yet, interestingly, also a significant number of the 'old EU' economies are located in this group: Austria, Denmark, Iceland, Ireland, Luxembourg, Netherlands, Norway, Portugal, Sweden and United Kingdom. We find only two transition countries in this cluster: Slovenia and Hungary. However, Hungarian results are clearly affected by its migration indicators: the country has been experiencing an inflow of ethnic Hungarians from the neighbouring countries.

The third cluster is characterized by average labour market performance. The mean unemployment rate is 10 per cent, working-age population dynamics is low, net migration rate is close to zero and dependency ratio is average. We find a significant number of both old-EU and transition economies in this group. Amongst the first, we see Belgium, Finland, France, Germany, Greece, Italy and Spain. Amongst the second, we find Czech Republic, Estonia, Kazakhstan, Latvia, Romania, Russia and Ukraine. One should emphasize however a lack of symmetry between the old-EU and transition economy group of countries in this cluster, even if labour market indicators are similar. Given that the labour market performance is generally weak in transition economies, we should consider those in this cluster as better labour market performers (in contrast with cluster one). On the other hand, the old-EU group is split between clusters two and three. Therefore, countries in this group, notably France, Germany and Italy should be seen as poor labour market performers, in contrast with the UK, Ireland, Netherlands and the Scandinavian countries.

Finally, cluster four consists of few labour market outliers, which face very dramatic labour market conditions characterized by extremely high rates of unemployment, high dependency ratio, fast growth in working-age population and migration rate very close to zero. The only European country (amongst those for which we have data) that we find in this group is Macedonia, which shares this cluster only with Algeria, Namibia, South Africa and West Bank and Gaza.

Structural characteristics of employment and labour force

Our second cross-section is based on the structural characteristics of employment and labour force. We take into account the share of both industry and services in employment, leaving agriculture as a benchmark-omitted category. To this we add the share of the micro-, small- and medium-size enterprises in total employment and finally an indicator of the educational level of the labour force, namely gross enrolment rate in tertiary education. Obviously, the key variable behind these indicators is the level of income *per capita*, as structures of employment are closely correlated with the level of development (Mickiewicz and Zalewska 2006). The same applies to education. However, omitting GDP *per capita* from our analysis has an advantage in that the we are able to identify the economies which are structurally more 'advanced' despite their level of development. Resulting groupings and average values of underlying variables are reported in Table 8.4. The number of countries we were able to include is significantly lower than the previous case due to data limitations.

The first cluster represents developing agricultural economies with small entrepreneurial sector and relatively low level of education. We find no countries of Central and Western Europe in this group, however, several CIS countries belong here, i.e.: Armenia, Azerbaijan, Georgia, Moldova and Ukraine.

The second cluster is where we found the significant number of European economies and also the US, amongst the non-European economies. It is characterized by small agricultural sector, medium size of the entrepreneurial sector and very high level of education. Amongst the transition countries we find the three Baltic republics, Poland, Slovenia and

Table 8.4 Structural characteristics of employment and labour force

Clusters	1	2	3	4
Cluster averages:				
Services in employment (%)	40.7	66.4	37.3	61.9
Industry in employment (%)	16.4	26.0	16.5	27.8
MSMEs in employment (%)	**18.7**	56.7	71.4	65.9
Enrolment in tertiary education (%)	35.2	**65.5**	19.4	38.0
Countries:	Armenia	Australia	Bangladesh	Brazil
	Azerbaijan	Austria	Ghana	Bulgaria
	Georgia	Belgium	Kyrgyzstan	Chile
	Moldova	Canada	Mexico	Colombia
	Thailand	Denmark	Philippines	Costa Rica
	Ukraine	Estonia	Turkey	Croatia
		Finland	Vietnam	Cyprus
		Greece		Czech Rep.
		Ireland		Hong Kong,
		Israel		China
		Korea,		Hungary
		Republic		Iceland
		Latvia		Italy
		Lithuania		Japan
		Netherlands		Portugal
		New Zealand		Slovak
		Norway		Republic
		Poland		Switzerland
		Russian		
		Federation		
		Slovenia		
		Sweden		
		UK		
		US		

last but not least the Russian Federation. Amongst the old-EU, Austria, Belgium, Denmark, Finland, Greece, Netherlands, Norway, Sweden and United Kingdom belong here.

The third cluster represents agricultural developing economies with low level of education, but exceptionally large share of the entrepreneurship in employment. Here we find only one transition economy, i.e. the Kyrgyzstan, which was for a long time seen as a relatively advanced reformed amongst the CIS economies (see EBRD 2006 for comparisons) – relatively early liberalization may help to explain the extent of entrepreneurship there.

Finally, cluster four may be directly compared with cluster two, as both contain most of the European economies. Both clusters have small agricultural sectors, but cluster four combines larger entrepreneurial sectors with less developed tertiary education sector. In this group we find South European old-EU economies (Italy, Portugal), Balkan economies (Bulgaria, Croatia), and three out of four Vysehrad countries (Czech Republic, Hungary, Slovak Republic).

When seen from the labour market performance point of view, the structural characteristics may interact with unemployment level in an interesting way. First, employment in agriculture may act as a substitute for unemployment. The most striking example in this respect is Romania, an economy which maintained a very high level of employment in agriculture combined with relatively moderate unemployment rates. Clearly, subsistence agriculture became an important, even if inefficient escape route from unemployment, or sometimes no less than means of survival (see previous chapter; Gerry, Kim and Li 2004; Mickiewicz and Bell 2000).

Second, both entrepreneurship and education may be seen as factors which improve labour market performance. It is interesting to notice that in the old-EU economies, those two factors appear – to some extent – as substitutes. At one end of the spectrum, Scandinavian countries (Sweden, Denmark, Norway, Finland) are characterized by relatively small MSMEs sectors and high level of education. At the other end, we find Italy and Portugal, with large MSMEs sectors and relatively smaller role of the educational system. This systemic difference is highlighted by our clusters two and four. It is interesting to notice however, that such a regularity does not apply to transition economies. In particular, amongst the new EU member states we find both countries with relatively high tertiary education sector and large MSMEs sector (Slovenia, Lithuania, Estonia, Poland), but also countries with small MSMEs sector and relatively lower size of the tertiary education sector (Slovakia in particular).

Labour market institutions

Finally, we look at the institutional indicators. Consistent with our discussion above, we take into account the index of industrial relations regulations, the social security index, and the employment rigidity index, following Botero *et al.* (2004) (however in the case of employment rigidity, the indicators are taken from World Bank 'Doing Business' version which follows the same methodology but offers a more extensive coverage). This is the same data we used in the previous section. We also include regulation of entry as proxied by the number of start-up

Table 8.5 Labour market institutions

Clusters	1	2	3	4
Cluster averages:				
Employment rigidity index	46.2	**64.0**	27.5	**8.2**
No of start-up procedures	10.1	9.7	8.9	**5.9**
Industrial relations regulation	**1.5**	**1.5**	1.1	**0.7**
Social security index	1.8	1.5	1.5	1.7
Countries:	Argentina	Burkina Faso	Armenia	Australia
	Austria	Latvia	Belgium	Canada
	Bolivia	Morocco	Chile	Denmark
	Brazil	Peru	China	Hong Kong,
	Bulgaria	Romania	Colombia	China
	Croatia	Senegal	Czech Republic	Jamaica
	Dominican	Spain	Ghana	Malaysia
	Republic	Tanzania	Hungary	New
	Ecuador	Venezuela	Ireland	Zealand
	Egypt		Israel	Singapore
	Finland		Japan	Thailand
	France		Jordan	Uganda
	Georgia		Kazakhstan	United
	Germany		Kenya	Kingdom
	Greece		Korea, Republic	United
	India		Lebanon	States
	Indonesia		Malawi	
	Italy		Mongolia	
	Kyrgyzstan		Nigeria	
	Lithuania		Sri Lanka	
	Madagascar		Switzerland	
	Mali		Uruguay	
	Mexico		Zambia	
	Mozambique		Zimbabwe	
	Netherlands			
	Norway			
	Pakistan			
	Panama			
	Philippines			
	Poland			
	Portugal			
	Russian			
	Federation			
	Slovak Republic			
	Slovenia			
	South Africa			
	Sweden			
	Tunisia			
	Turkey			
	Ukraine			
	Vietnam			

procedures required. As presented before, regulation of entry correlates with the rate of unemployment.

Again, we apply standard cluster analysis and chose a cut-off point generating four clusters. The results are presented below as Table 8.5.

Arguably, in light of our results on unemployment determinants, cluster four is the one that represents the most effective labour market institutions while cluster two represents the least efficient ones.

Cluster two is characterized by the highest level of employment regulation rigidity and high barriers to entrepreneurial entry. Regulation of industrial relations is also very high, but interestingly, the level of social security provision is not. In Europe (amongst the countries we have data on), cluster two is represented by Spain, Romania and Latvia. Indeed, Spanish labour market legal framework has been for the long time drawing attention of the researchers and has been criticized as ineffective, albeit reforms are being introduced. In particular, employment rigidity was noticed and its impact of unemployment interpreted in line with the insider-outsider theory (Bentolila *et al.* 1994; Teixeira 2001; Gil-Martin 2002). Romania is another interesting case, however, as already discussed, the impact of dysfunctional labour regulations could be masked by very high level of hidden unemployment in agriculture (see also previous chapter). Outside Europe, this institutional model is also very characteristic for the Latin American economies, including Argentina, Brazil and Mexico.

Cluster one has both high barriers to entrepreneurial entry and high level of industrial relations regulation. Where it differs from cluster two is that it has higher level of social security offered (the highest amongst the four clusters), but lower level of employment rigidity (medium-high range as compared with other clusters, see Table 8.5). Consistent with our regression results above we would classify this combination of labour market institutions as still an inefficient one, but considerably less so than in the case of the Spanish model (i.e. Cluster 1). We find most of the old-EU and transition countries in this group, including Germany, France, Italy, but also Poland and Russian Federation.

With cluster three, we move to the institutional framework with medium-low range of the employment regulations and medium range of both start-up barriers and industrial relations regulation. Social security provision is relatively low. We find a small number of old-EU countries and transition countries in this group, namely: Belgium, Ireland, Switzerland, and Czech Republic, Hungary and Kazakhstan. We also find Japan in the same group.

Finally, interpreted with the help of our findings on determinants of unemployment, we see cluster four as representing the most efficient combination of labour market institutions. Employment regulations are remarkably flexible, the start-up regulatory barriers are very low, and regulation of industrial relations is very limited. In short, this model represents deregulated labour markets which also facilitates entrepreneurial entry. Interestingly however, it is not coupled with low level of social security provision. The latter remains in medium-high range. Amongst the countries we have data on, we find that none of the new-EU countries belongs here, and only two old-EU labour markets are consistent with this model, that is Denmark and United Kingdom. Outside Europe, this cluster includes Australia, Canada, Hong Kong, Malaysia, New Zealand, Singapore, Thailand and United States.

Conclusions

We wish to highlight three key results.

First, consistent with Botero *et al.* (2004) and with the insider-outsider model of unemployment (Lindbeck and Snower 1988) we found that employment rigidity seems to be a dimension that correlates significantly with medium/longer-run equilibrium unemployment rates.

Second, we also find that barriers to self-employment and entrepreneurship are as important sources of unemployment as rigid employment regulations. Clearly, even where other people are unwilling to hire unemployed, many of the latter may create employment for themselves.

Third, from the labour market perspective, the transition economies look particularly troublesome. These nations suffer for two reasons. On the one hand, they go through the process of painful and sometimes misguided restructuring of their production and employment structures. On the other hand, from the command economy period, they inherited a particularly unhelpful institutional tradition, as defined both by formal and informal institutions (Chapters 1 and 2). Their labour markets tend to be over-regulated and characterized by interference from state administrations, themselves frequently inefficient and with deficient foundations in deeper level, constitutional order, that is with inadequate rule of law and property rights protection (see Chapter 3). The unemployment levels in transition countries remain high, and would be even higher if not for the mitigating effect of migration. However, while migration mitigates negative labour market outcomes it can also add to the problems as those individuals that are characterized by higher than average entrepreneurial potential may be first to leave.

9
Privatization: Speed, Efficiency, Distribution

This chapter is devoted to the key dimension of institutional change: privatization. Despite 20 years that passed since the collapse of the command economy, the process is far from completion in Central and East European economies. State sectors remain large as compared with economies in other parts of the world. In most of those countries the process took a long time to implement and is still not finished. In this chapter we will aim to understand what makes privatization such a challenge to implement.

The global context and the uniqueness of post-communist privatization; the trade-off between speed and efficiency

The word 'privatization' relates to the transfer of property from the government to private owners. It is a relatively new term; an earlier one, used before the 1980s, was 'denationalization', implying (correctly) that 'privatization' amounts typically to the reversal of an earlier process of nationalization. Yet, it does not have to be so; especially in the context of the former command economies, much of the property was created as state-owned. Yet, in many other cases, industrial property was confiscated; where it is returned to the (heirs of) the initial owners, we call it 're-privatization'.

While the transition programme has been unique, privatization has not. The corollary is that state ownership of industrial assets has not been confined to the command economy system. In particular, the two world wars fought in the 20th century were associated with the increased role of the state; this is not a historical coincidence. It is war where the elements of a command economy may prove most beneficial – since the system is at its best where economic objectives are few and well defined (maximization of a number of tanks, a well-defined objective of a space missile programme, etc.), and under the command system, economic resources are 'mobilized' and channelled towards the priorities. That can be achieved with or without formal nationalization (an example of the latter case is the rule of National Socialists in Germany, between 1933 and 1945). This example highlights the importance of the difference between nominal property rights and the economic concept of such rights. With key control rights transferred from the legal owners to government administrators or politicians, the economic difference between private and state ownership is narrow. Private owners with restricted rights to (1) use, (2) take benefits from and (3) transfer the assets are nominal private owners, yet no longer 'private owners' in an economic sense. With economic control rights restricted, any claim to residual value may become meaningless, as the latter can no longer be maximized (say, because of restrictions on price-setting or generally on freedom of contract).[1] Nevertheless, the economic role of the government increased significantly also in democratic developed countries during the First World War already. Some of these policies were abandoned after 1918, but were reinstalled and extended as a policy response to the economic depression of the 1930s and even more so as a necessary element of the war effort during the Second World War. The aftermath of the war saw a wave of nationalization in the industrialized democracies of the West, but the scale was typically limited and confined to a few 'strategic' industries. On the other hand, nationalization of the industrial assets owned by the colonial powers became a trademark for the low- and middle-income countries gaining independence. It was only in the early 1980s, following disappointing economic results of nationalizations, that the wave was reversed, producing a worldwide privatization drive (Megginson and Netter 2001, 2003). Thus, the transition programme should not be seen out of the global context. Without a change in the intellectual climate around 1980 it is unlikely that the idea of privatization would have gained such a wide popularity among the economists and experts who authored the reform blueprints.[2] And without the drive towards privatization, counterfactually, we could have more post-communist countries resembling Belarus instead of Estonia (taking as an example two geographically close economies with very different reform outcomes).

Economic policy choices around the world thus had an influence on the policy-makers who prepared the economic transition programmes at the end of the 1980s and the beginning of the 1990s. It is interesting to notice that, only ten years earlier, when the emergence of 'Solidarity' in

Poland led to an open and practically unrestricted discussion on economic reform, the independent reform proposals focused on self-government and independence of enterprises, but not on privatization *per se*. Only, in the late 1980s, in both Poland and Russia, were proposals of 'mass privatization' put forward as a key element of reform. These proposals took into account the fact that the task was qualitatively different from the privatization programmes implemented in other parts of the world: not just a small fraction, but the overwhelming majority of the industrial assets were state-owned at the start of the transition. The mass privatization programme, later to be put into practice in Czechoslovakia and subsequently in most other transition countries, was an innovative privatization technique, very different from the British-style privatization practised in the 1980s, which involved initial public offerings (IPOs) on the capital market.

More generally, the key dilemma related to the trade-off between the speed and quality of the privatization programme. Attempting to privatize rapidly, the policy-makers in the post-communist countries faced a similar problem as the administrators of the French revolution, who attempted to sell (i.e. privatize) the vast amount of land property (previously confiscated from the Church) and discovered that demand was insufficient to match supply. They were thus forced to lease property. The fundamental problem in both cases was the under-developed market for assets – i.e. the capital market. The market value of any asset is determined by the expected future net income flow, and the ratio of the value of capital to all production generated in the economy (GDP) is typically estimated by the capital markets at somewhere near or above 3:1. Nevertheless, any attempt at a one-off sale of the majority of those assets leads immediately to a liquidity problem. Demand for assets is insufficient, and the prices in privatization sales become depressed to such a degree that the privatization effectively amounts to the free transfer of a vast amount of wealth to a selected group of economic owners. This is risky from the political point of view, as such method of wealth redistribution it is likely to run against any socially accepted principles of justice, undermining not only the credibility of the government, but possibly even the legitimacy of the whole new economic system. Slower privatization is one alternative. However, slow privatization would mean that the behaviour of enterprises might remain inconsistent with the market environment created by liberalization, and reforms might not produce positive results.[3]

Privatization objectives: Efficiency, finance and political economy

Privatization is more than just an economic policy. A massive transfer of assets is involved and the character of the resulting ownership structures has implications not only for the distribution of income and wealth but also for the shape of the political structure and of the civic society. Accordingly, we will discuss the privatization objectives under three headings:

(1) economic efficiency,
(2) short-term economic objectives (related to financial market imperfections) and
(3) political economy arguments.

The discussion is summarized in Table 9.1.

Economic efficiency

The first issue relates to economic efficiency. The positive effects follow from tying together residual control rights and claims to residual returns, creating powerful incentives for value maximization (Milgrom and Roberts 1992). While this is achieved in full only in the entrepreneurial owner-manager firm, still, even in a modern corporation with separated ownership and management the link is far stronger than in a state-owned enterprise.[4] In other words, privatization leads to the reintroduction of a profit motive at the enterprise level. However there are some necessary conditions if the positive effects are to materialize in full.

First, the inherited economic structures are highly monopolistic; enterprises are big and, in a typical case, all firms operating on the particular product market are clustered together into wider industrial conglomerates. Breaking these monopolies at the time of privatization is an important task if full efficiency gains are to be achieved, but in many cases the simplest and quickest way of reintroducing competition effects is by opening the economy to imports. At the initial point of the command economy, the state sector is monopolized by definition, with one owner and one control structure, so privatization is a prerequisite for competition, not vice versa.

Secondly, in industries where external effects are strong, introduction of some regulatory or self-regulatory mechanism is needed. That

Table 9.1 Privatization objectives

Privatization objectives	Problem areas	Possible solutions
Economic efficiency:		
Tying together residual control rights and claims to residual returns to create incentives for profit maximization	Principal-agent issues	Corporate governance
Creating an efficient match between the resources and endowment of owners and managers and the firms assets	To achieve these objectives, the post-privatization property rights transfers are critical. However, the transaction costs of the latter may remain high, until the adequate institutional and legal framework is implemented, which may take time.	Attention should be paid to the initial distribution of property rights, as subsequent transfers of ownership may be slow
Creating the opportunity to introduce competition	High level of concentration in manufacturing, monopolies in utilities	Competition from imports; breaking-up large firms before privatization, regulation of natural monopolies
Innovations, adjustment, entrepreneurship (the latter especially important when the environment is uncertain)	Managers of state-run firms were chosen for their ability to implement plan and conformity, not for innovative skills	New private firms, outside ownership
Optimum wage and employment decisions	Insider interests	New private firms, outside ownership

Table 9.1 Privatization objectives – *continued*

Privatization objectives:	Problem areas	Possible solutions
Financial and fiscal objectives:		
Funds for restructuring/investment provided under hard budget constraint	Insufficient domestic capital	– Foreign Direct Investment – Leasing, delayed payments, – Contracts with explicit investment clauses
Raising revenue for the government	'Crowding-out effect': less money for private investment	Government investment in infrastructure
Political economy arguments:		
Reduce government interference in the economy Make lobbing for government support more difficult	Credibility of the declared 'hard budget constraint'	Stable government, Commitment, Speed, Legitimacy
To promote wider share ownership and create political support for the reform programme	Losers (impact of restructuring on employment and wage structure); Corruption, unjustified private gains leading to social dissatisfaction	Social safety net, Concessions for insiders Quality of public administration, adequate law and enforcement
Create foundation for democracy (the link between private property and political freedom)	Concentrated gains may create powerful economic actors that may not support democracy	Avoid both state capture and business capture

also relates to network industries, where marginal costs of supply may be decreasing over the feasible range (water, gas, electricity, railways etc.).

And, last but not least, the owners and the assets are heterogeneous, which implies that achieving an adequate match between the two is important. In the longer term, the problem does not exist if property rights are easily transferable – say, via a well-functioning capital market: assets will tend to be transferred to those able to make best use of them, as they will offer higher prices. However, this may not be the case in the transition economies, at least at the beginning of the transition period: informational asymmetries and transactions costs generated by cumbersome legal procedures may create frictions preventing efficient transfers to take place. It implies that the initial identity of the owners may matter and therefore different privatization methods may lead either to more or less efficient outcomes.

An important aspect of efficiency follows from wage and employment decisions. While discussing both recessions and labour markets, we already encountered different effects for different categories of emerging private owners. In particular, 'insider ownership' may lead to a low responsiveness of employment, both downwards and upwards.[5] The effects may be transformed from the micro level into general equilibrium effects if 'insider privatization' is the dominant method chosen and where both the entry of new firms and ownership transfers are slow.

'Insider privatization' may also be detrimental to the creation of capital markets as informational asymmetry coupled with potential opportunistic behaviour of the insider owners with relation to the outside minority investors may create disincentives for the latter group to acquire equity. In addition, in economies with inadequate protection of minority interests, the potential for opportunistic behaviour, in particular for realizing the private benefits of control by the managers (and dominant owners) may be high. In some types of privatizations, share transfers may be only internal, and it may be both relatively easy and in the interests of managers to prevent the transfer of shares from employees to outsiders. By doing so, they may preserve corporate control and the private benefits linked to it which are not shared with other employee owners; an effect that may be achieved with little capital investment by the managers.[6]

In general, the effects of privatization are conditional on institutional reform, and the existence of protected, enforceable and transferable property rights. Again, 'insider privatization' may not be associated with negative effects, where the institutional environment offers some degree of protection for external minority investors and facilitates transferability. However, where the ownership structures do not evolve after privatization, 'insider privatizations' can fail to over-come another major deficiency of state firms – i.e. problems with attracting external finance. While firms operate in the environment of private financial markets, that may lead to underinvestment, due to the informational asymmetry problems perceived by the providers of finance. An alternative is to continue to provide state-sponsored finance, and it may not be a coincidence that in transition economies, where transition programmes were dominated by 'insider privatiza-tion', the role of the government in shaping enterprise finance was also important, either by the provision of sponsored finance from state-owned banks, or by variation in the enforcement of tax collection. However, in most cases, informational asymmetry problems between the government and the enterprises are even worse than between the private providers of finance and insiders, the incentives of government officials are inadequate, the quality of administration is low and the likelihood of a 'soft' budget constraint is high.[7] This problem is not unique to transition economies; in both the UK and in other market economies, privatization programmes were typically first initiated for financial reasons. For example, with British Telecom – the archetypical case for many subsequent privatizations – it was practically impossible to raise the amount of debt finance needed to restructure the ageing physical capital and introduce modern telecommunication technolo-gies. It could be possible with explicit government guarantees, but with an investment programme of that size that would create significant risk for the government budget. Those examples reflect the same type of public finance risk that re-emerged with a wave of renationalizations of banks following the financial panics of 2008.

A final economic argument relates to a more elusive but nevertheless important effect of privatization on entrepreneurship and innovation. Managers of state firms were chosen for their ability to implement the plan and their conformity to the regime, not for their innovative skills. Transferring corporate control to outsiders may facilitate a change in management, but nevertheless a more basic problem remains: initially, there is no pool of managers with skills that are fully adequate for a market economy environment. The human and social capital endow-ment of the new entrants – i.e. entrepreneurs and new firms created from scratch – may be qualitatively different and more relevant for a market-orientated system. Yet on the other hand, different skills are needed to run start-up firms as opposed to large enterprises, so a problem remains. Importing managers from abroad may be a solution; however, the cost is high and they in turn will be hampered by a lack of knowledge of local conditions.

Short-term economic, financial and fiscal objectives

Again, both types of privatization and the environmental institutional characteristics affect access to finance. With capital markets in a nascent state and few savings available, there is insufficient supply of funds. Here, we come back to the issue of the speed-quality trade-off. Selling fast means not only selling under-priced assets, but also selling to economic agents with no effective opportunity to raise the funds required for restructuring. The limited financial resources of potential buyers coupled with constraints in access to finance imply a trade-off between the price paid for privatized assets and the value of the remaining funds available for investment and restructuring. Leasing and delayed payments may be a solution in this case. Explicit investment clauses may also be introduced as part of privatization contracts. However, in the case of large firms, the best source of finance,[8] but also for the inflow of other tangible and intangible resources, including managerial skills, may be foreign direct investment (FDI). FDI creates more stable links and reduces the risk of speculative outflows and the destabilizing impact of changes to the exchange rate, unlike other sources of finance from abroad, a feature that become critical for economic performance during the 2008–2009 crisis. However, with excess of asset supply over demand, and high risk premium, the low prices received for assets during a foreign-led privatization may lead to political controversy. Again, where the transaction costs of property rights transfers are relatively low, the initial preference given to domestic players may be followed by subsequent transfer of ownership to foreigners. The only difference is that instead of the state budget, domestic investors cash in on the price premium when selling to foreigners. The Czech Republic may be an example of this kind of evolution in ownership structure.

The issue of FDI leads us to another privatization objective – i.e. raising fiscal revenue for the government. This is no longer an argument based on the efficiency of private firms. Its validity rests on financial market imperfections and the difficulty for the government to smooth its revenue and spending over time. Fiscal problems may be particularly acute at the time of institutional reform, which may both affect capacity of the government to raise tax revenue and result in some temporary increase in spending. This is where privatization revenues can make a difference. In Central Eastern Europe domestic savings are low and, as already discussed, selling to domestic investors may result in the risk that their funds will be used to pay for privatized assets instead of subsequent investment in privatized firms. This situation has been typical for many employee buyouts, where company funds were channelled as loans to employees to finance the privatization. From this point of view, the choice of foreign investors, who have easy access to lower-cost finance available on the foreign financial markets, is attractive. Indeed, there is clear empirical evidence of the link between the amount of government revenue generated from privatization and the involvement of foreign investors in privatization (see EBRD 2000: 84; Hungary is the country with both the highest cumulative privatization revenues *per capita* and the highest cumulative FDI *per capita* over 1989–99; at the other end of the spectrum we find Uzbekistan).

While privatization can generate a substantial amount of fiscal revenue, how these funds are spent by the government is also important. Fiscal policy may be most efficient if the government channels the funds obtained towards productivity-enhancing public infrastructure. Another option is to use temporary privatization revenues to fund a temporary increase in welfare spending resulting from a temporary, restructuring-induced increase in unemployment.

Political economy

In addition to pure economic and finance arguments, some privatization objectives may also be defined in terms of political economy. Delimitation of border lines between the state administration and industry is far easier when firms are privately owned. It makes lobbying more visible and therefore more difficult, and therefore improves the overall efficiency of public finance. Here, however, the argument supports faster, not slower, privatization, in direct contradiction to some of the financial and economic reasons presented above. Leaving many firms in the state sector may result in the subsequent entrenchment of insiders and stagnation.

In a broader sense, there is also a link between the economic and political system. Privatization with many beneficiaries may create political support for market democracy, while an economy dominated by state ownership is hardly consistent with political pluralism. With control over economic property, the incumbent government gains an enormous means of economic control over its citizens, including their employment and income. It is not by chance that the extensive state ownership in the economy is typically mirrored by more or less acute forms of authoritarianism, typically hidden behind façades of democracy.

The political economy argument for fast-paced privatization played a key role in the heated debate on privatization in Russia. As was argued, the only fast privatization path implied transfer of ownership to insiders. The proponents of this point of view argued that insiders were already endowed with control rights at the onset of the transition, and the formal transfer of ownership to them could lead to a widespread legitimization of private property (Boycko, Shleifer and Vishny 1995; see also Åslund 2002). According to this point of view, the expected positive effects of the reforms on political legitimization outweighed the (hopefully short-term) economic efficiency costs of the chosen privatization strategy.

However, the political results of the programme in Russia were not as positive as expected. The major problems resulted not necessarily from the mass privatization programme, but from the subsequent 'loans-for-equity' privatization scheme which was introduced in 1995, generating funds that helped Boris Yeltsin to win the presidential elections the year after. The 'loans-for-equity' programme led to an enormous transfer of wealth (in particular: assets in the natural resources sector) to a narrow group of people with strong political connections; this contributed strongly to the creation a group of 'oligarchs', and to corruption, creating foundations for political capitalism. While the power balance between politicians and business 'oligarchs' evolved over time in Russia, the close relations between the two groups remains a defining feature of Russian capitalism. The problems Russia faces may be seen as an example of a 'political resource curse' – i.e. a situation when a rich endowment in natural resources has not only positive effects on the economy (as for instance exemplified by the fact, that Russia was able to accumulate financial reserves that helped it to accommodate the impact of 2008–2009 economic crises), but it also amplifies corruption (Buccellato and Mickiewicz 2009). Thus, fast privatization may be damaging when the value of assets is very high and involves a non-equivalent transfer of wealth to a narrow group of owners, since it may decrease political support for private property instead of increasing it (empirical evidence on the 'political resource' course is provided by Kronenberg 2004).

Privatization objectives may thus be summarized under three headings: economic efficiency, finance and political economy. The optimum choice of faster, or slower privatization, and the related choice of privatization method, are conditional on the weights we attach to each category of objectives. Economic efficiency and finance arguments suggest that the best method of privatization may be a technically slow privatization to outsiders, with a prominent role played by foreign investors. If political economy arguments imply a fast privatization, then the only feasible solution is either to follow a mass privatization programme (voucher privatizations) or transfer corporate control to insiders. However, a first best solution may in fact be a combination of both, or what may be called a 'pecking order of privatization' (Mickiewicz 2009): where strong demand exists assets are sold to highest bidders, but assets that find no strong demand are privatized using mass privatization methods. Czech Republic comes close to representing such a strategy.

Trade-offs among privatization methods and secondary ownership transfers

Privatization, as we have seen, is defined as the transfer of ownership of assets from the government to private owners. From the legal point of view, the situation is clear: firms where over 50 per cent of equity is held by private owners are considered private (i.e. either a privatized or a new private firm). However, it is sometimes not easy to establish this in practice. While state firms are typically prevented from buying assets of other privatized companies, it is not always the case. In reality, the majority equity stakes in 'privatized' companies were sometimes held by some other state companies. Three main issues matter from the economic efficiency point of view – if there is:

(1) adequate monitoring by owners or their representatives,
(2) a positive change in the way a company is managed and
(3) access to resources is widened.

In this respect, some secondary ownership transfers resulting in majority stakes held by other state companies may not bring negative results, provided that the company is exposed to capital market discipline implying that minority block-holders can contribute to effective monitoring.

However, a different situation arises when apparent privatization is in fact a disguised transfer within the state sector. A good example of such a situation is the bank-led restructuring programmes which in some cases led to solutions where debt-equity swaps resulted in majority shares being transferred to state-owned banks, awaiting their own privatization. One well-known example is the Szczecin shipyard in north west Poland, announced as a prominent case of successful restructuring without a dominant role for outside private strategic investors which only a few years later proved to be an example of managerial failure and fraud due to insufficient corporate control by the absent owners. While possibly less spectacular, the results of other firms 'privatized' by bank restructuring programmes were no better (Chudzik 2000).

This example indicates that concern should not be about a formal act of privatization, but about an efficient transfer of control rights to investors (owners) capable of imposing a new set of objectives and strategies on the privatized company and also of providing new resources. In this case, the positive effects of privatization may appear even before the nominal transfer of ownership: incumbent managers may improve their performance in order to secure an extension of their contract from the new owners (in addition, they may also receive shares as part of the privatization deal, thus improved performance may be transformed into subsequent wealth increase for them, provided that the price of shares for the privatization sale is not pushed upwards, being based on the accounting value of assets; see Pinto Belka and Krajewski 1993).

In addition, from the corporate control point of view, it is important to describe the starting point correctly (see Figure 9.1 below). Dissolution

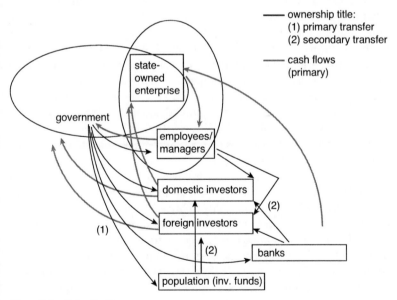

Figure 9.1   Privatization

of the central planning administration led to a vacuum, where effective control of thousands of state companies was left to insiders. In different transition countries, the balance of power between managers and workers differed. In Hungary, Poland and Yugoslavia, the role of workers' councils at a time of systemic change was relatively strong, with influence on managerial appointments and the distribution of profits. In Poland, and later on in Bulgaria, strong independent unions emerged, with well-organized structures able to counterbalance the managers' position. In both cases, due to the initial control void, the impact of trade unions was ambiguous. On the one hand, employment decisions driven by employee interests could work against efficient restructuring; on the other, the unions could provide the only effective mechanism blocking managerial theft, for which incentives had been created by endowing managers with effective control rights without residual claims (and inadequate monitoring and legal enforcement) (Bałtowski and Mickiewicz 2000; Mickiewicz and Bałtowski 2003).

The paradoxical feature of the command economy was that the ownership status of the 'state-owned companies' was blurred. Instead of being owned by the treasury, they were ambiguously described as 'socialist enterprises'. Key control rights remained with the economic administration and branch ministries, which were in turn supervised by the communist party structures. As already mentioned, dismantling of the latter led to insiders being endowed with effective control rights. This left policy-makers with two choices: either accept the status quo and privatize in the form of employee and managerial buyouts (typically based on heavily discounted prices of assets) or 'nationalize' before initiating a privatization aimed at outside owners. The latter option is usually described by the term 'corporatization', where the 'socialist' enterprises were turned into (state-owned) standard limited liability companies by issuing equity shares. The problem with this solution was that the insiders lost important control rights and as compensation they were typically offered minority shares (up to 20 per cent).

One particular issue related to employee buyouts was that even with discounted prices of assets and payments by instalments, it was difficult for employees to raise the necessary finance. The financial sector was not developed enough to participate in the operation. In practice, the only available source of finance was the company cash flow. Paying themselves higher wages was a costly option, given that much of the transfer would be captured by taxes. Thus, a typical scheme consisted of loans offered by the company to the employees, who could (partly) pay with them for the privatized assets. This explains why many employee buyouts left companies with insufficient cash and could result in initial deterioration of performance instead of improvement after privatization. To make things worse, the ownership of assets of the privatized companies was typically not transferred to the new private company organized by the employees until more than half of the privatization price had been repaid in subsequent instalments. Thus, the assets were leased and could not serve as a collateral for new finance.[9]

In many cases, policy-makers were aware of the potential problems related to 'insider privatization'. For two early reformers (Hungary and Poland), the initial policy choice was to privatize to outsiders via newly created stock exchanges ('capital privatization') using IPOs, a solution copied from standard British and other Western European methods. However, within the first two years of the reform programme only five privatizations were completed via this method in Poland and four in Hungary. The implementation of the programme turned out to be time-consuming, for several reasons. First, the prerequisite for floatation was a mandatory initial valuation. With accounting systems inherited from a command economy, where finance played only a secondary role, valuation by hired international auditors turned out to be very difficult. Secondly, while for political reasons the government agencies were aiming at high prices, the demand for privatized shares was low, given the transitional recession and uncertainty about the future. As a result, a mixture of various privatization methods was adopted in both countries (Frydman, Rapaczynski and Earle 1993; Mickiewicz and Bałtowski 2003; Mihalyi 2000).

In general, where the choice was to privatize to outsiders, policy-makers were left with four major options:

1. domestic investors,
2. foreign (corporate) investors,
3. financial institutions and
4. the population at large.

Typically, where financial institutions emerged as dominant owners it was as a result of bad debt problems and debt-equity swaps. Domestic investors played a more important role in the case of small- and medium-size firms (SMEs) and a less important role in case of large firms, at least in the initial stages of privatization. There were simply insufficient numbers of domestic investors. Moreover, to choose outside domestic investors was not always the most attractive option from the political point of view. This is because much of the domestic wealth before transition was held by nomenklatura members: it was not unusual to see 'red' directors coming back as new private capitalists, provoking public dissatisfaction.[10] In turn, foreign investors were typically capable of paying the highest privatization prices and bringing in financial, managerial and other intangible and tangible resources essential for restructuring. Nevertheless, the dominant role of foreign owners was not always politically expedient either, as governments were criticized for selling national assets for depressed prices. That led many policy-makers to adopt another option – to transfer the assets to the population at large. Those schemes, known as 'mass privatization', became a trademark and a unique feature of the transition programmes. First applied in Czechoslovakia in 1991, they were implemented to a different extent in all the transition countries apart from Hungary (Coffee 1996; Estrin and Stone 1996; Takla 1999; Havrda 2003; Mejstrik 2003; Zemplinerova and Machacek 2003).

The basic idea of mass privatization is to issue coupons, available to all citizens, which in the next stage may be exchanged for the equity of privatized companies, typically in auctions, which determine the price of equity in terms of the coupons. The schemes led to the emergence of privatization investment funds, which could make investment decisions on behalf of individual investors.[11] In some cases (in particular, Russia), the mass privatization schemes were combined with 'insider privatization' in such a way that the latter dominated. In effect, these privatizations ended up being 'insider privatizations'.

In terms of control rights, the mass privatization schemes achieved very little in the short term. Dispersed private owners could neither counterbalance the insiders' influence nor were they capable of or willing to provide new finance for restructuring. The investment funds were also not well prepared for efficient monitoring (in contrast to strategic corporate investors), and had no access to new finance. In addition, in Czechoslovakia and in some other cases, specific restrictions were imposed on investment funds so that they did not acquire dominant stakes in the privatized companies. As a result, the control vacuum inherited from the initial point of transition continued for several more years, with protracted stalemates between investment funds and insider managers, and with the rights of minority individual investors neglected altogether. In the longer term, however, the evolution of ownership structures started, with some funds and other investors focusing on the middleman role, specializing in acquiring controlling stakes to sell later to strategic investors.

However, any privatization method needs to be assessed against feasible alternatives. The main advantage of mass privatizations was that it separated the industry from the political sphere much better than in the case of state companies. This in turn helped to diminish effects of selective soft financing of firms and of other forms of political favouritism that destroy efficiency effects of competition. Indeed, Bennett, Estrin and Urga (2007) demonstrated that mass privatization was associated with stronger economic growth in Central and Eastern European economies.[12]

Table 9.2 below summarizes the discussion on the immediate impact of privatization methods. However, there were subsequent transfers between the categories and after a decade of privatization programmes the resulting ownership structures of the CE industries is surprisingly similar, with a dominant role played by foreign capital. On the other hand, much of Russian and CIS enterprises remain controlled by insiders (Filatotchev, Wright and Bleaney 1999; Mickiewicz and Bałtowski 2003; Voszka 2003; Zemplinerova and Machacek 2003; Mickiewicz 2006). From the point of view of capital market efficiency, the subsequent transferability of ownership shares coupled with adequate protection of ownership rights were important conditions if any privatization method was to produce efficient results.

Table 9.2   Trade-offs among privatization methods

Objectives	Better corporate governance	Speed and feasibility	Widened access to skills and capital	Increase in government Revenue	Greater fairness
Method:					
Sale to outsiders	+	–	+	+	–
Management buyouts	–	+	–	–	–
Employee buyouts (and mass privatization to insiders)	–	+	–	–	–/+
Mass privatization (equal access)	–	+	–	–	+
Re-privatization	?	–	–	–	+

Notes: + = positive effect; – = negative effect; ? = ambiguous effect

The microeconomic impact of privatization

The impact of privatization may be considered on both the macro and the micro levels. On the macro level, there are synergies between the different elements of the reforms: the effect of privatization is conditional on other elements of reforms being implemented either first or at the same time. Price-setting, and freedom to export and import are key elements of control rights, without which formal property rights are devoid of economic sense. Where those restrictions were not removed, no significant changes in the behaviour of economic agents resulted. For instance, rent controls in tenement houses below equilibrium level led to underinvestment and a gradual deterioration of stock and impeded the development of the housing market. In the sectors with technological reasons for entry difficulties, competition policy and anti-monopoly regulation is needed. The major state telecommunication operator may be privatized to a strategic foreign investor without generating fast development of services if the investor secures a monopolistic position as part of the purchase contract (typically for some specific period of time). Without proper regulation and freedom of entry, the foreign monopolist will remain orientated on maintaining high prices and taking over monopolistic rents.

However, assuming freedom of decision-making and competitive frameworks including free entry, the key issues relate to the improvement in microeconomic efficiency resulting from the transfer of corporate controls to new owners. By now, there is a well-established methodology of empirical studies on the performance of firms after privatization (see especially Megginson and Netter 2001); however, there are caveats to be considered. Five key identification problems can be isolated:

(1) The period of time may be too short. Some effects of privatization may emerge with a delay, after a few years. The time path following the restructuring effort may resemble a 'J-curve', with an initial deterioration in financial indicators resulting from reorganization. The issue is not trivial, as can be easily seen by a proliferation of early studies on performance, based on the first-second year after privatization. A lot of attention was given to the results, which production and dissemination may now be justified only by policy-makers' pressure to have reports on the impact of privatization programmes.[13] That leads to the underestimation of privatization effects.

(2) As mentioned earlier, change in expectations may already lead to the improvement of performance of managers. As documented by Pinto, Belka and Krajewski (1993), 'managers believe that good performance will be rewarded at the time of privatization and that their reputation, and hence compensation, will depend upon their performance today' (1993: 255) It is not only that they may aim at keeping their jobs after the takeover of control and expect to be rewarded. It is also due to the fact that the emergence of private firms creates a labour market for managerial talent, which has beneficial effects on the performance of those enterprises which remain state-owned. Positive incentives for managers appear, because they care for their reputation and career prospect. We may thus have external positive effects of privatization; they may apply to companies not yet privatized. In each case, the effect will undermine the empirical evidence on the gains from individual privatizations if the comparison is cross-sectional, between the privatized and non-privatized firms.

(3) However, the opposite effect may take place in the case of 'insider privatizations'. It may be profitable for insiders to hide the good results of their firms before privatization to achieve a lower privatization price. The positive effect of 'insider privatizations' may thus be overestimated in empirical studies.

(4) Reliability of information. For tax reasons, firms manipulate profit and investment figures. While state firms had incentives to exaggerate their results, private firms, especially those which are not publicly quoted and do not crucially rely on external finance, have an incentive to hide profits and investments, as inflating current cost becomes important where corporate income taxes are high. The quality of accounting and audit improved, but it was particularly poor in the initial period of transition. As a result, privatization results may have been underestimated. That would apply more strongly to companies privatized in countries where institutional environment is weak (see our earlier discussion on the latter).

(5) Selection bias. This bias may operate in both directions, depending on the circumstances. In companies with high rents and a high value of capital, insiders may block privatization efforts as they may not have sufficient funds for employee buyouts. By doing that they will continue to extract rents under state ownership. In contrast, in badly performing firms, the insiders may put pressure on the state administration to help them find investors who may save the company, provided that the threat of bankruptcy is credible.

Both those effects can result in inefficient companies being chosen for privatization, especially in the initial phase.

On the other hand, external investors, especially foreign investors, may be interested in picking up the best companies; here the resulting bias in empirical estimation of privatization results to foreign investors may be positive. Where a battery of privatization methods is available, it is likely that those firms that cannot attract the interest of strategic investors will be dumped into a wide pool of mass privatization, which may result in the negative selection bias there.

With these caveats, the list of microeconomic performance indicators opens with productivity measures. Total factor productivity (TFP) may be estimated from the production function, although good data on the value of assets has been missing in early period, making the estimates problematic initially. For that reason, many empirical studies focused on labour productivity approximated by the sales/employment ratio. Albeit popular, the measure is misleading. A company (say, a new firm), which increases employment following the increase in sales is recorded as one with deteriorating performance, while another (say, an insider-dominated company) maximizing rents per head and blocking employment increase seems to be more efficient.

With time, the quality of financial information improves, and studies relying on more recent data increasingly use standard financial indicators of performance, such as return on equity (RoE) or assets (RoA). Again, because data on the value of assets is problematic, profits per worker is another statistic often used. Servicing of external financial obligations and no default on debt may be another measure, as are indicators of a 'hard' budget *vis-à-vis* the government (no tax arrears, etc.). Sometimes, an external 'soft' budget was replaced by a form of internal 'soft' budget in a form of wage arrears, the lack of which may also be included as a performance measure. However, the limited reliability and high volatility of purely financial measures over time led many researchers to rely on simple output (revenues, sales) dynamics, which are typically highly correlated with earnings/ profits smoothed over time. Finally, given the short time horizon, studies with access to survey data may rely on some direct indicators of restructuring (quantitative and qualitative). These include indicators of the renovation/restructuring of capital and machinery, the innovativeness/ creation of new products and the employment policies, including the restructuring of employment. Djankov and Murrell (2002) provide an extensive meta analysis, which summarizes empirical studies on the performance of privatized companies. Table 9.3 reproduces one of their results: a compar-

Table 9.3 Djankov and Murell results: Testing if change of ownership and organizational form brought improvement in performance, as compared with state firms

Category of firm/owners	Significant evidence of improvement	Significance (t-statistics) from meta study
Workers	No	–
Diffuse individual owners	No	0.50
Managers	No	0.90
Insiders (as a composite group)	Yes	2.61
Banks	Yes	3.42
Outsiders (as a composite group)	Yes	3.45
State firms after corporatization	Yes	5.69
Investment funds	Yes	7.05
Domestic block-holders	Yes	7.73
Foreign investors	Yes	7.82

Source: Adapted from Djankov and Murrell (2002).

ison of the performance change brought about by different forms of privatization – i.e. in comparison with the traditional SOE. It is interesting to note that there is little improvement in firms owned either by insiders or by diffuse corporate owners. The latter seem unable to affect the internal control structures, given the underdeveloped capital markets and inadequate legal protection of minority shareholders. Financial institutions as owners are in the middle range. So are firms, not yet fully privatized, in the initial phase of preparation – that is, 'corporatized'; it seems that the positive impact of the privatization process may already appear prior to the final formal privatization date. Finally, strategic private investors, both domestic and foreign, appear as most effective in imposing the necessary efficiency-enhancing restructuring. One may note that the difference between the domestic and foreign corporate players performing the investment role is not that significant. Thus, the important role of foreign investors may result more from the fact that there was a limited number of domestic industrial players that could participate in the privatization process, not that their capacities were lower.

Private sector, privatization revenue and the pecking order of privatization

Figure 9.2 present a most recent assessment of the two key privatization parameters. On the horizontal axis we find the approximate share of the

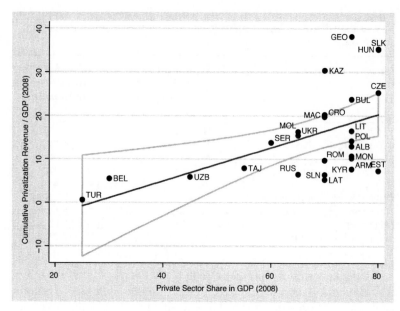

Figure 9.2 Private sector share in GDP and cumulative privatization revenue over GDP (2008)

Source: EBRD.

private sector in GDP (resulting both from the privatization processes, but also from new entry of private firms, and shrinking or expanding of the remaining state companies). On the vertical axis we find cumulative privatization revenues scaled by GDP. Obviously, the two are related: there is a positive correlation between the size of the private sector and the privatization revenues accumulated over time. It is more interesting therefore to focus on countries that are above the estimated least square line (linking size of the private sector and privatization revenues): those are countries that maximized the revenues from privatization.

High privatization revenues may be important from the fiscal point of view. However, they may also be important as an indicator of the quality of the privatization programmes: high privatization prices indicate that assets were transferred to those who can make most efficient use, as indicated by their willingness to pay. As already discussed, high privatization revenues are typically associated with participation of strategic outside investors, foreign investors in particular, and their presence tend to be associated with better governance structures and with better performance. Using terminology of Bałtowski and Mickiewicz (2000) we may label such privatizations as 'equivalent', in contrast of 'non-equivalent' privatizations, either to insiders or to general public.

Hungary, which never implemented a mass privatization programme, and from the very beginning opened its industry to foreign investors, is both one of the few transition countries with smallest residual state sector and which accumulated largest privatization revenues relative to the size of the economy.[14] Georgia's position is very similar. More interestingly however, we see Slovak Republic not far away, and the position of the Czech Republic is also good with respect to use of equivalent privatization techniques. This is revealing if we take into account that those two nations started first mass privatization programmes early on. Clearly, especially in the case of Czech Republic (as Slovak privatization was slowed down in mid-1990s), we can see there is not necessary an inherent contradiction between speed and quality. The key policy choice is to apply 'equivalent' direct sales (or stock exchange flotations) where strong demand is visible and to privatize the remaining assets using 'non-equivalent' techniques. This way, where the efficient owners can be found quickly, property is being transferred to them. Where this is not possible, fast privatization is preferable as it restores a relatively more effective barrier between the government and business assets making soft budgeting and other distortions of competition less likely. This is the pecking order of privatization (Mickiewicz 2009). However, as even in countries where the process has been most advanced, the share of government in production still remains around 20 per cent – high by international comparisons – the privatization business clearly remains unfinished.

10
The Order of Financial Liberalization

This chapter begins with an overview of the functions of financial inter-mediation and possible sources of inefficiency, as seen in the context of transition economies of Central and Eastern Europe. We discuss the order of financial liberalization. Next, we ask how the transition economies in general, and the more narrowly defined regions within this group, differ amongst themselves and from other comparator economies along basic financial dimensions. We discuss how the financial reforms implemented in the transition countries affected the characteristics of their financial systems, distinguishing between immediate effects and those that came with a time lag. We then draw some brief conclusions.

Financial intermediation and transition

Financial intermediation

It may be useful to start our discussion with the basics. Reforms intro-duced in Central and Eastern Europe and Central Asia aimed at rebuild-ing the basic functions of financial intermediation, most of which were simply not performed under the old regime. Borrowing from Stiglitz (1992) and expanding, we may distinguish five key roles of financial intermediation:

- First, the financial sector facilitates the transfer of 'resources (capital) from those who have it (savers) to those who can make use of it (borrowers, or investors)' (Stiglitz 1992: 163). This is possible due to credible financial contracting: the investors expect future returns, with net present value no smaller than the invested funds. Finance is always thus linked to inter-temporal choice and to the willingness of some economic agents to trade present for future consumption. In addition to transfers, the financial institutions facilitate cooperation between individual investors in agglomerating capital for a given investment project. This is important, as many projects 'require more capital than that of any of one saver or any small set of savers' (Stiglitz 1992: 163).

- This links to the next point – i.e. risk management. Because all financial transactions involve time, they also involve risk, as the future is always uncertain. The risk varies between one project and another, and the financial sector creates a possibility to match alternative projects with investors characterized by different preferences towards risk. Moreover, financial intermediation reduces the overall level of risk for any investor, by creating opportunities for pooling risks and creating diversified investment portfolios for which the idiosyncratic risks of individual projects balance each other.

- Financial institutions are also responsible for selecting the projects and choosing the structure of financial contracts that maximizes efficiency for a given type of project. It is not always the case that individual borrowers have sufficient knowledge to arrive at a realistic assessment of the value of their projects. Moreover, they may be motivated to misrepresent the information they offer to the providers of finance (pre-contractual opportunism or the adverse selection problem, Stiglitz and Weiss 1981). The incentive to do so results from the fact that in many financial contracts we see an asymmetry of benefits and costs from possible outcomes of the project. If the financial contract is based on fixed claims (such as an ordinary bank loan), the borrower may be tempted to choose a risky project which may yield high returns in the case of success. The (mean) expected PV of the project could be negative, but it may still be attractive to the borrower, who will get all the residual value (after paying fixed returns to the lender) in the case of a positive outcome, but will be limited in her losses to her initial share if things go wrong. An alternative category of financial contract is equity. Here, the provider of the finance shares the residual value. That may reduce pre-contractual opportunism, but can increase post-contractual opportunism (the agency problem). The latter issue stems from the fact that while residual claims are shared between insiders and outsiders, much of the effective control rights remain with insiders (managers). As a result, the value of the project (the firm) is no longer fixed. It depends on the actions of managers, who may pursue some private benefits of control (Jensen and Meckling 1976; see also Hart 2001).

- That leads us to the next point. The efficient outcome will be achieved by combining an adequate financial contract and monitoring (which ensures that funds are used in the way the receivers of finance committed themselves to, i.e. counteract post-contractual opportunism – the agency problem). Thus, efficiency is increased via both the expertise of the financial sector in monitoring and via effective financial regulations, which make monitoring more easy.
- And, finally, contracts have to be enforceable, so that those who have obtained the funds transfer back the resources in the way specified by the contract. Effective bankruptcy procedures are part of the solution here.

Institutional and legal environment

These last comments indicate that the efficiency of financial contracts is affected not only by the actions of the parties directly involved, but also by the institutional and legal environment. Some of those common arrangements result from self-regulation (for instance, on some major stock exchanges), and in many cases reputation may be the strongest single mechanism enforcing compliance. However, in the transition environment waiting for the natural 'bottom-up' construction of self-regulatory mechanisms by market participants may be an unrealistic option, as reputational effects may be slow to build and incentives to free ride may remain strong. Relevant behavioural mechanisms may take decades to build, as exemplified by the history of self-regulatory financial institutions. It is typically thus the government administration – an institution endowed with the right of coercion – which plays an important role in preventing fraud and deception and building a institutional framework for the financial sector.

An important function of efficient regulation is to increase the amount of information available to the relevant parties. That comes in the form of disclosure laws, in particular, so that investors can adequately assess risk. Because of the large number of dispersed investors, a free rider problem may arise, and there is thus a need for centralized monitoring and regulation of financial institutions. The key functions of the government (or alternatively of other forms of collective action, including self-regulation) are the following.

A fundamental task of any government is to protect property rights to assets and the contracts that link those assets with different users. At the same time, the government needs to impose some credible constraints on itself, so that expropriation of financial assets by excessive taxation or outright nationalization are not seen as threats discouraging the expansion of the financial sector. Equally importantly, the government provides protection against expropriation by other individuals and private institutions, in particular by combating fraud and outright deception. This function does not differentiate the financial sector from any other types of economic activity, except that the financial contracts are more complex and therefore protection against expropriation is more challenging.

Second, the government may increase the overall efficiency of the financial sector by competition policies, as in other sectors of the economic system. Oligopolistic banking sector, closed to competition from both inside the country and from foreign entry creates rents for incumbent players, at cost of more expensive finance for outside users and lower rewards to the providers of finance, including savers.

Third, the importance of the government for the financial sector also relates to the fact that the financial sector is strongly affected by the macroeconomic performance of the economy, and vice versa – problems in the financial sector may have detrimental effects on the rest of the economy. The first issue leads to the simple observation that maintaining overall macroeconomic stability may decrease the cost of finance, expanding the volume of financial intermediation and leading to more investment and growth. A high inflation rate is typically associated with more variation and more risk with a detrimental effect on any long-term investments.

On the other hand, financial crises and the collapse of financial intermediation have a strong negative effect on economic activity – i.e. they may lead to recession and even to prolonged slump. For that reason, the government typically plays the role of the lender of last resort (LOLR), using deposit insurance and guarantee funds. However, such public insurance may again result in opportunistic behaviour (moral hazard). In particular, as was clear during the 2008–2009 global crisis, large financial institutions create a moral hazard problem: they become so big that they may safely assume they will be always rescued by the government. That may lead to reckless financial strategies, and lack of proper care in financial investment. The ultimate cost of this comes in a form of public spending on rescue packages, ultimately always financed by taxpayers.

Insurance may decrease the monitoring effort by the ultimate providers of finance. It thus works only if some public agency offers an efficient replacement for monitoring, which leads us back to the issue of public regulation. The government needs to impose a system which minimizes the risk of financial meltdown, in particular by imposing adequate reserves requirements on banks. However, while important, such reserve requirements, and other forms of 'financial repression', increase the cost of finance, as they lead to a larger wedge between the loan and the deposit rate (McKinnon 1993). In addition, without high quality administration, this regulatory effort is not only likely to be ineffective, it may be become counter-productive: endowing an inefficient government with more regulatory powers will not improve the situation. To understand this we need to reach beyond the old, traditional 'public interest' view of the government, which assumes the government has both capabilities but also incentives to implement efficient policies and regulation. Consistent with this view, if efficient solutions are not implemented, the problems must be purely of technical nature, they imply technical mistakes or lack of technical knowledge. This technocratic view of government is questioned by the 'private interest' approach. It accounts for the possibility that politicians and regulators may act opportunistically. Regulation may be captured by those that are supposed to be regulated ('regulatory capture'), or it may be driven by political interests ('political capture'). As a result, financial institutions may be pressed to channel credit to firms that are chosen on political not on efficiency basis, or simply to subsidize government spending below the real opportunity cost. In particular, the regulators may be pressed to maintain low-interest rates to make government borrowing easier, a pattern that was clear in many countries in build-up to the financial crisis of 2008–2009. In general, regulation may maximize the welfare of politicians and bureaucrats instead of public welfare (Barth, Caprio and Levine 2006).

All this has important implications for Central East European economies. As already discussed, generally the quality of public administration is lower, and if this is not taken into account, endowing the executive branch of the government with the same monitoring and regulatory powers as in some of the most advanced, institutionally strong Western economies may be counter-productive. The challenge is to build genuinely independent monitoring institutions that could be isolated from political influence, with strong legal foundations based on real and not on apparent constitutional guarantees of independence. That relates to the functions of Central Bank in particular.

Finance in the transition economies

The quality of financial market regulation correlates with the general level of economic development.[1] Djankov, McLiesh and Shleifer (2005) demonstrate a clear-cut link between the level of GDP *per capita* and the index of creditors' rights.[2] In the same paper, the authors also distinguish between five legal traditions: English, French, German, Nordic and Socialist. In the French and Nordic legal traditions, creditors' rights are protected less than in the English one. The comparison of the latter with both German and Socialist legal traditions is less clear-cut. It is interesting to note that the transition economies are not included in one legal tradition category. While all 12 CIS countries, for which the communist period lasted for about seventy years, are included in the 'Socialist' legal tradition category, the remaining 15 transition economies are not. In the latter group, the communist system was imposed within the timespan of a few years after the Second Word War and lasted for about 40 years. Even more importantly, it overlapped with only the few final years of the Stalinist era, when the process of eradication of market institutions was most radical. More importantly, all economies in the latter group (non-CIS) were able to reinstall their pre-1939 legal regulations, without the necessity of creating or importing their business law from abroad. That gave them a clear advantage in terms of financial markets regulation and meant that they could introduce more advanced reforms faster. We shall discuss the differences between both groups; before that, however, it is worthwhile making few comments on the appropriate order of financial reforms.

Before transition, the banks merely executed the plan, and never exercised any monitoring or risk assessment role. Thus, at the beginning of the transition, the banks had to develop monitoring skills, build up information on their customers and learn how to assess risk. To complicate the task even further, the past performance of the clients was not relevant for the assessment of future performance, as firms were operating under a very different set of incentives, and different skills were rewarded (Chapter 1). Even if the banks had had long-term relationships with some firms, the nature of economic change made this past knowledge mostly redundant from the point of view of financial assessment. Neither was present performance a good indicator of future performance, due to the high level of economic instability. According to Colombo and Driffill (2003), initial imperfections in the credit financial market particularly affected three aspects of the transition processes:

- Restructuring of the state-owned and privatized companies
- Growth of the new entrepreneurial firms
- Privatizing those companies – i.e. pricing the firms and channelling the demand for assets.

We have already discussed the first two issues in the context of the explanation of 'transitional recessions' (Chapter 6). The third was discussed in

Chapter 9.[3] The theme we focus on here is the policy trade-off between expanding finance (which may facilitate both restructuring and expansion of the new sector) and minimizing the risk of financial crisis, likely when the pace of financial liberalization is faster than the related creation of a regulatory environment. This issue is discussed in detail in a seminal book by McKinnon (1993: first edn, 1991; see also his 1992 paper) and while there is no need to reproduce the whole argument, the main line of reasoning is worth bearing in mind.

McKinnon (1992, 1993) draws attention to the interdependence between financial sector reforms, macroeconomic stabilization and privatization. He argues that there is an appropriate order of financial liberalization, and that more advanced steps should not be implemented before the previous ones are in place. This is not necessarily an argument for gradualism and sequencing. Subsequent elements can be introduced faster or even contemporaneously, as long as we are sure that the most fundamental elements are already in place.

The first issue to note is that macroeconomic stabilization is a necessary condition for both financial and fiscal reform. Persistent high inflation may result in a high real cost of credit (see p. 152). McKinnon (1993) argues that, in turn, the high cost of credit provides a strong motivation for the government to subsidize enterprises. The financial source comes typically in the form of an inflation tax (imposed on the banking sector in particular) and a vicious circle of 'non-reform' is created. That leads us naturally to the reform of government finances (both removal of 'soft' budgeting and tax reform) as a second necessary condition for a sustainable expansion of the financial sector and macroeconomic stabilization.

In the sequencing of bank reforms McKinnon (1993) accentuates the role of positive real interest rates triggered by their early liberalization, and argues that an initial high relative cost of finance may be less harmful than it appears, as long as high lending rates are accompanied by an increase in deposit rates. The first argument is that much of enterprise finance for development relies on retained earnings, which are deposited within the banking sector; positive rates on deposit therefore play a critical role in encouraging financial accumulation in successful companies. Second, high deposit rates are instrumental in rebuilding domestic savings, and increasing the supply of credit for good projects.

McKinnon (1993) argues that high lending rates and a large spread between lending and deposit interest rates in the early period of reform may be a necessary price to pay for the preservation of financial system stability. If moral hazard in bank lending is significant (so that past loans are not repaid), it is better to force banks to create reserves to protect against bad debts and impose a regulatory regime which will increase the cost and supply of credit than to risk financial meltdown.

However, while an efficient regulatory regime may arrest the development of bad debts and prevent banking crises, it cannot by itself guarantee that the process of financial intermediation is efficient. For the latter, both the objective function of the financial institutions and their technical capacities have to change. Adequate privatization may result in the objectives of the banks becoming consistent with economic efficiency and may provide the know-how, human capital and managerial skills and resources for investment. The most realistic opportunity for such investment relates to the inflow of foreign capital and the takeover of banks by foreign owners. Fries, Neven and Seabright (2004) demonstrate that the foreign-owned banks initially had a cost advantage in the transition, albeit the effect vanished in the latter stages, possibly due to spillover learning effects. Yet, privatization must be accompanied by a competition policy, which is again particularly important to ensure the critical effect of positive deposit rates.

Transition economies in comparative perspective

The size and the quality of the financial sectors in comparative perspective

Gros and Steinherr (2004)[4] compare the transition economies with other countries, using a 1997 cross-section of countries. Their methodology relies on regressing an indicator of interest on GDP *per capita*, GDP *per capita* squared and dummies representing three subgroups of the transition economies: twelve CIS countries, eight economies that joined the EU in 2004 (CE8) and the remaining group of transition economies, all in South Eastern Europe (SEE, the Balkans). They report results for the following three financial indicators:

(1) The ratio of broad money (M2) to GDP. This indicator approximates the size of the banking sector. The results are that the dummy for the CIS is negative and significant; for the CE8, it is negative and insignificant.
(2) Credit to the private sector as a percentage of GDP. This is the same measure as used by Djankov, McLiesh and Shleifer (2005). It may be a better measure of the financial sector as it excludes the financing of the government, which adds nothing to the task of financial intermediation. On the other hand, it does not distinguish between two effects: the size of the financial sector and

the size of the private sector. The results were that all three groups of transition countries were significantly different from comparator countries in 1997.

(3) The spread between lending and deposit rates, an indicator which measures the efficiency of the financial system (a high spread may be caused by monopolistic banking structures, but also by an unstable macroeconomic environment and high inflation (see McKinnon 1993). The results are that the CIS dummy is highly significant, and the dummies for the two other groups are insignificant, due to a large variation within those groups. In particular, Hungary was identified as a positive outlier.

The results of a similar exercise based on more recent data with a slight variation in methodology are reported by Mickiewicz (2005: 154–6). The 1997 groupings of transition economies (CIS, CE8, remaining SEE) is no longer adequate in the more recent period. In general, we face further polarization of the transition economies. Out of the residual group, two more economies joined the EU in 2007 (Bulgaria and Romania), which reflects the advanced level of reform and adjustment in the more recent period. Similarly, Croatia is advanced in its reforms, and at the time of writing the EU accession negotiations are going on. Macedonia is another official candidate, and Albania, Montenegro and Serbia all applied for EU membership. Thus, most of the SEE (Balkan countries) group is gradually being moved to a 'new and prospective EU' group.

Mickiewicz (2005) confirms that in the more recent period the group of transition countries as a whole has been still distinguishable from the rest of the world in terms of finance. Combining the results on the size and efficiency of the financial sector, we may say the following: in early 2000s, the transition economies have not had sufficient time to build a sufficiently wide financial sector. However, in those economies which were more successful in their reforms in terms of the efficiency of the financial sector, the results were already better than for a comparator group of countries with similar level of GDP *per capita*.

Quality turned out to be easier to achieve than quantity: during the 2008–2009 global crisis most of the Central Eastern Europe faced little problems caused by its financial sectors; in those economies which were seriously affected by the crisis, the sources of problems were either on the fiscal side or related to too much exposure to financing from abroad.

Differences within Central Eastern Europe

We may get more insights looking at a more specific country-level comparison within the Central and Eastern European region. Figure 10.1

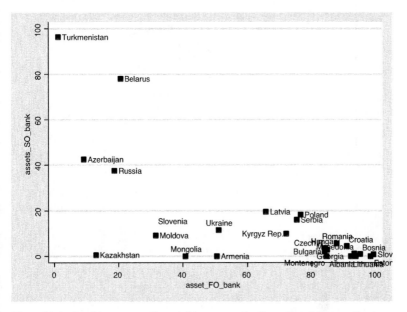

Figure 10.1   Banking sector: Ownership pattern in Central and Eastern Europe

presents the basic ownership structure of the banking sector, focusing on foreign ownership share (horizontal axis) and state ownership share (vertical axis). By 2008 the share of state ownership has been relatively low, with two notable exceptions of Turkmenistan and Belarus. On the other hand the share of foreign ownership of the banking sector, especially in the EU member states and those countries that are already included in the integration process, apart from Slovenia. The high foreign ownership share in banking turned out to be an important stabilizing factor during the 2008–2009 crisis, thanks to additional financial guarantees and imported credibility.

We may now turn to the measures of banking sector quality. Figure 10.2 presents lending rates, which capture the inefficiency of the banking sector, the inefficiency of the macroeconomic policy (inflation), but should also be corrected for the strength of demand for credit (which is not implemented here). Generally, lending interest rates are lower in countries that implemented banking reforms more thoroughly, again with the new EU member states benefiting additionally from imported credibility of their financial system. However, Belarus is a remarkable exception. Low interest rates on loans are driven not by the markets but by government policies implemented in the state bank sector. Given that the allocation of credit remains problematic there, this is not necessary a positive sign:

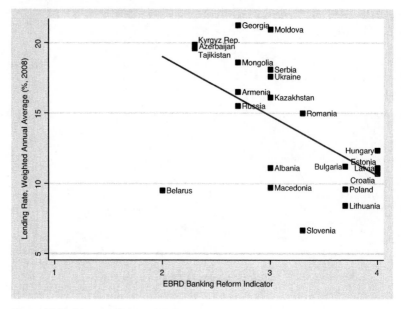

Figure 10.2   Interest rates on loans

financial repression results in subsidized credit being channelled to the state-owned companies generating no structural change.

Figure 10.3 below also focuses on interest rates, but this time presents the wedge between interest rates on loans and deposits, capturing efficiency of the banking sector more directly. Again, the link with banking reforms is very clear, with Belarus being an outlier due to its low interest rates imposed on the state banking sector by the government.

The share of non-performing loans in the banking sector may also be taken as another important dimension of quality, which relates to the inherent risk in the banking sector. If the share is large, the stability of the banking sector may be in danger. What is interesting to notice is that the banking sector reforms seem to have a non-linear effect (Figure 10.4): non-reformed banking sectors (Turkmenistan, Belarus) come with low risk of default, it appears. On the other hand, economies where the reform process resulted in both strong regulatory frameworks and in corporate governance structures that jointly guarantee efficient credit policies, the amount of bad loans also goes down. It seems that the worst situation is where reforms were partial: some liberalization was attempted, but the banks remained protected from competition and may continue to be

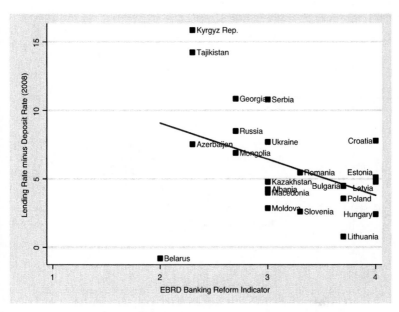

Figure 10.3 The difference between interest rates on loans and deposits

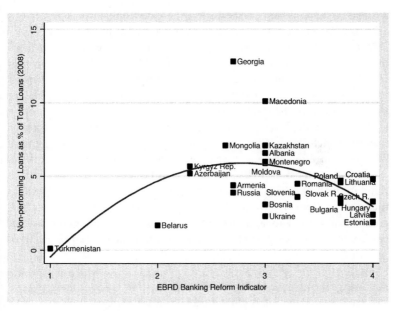

Figure 10.4 Non-performing loans

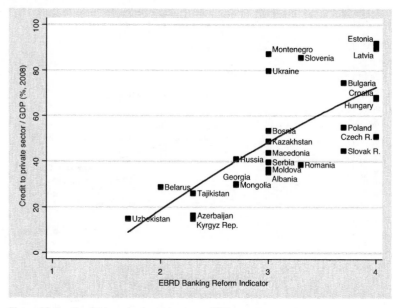

Figure 10.5   Credit to private sector over GDP

influenced by politicians, which affect their crediting choices negatively. This conclusion is not far from the one we arrived at in Chapter 6.

Last but not least, we present data on availability of finance as proxied by the ratio of credit to private sector over GDP (Figure 10.5). In Belarus, Uzbekistan and Tajikistan the share of private sector in production remains below 50 per cent and it comes as no surprise that most of finance takes place within the state sector. In few other Asian transition countries credit is also underdeveloped, despite larger levels of private sector activity. Countries included in the EU integration process are at the other end of the spectrum. However, for small open economies there are dangers associated with extensive credit provision, if it becomes too dependent on flows from abroad. This may come at cost of wide variation in output, as the world economy follows its all credit cycle, as documented by 2008–2009 crisis. Estonia and Latvia, with the highest position on our graph, are the two countries in case. We will come back to this issue in Chapter 12.

Determinants of financial characteristics

Following empirical illustration, our next question is about more systematic findings on the links between the reforms, the macroeconomic environment and our proxies of size and efficiency of the financial system.

First, we expect that both macroeconomic instability and lax public finance may exert a negative impact on the financial sector. We approximate the former by the inflation rate and the latter by the government balance (expecting a negative sign of the coefficient).

Secondly, following McKinnon (1993), we expect that the initial 'hardening' of the budget constraint may be accompanied by 'financial repression' higher interest rates, higher reserve requirements and other measures that may lead to a shrinkage in the volume of credit and finance. Again, however, following the appropriate order of financial liberalization, the effect should be temporary and after establishing some rudimentary financial control, the expansion of finance may again follow. Our primary proxy of this initial financial 'hardening' is the EBRD liberalization index, which includes measures of the 'soft' budget control.

Thirdly, the structural reforms in the banking system should be expected to bring positive results. A better corporate governance legal framework should result in lower agency problems and lead to an increase in supply of finance. The proxies are the EBRD indicators for 'Bank reform' and 'Governance and enterprise restructuring'. In addition, EBRD data permits us to investigate the impact of both the ownership composition of the banking sector and the number of banks operating in a given economy. The latter may be used as an (imperfect) proxy for competition in the banking sector. The measure is very crude – as, for instance, a situation with one dominant bank and large number of very small banks is clearly not equivalent to a competitive structure – however, we have no better indicator. Regarding ownership, the share of the state sector in the banking sector may be a proxy for less advanced reforms associated with a smaller size of financial sector. The opposite may be true in relation to the share of foreign banks. Finally, we expect the number of banks to be positively related to the size of the financial sector, albeit the relationship may be non-linear: a very large number of small banks may be an indicator of lax regulations, with counter-productive effects on the financial system.

In addition to the variables discussed above, the size of the financial sector (private credit/GDP ratio and M2 over GDP) may also be affected by the size of GDP. For the interest rate spread, GDP growth rate may be a more appropriate control variable, proxing for the strength of demand for finance relative to supply. In addition, the EBRD publishes the estimates of the private sector share in GDP. This is convenient, as we may control directly for the obvious effect on private credit of the size of private sector.

Taking this into account, both Fries and Taci (2002) and Mickiewicz (2005) estimated the growth of credit offered by banks. Fries and Taci (2002) estimated separate models for high-reform and low-reform economies. The results were stronger for the first group. GDP growth was associated with the expansion of credit and the budget deficit and inflation had the opposite effect. For low-reform countries, only the negative effect of inflation is significant.

Mickiewicz (2005) applied the Arrelano-Bond GMM dynamic panel estimator. Not surprisingly, both the size of GDP and the size of the private sector in GDP were positively and significantly associated with the size of credit to private sector. The impact of the government balance on the size of the financial sector was significant and positive. Inflation has a negative impact, again as expected, but the coefficient was insignificant. Generally, macroeconomic instability had negative influence on the size of finance. An interesting pattern emerged in relation to reform. Price liberalization (which may also serve as a proxy for the cluster of most fundamental reforms) has a mild immediate negative impact on the volume of credit. However, this effect was more than counterbalanced by the far stronger positive influence that came with a one-year delay.[5] Interestingly, a similar pattern appears with relation to the EBRD measure of bank reforms and interest rate liberalization. As described by McKinnon (1993), interest rate liberalization leads to an initial restriction in credit, as lending rates adjust up to higher levels, which are positive in real terms. Later on, there is a weak positive response of credit to reforms, but it is not significant.

The results relating to private credit were corroborated by estimates of broad money (M2). The macroeconomic variables turned out to be highly insignificant. On the other hand, the J-curve-type response to reform was apparent. Price liberalization, which includes elimination of state procurement at non-market prices, affects broad money first negatively and then positively with a one-year lag. Both effects remain significant. On the other hand, the impact of banking reforms seems dominated by an 'enterprise reform' indicator, which measures improvement in corporate governance framework and elimination of 'soft' budgeting at the enterprise level. There is a clear-cut positive and significant effect, which appears with a one-year lag. The result implies that legal framework which alleviates agency problems is conducive to the expansion of the financial sector.

In addition, the share of the state sector has a negative impact on the size of the financial sector, but the coefficient was marginally insignificant. The number of banks was positively associated with the size of the financial sector, but the impact was non-linear – i.e. when the number of banks grows, the marginal effects becomes negligible.[6]

Finally, inflation has been clearly associated with a wider interest rate spread – i.e. it leads to lower efficiency of financial intermediation.

Conclusion

Empirical results we report seem to be consistent with the intuitions offered by McKinnon's (1993) seminal book on the appropriate order of economic liberalization. As with so many other transition phenomena, we observe a J-curve-type response of the volume of credit to reforms. Successful reforms lead to an initial tightening, necessary to overcome the inherited 'soft' budget constraint. This is followed, however, by an expansion of credit.

An important additional detail is that it is not only liberalization, including interest rate liberalization, which matters. One of our results is that the enterprise reforms and corporate governance framework have a positive effect on the finance sector. The latter implies the need to alleviate the agency problems between the providers of finance and enterprises. The link between corporate governance and finance is close.

In line with McKinnon's (1993) argument, macroeconomic destabilization and a government budget deficit have detrimental effects on the financial sector.

And, finally, bank reforms have an unambiguous negative effect on the interest rate spread, increasing the efficiency of the banking sector. They also produce lower share of non-performing loans. However, the policy problem relates to the fact that partial reforms are dangerous as illustrated by Figure 10.4. As such limited reform attempts may produce negative results, the reversals in bank liberalization policies are likely to follow from that. As a result, some governments may be stuck with non-reform equilibria because when the reforms are attempted, in the initial phase they come with serious risk that things may go wrong in the short run. It is the memory of the aborted episodes of bank liberalization that can make some government disinclined to liberalize. That however comes at cost of substandard allocation of credit (and related structural inertia), and of high cost of credit and its lower availability.

11
Public Finance: Size and Efficiency of the Government

As nations like Ukraine are learning hard way during the 2008–2009 economic crisis (and as we will discuss in the next chapter), a country can pay dearly for poor fiscal policy. Poor fiscal policy is the one based on extensive redistribution by the government, with no smoothing of expenses over time (i.e. with no adequate reserves created during good times), it is also one, which is characterized by problems with both collecting taxes and with spending money efficiently. Those effects are costly in terms of economic performance, growth and prospects for alleviating poverty. Thus both inefficient and inflated government spending and inadequate and ill-targeted tax collection result in problems. The latter case relates to a number of nations that regained independence after the Soviet oppression and faced a difficult challenge of building their own government institutions and of stabilizing politically, suppressing ethnic hatred and violence. As an outcome, both tax collection and as a result also government spending virtually collapsed in some of those countries, especially in the Caucasus region, resulting in infrastructure falling apart and wiping out any effective assistance for the poor.

In the longer run, macroeconomic stabilization is not sustainable without sound public finance. And with recurring fiscal destabilization, the positive impact of economic liberalization is also dampened. This makes fiscal issues a key to the overall success of the transition programme. However, fiscal reorganization is the area of institutional reforms, which are slower and more difficult to implement, as they require changes in the law and implementation. The latter relies on the adequate functioning of the public administration, which in turn implies an improvement in human and social capital, a change in attitudes and practices – a new pattern of behaviour.

Moreover, the reforms, liberalization in particular, may lead to a temporary fiscal tension. These feedback effects may potentially cause a threat to the overall success and pace of the institutional change programme. Reversals of reform happen and can produce some stable non-reform equilibria.

We first look briefly at the inheritance from the old regime. We then sketch the key issues related to fiscal reform. Subsequently, we present results of empirical tests, investigating if and how the fiscal balance was affected by the components of the liberalization programme and contrast the results with transition theory. Finally, we bring together public finance and the rule of law to discuss their interdependence.

The inheritance

Under the old regime, tax collection was a simple task. The state administration was neither restricted by legislative process and courts, nor media, and arbitrary decisions were commonplace. One could even argue that in the era of the command economy it was not meaningful to speak of 'fiscal policy' and 'public finance', because:

> The existence of *public* finance presupposes that of *private* finance. The countries did not need market-type tax systems to raise public revenue because the government could simply appropriate the share of total, and mostly public, production for its own needs. (Tanzi and Tsibouris 2000: 3–4, emphasis in the original)

Before the transformation began, all was, in a way, public. Moreover, many fiscal functions, as these are defined in market economies, were not carried out by the government but by state enterprises.

In particular, most taxes were collected directly from the SOEs, and the process was largely not visible to the general public – i.e. to the ultimate individual taxpayers. The flows between the state-owned firms and the treasury were all within the state sector; they caused relatively little friction and did not require any level of the sophisticated tax administration one finds in developed market economies. Explicit taxation consisted of wage taxes, national insurance contributions (paid by enterprises on behalf of the workers) and a turnover tax levied on final consump-tion. The latter was a primary source of income and (unlike value added tax (VAT)) its rates varied for different categories of products, with the number of categories running into hundreds or even thousands. For that reason, it had highly distortionary effects (Gregory and Stuart 1995).

The explicit taxes were complemented by implicit taxes. Administrative transfer prices resulted in taxing profits away from some enterprises and redirecting them towards firms which would have been loss-making had market prices and 'hard' budgeting prevailed. As wages were under administrative control, simply keeping them at a low level was equivalent to the taxation of income, as the value-added retained within the enterprise could be easily transferred elsewhere by economic administrative decision. This implicit tax collection at the enterprise level was supplemented by related additional mechanisms. First, savings were implicitly taxed by maintaining negative real deposit rates within the mono-bank system (and, again, on the other hand, some firms were subsidized via the low cost of finance). Second, the shortage of consumer goods at prevailing administrative prices was another characteristic which supported implicit taxation via negative interest rates, since it forced many individuals to save.

While serious problems existed on the revenue side of public finance, the expenditure side was no better. The SOEs were not only production units; they were also providers of welfare. Somewhat paradoxically, some elements of the specialized institutions of the modern welfare state were therefore underdeveloped under communism. They were substituted by the provision offered to workers and their families by state-owned companies, including housing, health care, child care, recreational facilities and various benefits in kind. Rein, Friedman and Wörgötter (1997) report that the share of these in labour costs ranged between 10 per cent in Hungary and a staggering 35 per cent in Russia. This pattern of welfare provision was both inefficient and incompatible with the new market environment. Yet, creating the new institutions of a specialized governmental welfare system was a challenge, compounded by the emergence of open unemployment and growing income inequality. The increase of spending on welfare had to be matched by a decrease in enterprise subsidies if a fiscal crisis was to be avoided. In general, the measured, explicit levels of taxation and public spending were both very high, especially when the transition economies are compared with the middle-income group of countries to which they belong. For several economies (Bulgaria, Czechoslovakia, Hungary and Romania), the ratio of government revenue to GDP exceeded 50 per cent at the onset of the reforms.[1] The overall level of transfers, implicit spending and taxation included, was even higher, in particular if we take into account the social and fiscal roles of the state enterprises which substituted the government: some redistribution had already occurred at the enterprise level, where social welfare provision was financed via lower wages.

Reforms and fiscal imbalance during the transition

The setting up of tax systems broadly similar to those prevailing in Western Europe was a common goal of the transition economies. This benchmark system relied on (1) individual personal taxation which included both income tax and social security contributions/payroll taxes collected from both employers and employees; (2) taxation of enterprises (corporate income tax); (3) indirect taxation in the form of VAT and some excise taxes; and (4) some taxation of wealth (property taxes and inheritance taxes; both were typically limited in the transition economies). To transform the old system based on the direct taxation of wages and on a turnover tax in the new system required new legislation – the enactment of the many rules and regulations that accompany a modern tax system and that make the administration of that system possible, and the setting up of an appropriate tax administration. Application of these laws requires skills in both compliance and enforcement, and these skills were slowly enhanced during the transition. The task was further complicated in comparison with the Western economies, where tax systems operate in a relatively unchanging environment (stable inflation, small fluctuation of output, stable structures of production). In general, a well-functioning tax administration requires adequate staffing, computerization and adequate software including the establishment of a modern taxpayer and national insurance identification system and master files, modern registration and collection procedures, information systems for tax payers, internal monitoring and audit, limited arbitrariness, transparency and other anti-corruption measures (Tanzi and Tsibouris 2000). Introduction of all these elements requires time, knowledge and specialized resources.

In those countries which faced the most dramatic decrease in revenues, poor tax collection often had its roots in the poor design and administration of taxes. The definition of tax bases remained problematic throughout the CIS, taxes also tended to change frequently without due notification, and were sometimes applied retroactively. The tax law was complicated and unclear, some of the marginal rates very high, but were hardly ever applied due to widespread exemptions and tax credits that eroded the tax base. The end result was widespread arbitrariness by tax administrators and a lot of management time dedicated to the avoidance or evasion of taxes. Continued use of barter exchange and the accumulation of payment arrears (whereby a large share of transactions and income effectively escaped taxation) was partly associated with tax evasion and remained a major cause of poor tax revenues, particularly in the CIS throughout the 1990s.

The ratio of effective to statutory taxation offered an aggregate indicator of the distortions in the tax structure and its overall quality. As shown by Schaffer and Turley (2001), in the late 1990s the rates were generally lower for the CIS and higher for Central Europe, ranging between 9 per cent for the non-reformed economy of Tajikistan, where tax decisions were clearly left almost entirely to the discretion of the government administration, and 68 per cent for Estonia, with consistent and transparent tax rules on a par with some of the best instances of the high-income non-transition economies.

On the expenditure side, the critical issues were to introduce unemployment benefits and strengthen the social safety net; to reduce and streamline social expenditure for some occupational groups, privileged under the former regime; to eliminate the system of direct subsidization of loss-making enterprises; to reduce military expenditure; to create an efficient balance between central government, specialized government agencies and local government; to reform the pension system and the educational system.

Those issues are relatively well covered in the transition literature, and a good account can be found in Barr (1994, 2001) and Funck and Pizzati (2002). Since we have no real hope of adding anything new on these topics, we turn our attention to another issue: the interplay between liberalization and fiscal balance.

Liberalization, fiscal revenue and expenditure

Liberalization and fiscal balance: expected effects

The removal of subsidies is an integral part of the price liberalization, and as a result many large SOEs move into a period of low or negative profit. On the other hand, the emerging small enterprises in the new private sector are paying no corporate income tax, as they also go through an initial period of zero or low profits, albeit for different reasons, consistent with the early stage of the 'life-cycle' pattern of companies. This combination suggests an initial negative shock to government revenues, as the tax base for 'old' taxes is shrinking, without being counterbalanced by the 'new' sector.

Similarly, foreign trade liberalization led to increased competition, and the price shocks faced by the 'old' sector are enhanced. The immediate impact on tax revenue is to be negative, parallel to internal price liberalization. Yet, the negative effect of price liberalization on tax revenues is likely to be matched by its dampening effect on expenditure, as the removal of subsidies leads to smaller government budgets. Price liberalization is thus likely to result in an immediate scaling down of the government budget, with its effect on the budget balance remaining ambiguous and dependent on the relative magnitude of the balancing revenue and expenditure effects. Unlike immediate effects, subsequently, the effect of the reforms on expenditure is likely to change from negative to positive. All three elements of liberalization – internal prices, external liberalization and freedom of entry – lead to an increase in income inequality and unemployment.[2] With the social functions of SOEs scaled down, the social safety net system had to be developed as a response, leading to an increase in government expenditure. Thus, it is not the case that the overall level of government expenditure is reduced with successful reforms, but rather that its structure is rationalized, with subsidization of loss-making state enterprises being replaced by increased direct social transfers.[3]

Changes in revenues and expenditure can be also interpreted in a manner consistent with a traditional cyclical pattern – while economies shrank during the prolonged post-communist recessions, parts of the tax base (such as profit and income taxes) is eroded. On the other hand, growing unemployment may result in a countercyclical increase in expenditure. The same pattern is visible again during the 2008–2009 crisis.

The interesting empirical question is to see if the direct impact of liberalization on taxes, expenditure and fiscal balance can be disentangled from the effects working through both GDP and the unemployment path. This is an issue we shall investigate next.

Econometric results

Pirttilä (2001) examined the determinants of the government balance using panel data for 25 transition countries for the period 1990–7. The set of explanatory variables includes both standard macroeconomic variables – GDP growth and the unemployment rate – and the three EBRD measures assessing the components of liberalization: (1) Internal price liberalization, (2) External liberalization and (3) Freedom of entry and small-scale privatization. In estimations reported in more detail in Mickiewicz (2005), in addition to the fiscal balance, separate models for both expenditure and revenues were estimated. As follows from the discussion in the previous section, the expectation was that the reforms may result in parallel shifts of both revenues and expenditure, making interpretation of the resulting impact on the fiscal position difficult to understand without looking at the two sides of the budget statement separately.

Below we discuss the results of those test. We shall start with expenditure, then fiscal revenue and finally the government balance.

First, there is considerable and significant persistence in the government expenditure share in GDP. Next, GDP growth dominates the impact of all the other explanatory variables on government expenditure. There is a strong contemporaneous negative effect of GDP growth on the share of expenditure in GDP. This negative effect is still significant, but weaker, after one year; however, it changes sign after two years, where it turns into weak positive effect. Given that expenditure is measured as a ratio to GDP and that not all expenditure items adjust automatically to GDP, the clear-cut negative effects – both contemporaneous and with a one-year lag – are not surprising. It seems, however, that sustainable growth triggers policy response and a small upward adjustment in expenditure, typically after a delay of two years.

On the other hand, the effects of unemployment are all insignificant. This may be seen as an important result when compared with theoretical models of the institutional reform based on the interaction between fiscal variables and unemployment (see especially the seminal paper by Aghion and Blanchard 1994). The discrepancy between the theory and the empirical results may be explained by the relatively modest role of social support for the unemployed in many transition countries (Mickiewicz and Bell 2000; Golinowska 2001). In fact, Aghion and Blanchard (1994) declare that their model applies to CE economies where the responsiveness of expenditure to unemployment may be stronger. Our empirical results are based on the sample of all 27 transition economies. And last but not least, while in the theoretical model all the social effects of restructuring are captured by unemployment, in practice outflows into economic inactivity or subsistence agriculture makes unemployment a very imperfect proxy of the increase in social spending triggered by the liberalization.

The components of the liberalization programme have some significant impact on government expenditure, as expected. First, price liberalization leads to a contemporaneous decrease in government expenditure. The result is consistent with the expected impact of removal of subsidies and, generally, with 'hardening' of the budget constraint, which is a defining element of price liberalization and equalization. External liberalization is also associated with a contemporaneous decrease in expenditure; however, the effect changes sign (significant) after one year, similarly to internal price liberalization (insignificant). Similarly, reforms related to the freedom of entry produce a significant increase in expenditure with a one-year lag, and we obtain the same result when the aggregate measure of liberalization replaces individual components. Thus, a J-curve pattern emerges, on which we may impose the following speculative interpretation:[4] Liberalization leads to an immediate reduction in government spending due to the elimination of subsidies and a general 'hardening' of the budget constraint (which also includes items such as subsidization of bank credit). At the same time, liberalization increases pressure on the 'old' sector, restructuring is triggered, factories start to shed excessive labour, wage dispersion increases and enterprises are forced to cut down the provision of social benefits and concentrate on their core activities. All that leads to an increase in government spending, which we clearly detect as emerging with a one-year lag. Thus, in this wider interpretation, the link between reforms and government spending is restored, consistent with Aghion and Blanchard (1994) and Blanchard (1997). Yet, an important new detail derived from the empirical analysis is timing: the positive and negative effects of reforms on government spending are not yet synchronized. Reforms imply an immediate reduction in government spending, an effect which is reversed later, being triggered by the impact of restructuring working through the economic system.

We may now turn to the determinants of government revenue. The first thing to note is that there is less persistence in government revenue: the coefficients on the lagged dependent variable are less significant and the values are about twice as small as for expenditure. In addition, the share of revenues in GDP does not respond to GDP growth, and the corresponding coefficients are close to zero. And the impact of unemployment is ambiguous.

In contrast, there are some clear-cut and stable results related to the liberalization indicators. The contemporaneous impact of both internal and external liberalization on government revenue is negative and significant. Interestingly, however, when we allow for a longer lag structure, liberalization has a strong positive impact on revenue, emerging with a two-year lag; taken together, the positive effects clearly more than counterbalance the initial negative effects. This result may be combined with the findings on the impact of reform on the dynamics of expenditure. If the reform implies that the protection of the 'old' sector (in terms of a 'soft' budget, foreign trade barriers and entry barriers) is removed, that may produce a sequence of a fall in both expenditure and revenue first, an increase in expenditure next and finally an increase in revenue. The time pattern detected is consistent with the following stylized interpretation. First, the 'old' sector firms face a negative shock affecting their revenues and a decrease in government revenue appears. Second, after a while, continuing competitive pressure results in an employment reduction, the cutting of the enterprise-level social spending and other adjustment measures. All that calls for a response from the government, and spending increases. Finally, after about two years, the positive effects on government revenue start to prevail, as the taxes from the emerging 'new' sector finally counterbalance the decrease in revenue from the 'old' sector. Government revenue increases again. Taken together, we can observe a clear J-curve time pattern in government revenue.

An alternative interpretation could be offered in the spirit of Aghion and Blanchard's (1994) paper. In their model, restructuring triggered by the reform leads to an increase in social expenditure, which has a subsequent impact on the increase in taxation, as the government is forced to match expenditure with taxation, facing a limited possibility of debt financing.

What makes this interpretation marginally less convincing is the fact that we should see a parallel effect on economic growth. Yet, as may be seen from the results in Chapter 6, faster and more radical reforms result in shorter recessions. Thus, it is more likely that the empirically observed increase in revenues comes from the 'new' sector firms, instead of being a sign of bad equilibrium resulting from too much liberalization.

Where our empirical results may contribute to the discussion is to demonstrate that the fiscal effects are never instantaneous and that there are important time lags built into both the response of enterprises and the response of the government to liberalization shocks.

Finally, we may look at the estimates of the budget balance, which enable us to compare some of the results of Mickiewicz (2005) with those obtained by Pirttilä (2001). First, similar to expenditures, but unlike revenue, the government balance exhibits a relatively strong persistence. The growth of GDP improves the government's fiscal position (both a contemporaneous positive effect, as in Pirttilä (2001), and also with a one-year lag), but later on tends to have some correcting, weak negative effect on the fiscal balance (two years after economic growth appears). The latter effect is clearly driven by the increase in expenditure. Some speculative political economic arguments may be applied here. Economic growth may ease the government budget constraint and lead to more expenditure, an effect which is not only transition-specific, but likely to have a more universal character.

Again, similarly to Pirttilä (2001), the effects of unemployment on the fiscal balance in Mickiewicz (2005) are ambiguous; in the case of the longer lag structure, adding up all the corresponding coefficients the net impact is negative – i.e. on balance, higher unemployment results in a deterioration in the fiscal position. The effect with a two-year lag is unambiguously negative; the mixed results for the contemporaneous and one-year impact may be attributed to the fact that unemployment may be a proxy for efficient restructuring and elimination of 'soft' budget government financing, as indicated by consistently positive (albeit insignificant) contemporaneous sign of unemployment.

Looking at the impact of the reforms on the fiscal balance, two main results emerge. First, we have a strong and robust positive effect of price liberalization on the government balance after a one-year lag. This may be contrasted with the ambiguous contemporaneous effect. Second, a closer inspection reveals that after a one-year lag, price liberalization results in an increase in expenditure, but revenues also start to recover. Clearly, the positive effect of revenue on the fiscal balance dominates.

Quality of institutions and public finance

Figure 11.1 below presents a scatter diagram of the ratio of government expenses to GDP (WB WDI data, 2007) and freedom from corruption (based on Transparency International, Corruption Perception Index) for 35 countries with largest population in the world (which include three transition economies: Russia, Ukraine and Poland). We find France

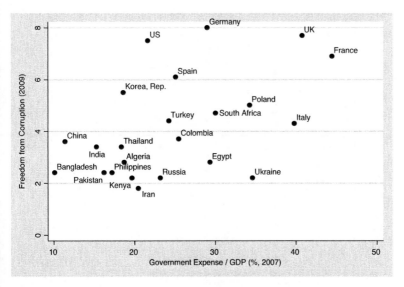

Figure 11.1 Government expenses and freedom from corruption: Largest countries

located in the upper right corner with a strong rule of law and an extensive state sector. By 2007, UK position become very similar to France, as the size of the government in the country increased dramatically since mid-1990s. In contrast, the US and South Korea are the two countries which combine the rule of law with a small state sector. Hong Kong and Singapore (not on the graph) are the two economies that would be even closer to the right hand side corner. In contrast, China, India, Pakistan, Bangladesh and few others are all countries where the size of government spending and taxation remains low, but rule of law is weak. Finally, there are not that many countries with large state sector and weak institutions, but Ukraine – for transition countries, and Italy – for developed countries, come close.

Based on the whole world sample we can fit a non-linear relationship between government expense and freedom of corruption (Figure 11.2 below). However, it is not easy to disentangle the problem of both-ways causality between the two dimensions. The positive correlation between the two factors on the left hand side of the graph is probably driven by the fact that a large state sector is difficult to build where basic institutional quality is low, because the latter affects the state's capacity to collect taxes. The sign of the correlation in this range contradicts the

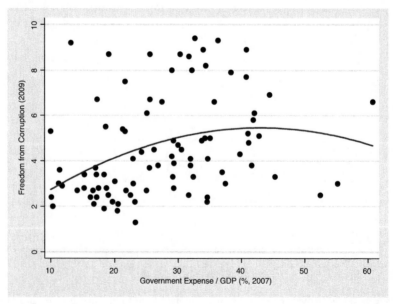

Figure 11.2   Government expenses and freedom from corruption: All countries

theoretical prediction of the theoretical model by Acemoglu and Verdier (2000), who argue that while state intervention may have a positive impact, it comes at cost: some corruption may be unavoidable. According to them, balancing a positive effect of spending against the cost of corruption, implies that an efficient outcome in the feasible range may be where some degree of corruption is unavoidable. On our graph, this theory would imply a positive correlation between the two factors. Yet this emerges only over a section of the distribution: just above the level where government expenses are very high, exceeding 40 per cent of GDP, like in France, Italy and the UK. It is in only in this region that the larger state sector becomes associated with greater corruption leading to an ordering of observations along the negative trend. However, this is not what we observe for most of the actual range. Rather, the findings in Figure 11.2 suggest that for most of the countries, the relationship is a positive one. As indicated above, one explanation is that poor institutional quality affect government capacity to collect taxes. Another is that, consistent with Hellman *et al.* (2003), in the countries with a large state sector, corruption may be lower because special interests become directly embedded within the state sector so that special interests become institutionalized and are no longer seen as corruption. In other words, corruption becomes more visible, where boundaries of the state become more clear-cut (see also: Mickiewicz 2009).

Acemoglu and Verdier's (2000) perspective we just discussed is motivated by the efficiency theory of institutions, which assumes that observed institutional outcomes have some traits of efficient feasible solutions. In contrast, Botero *et al.* (2004) argue that the institutional outcome may also be explained by politics, as institutional design may reflect some entrenched special interests, and also by institutional inertia (for instance, as represented by legal origin) (see also, Olson 2000): institutions are difficult to change and therefore inefficient economic institutions may persist, even where they outlived their functionality given the surrounding technological and economic condition change. Thus, apart from efficiency-based theory of institutions, both political factors and institutional continuity can contribute to the explanation, and the latter two approaches seem to tell us more about the corruption – size of the state nexus.

Efficiency of public spending and the size of the state

From the point of view of public finance, it is critical what is the efficiency of public spending, given that any government taxation is distortionary therefore comes at cost. It implies that it is in a country where institutions are weak that large state sectors are particularly disruptive. For example, the efficiency cost of big government in the UK may continue to be relatively limited as long as the underlying quality of institutions is not affected. However with lower institutional quality, we are moving to the case like Italy: we may assume that corruption will affect the efficiency of spending. At the same time low institutional quality will imply that the distortionary cost of taxation is also likely to be high.

Having this in mind we may now take a closer look at the transition economies (Figure 11.3). We find the same non-linear relationship between freedom of corruption and the size of the government. Assuming our intuition is correct, it is corruption that limits the possibility of raising revenues on the left hand side of the graph, while above approximately 40 per cent level of ratio of expenses to GDP, the causation may reverse: increase in the size of the government is associated with more corruption. Here, position of Ukraine, Belarus, Bosnia and Herzegovina, and Serbia is particularly problematic. They all have extensive state sectors, while widespread corruption they experience suggests that resources which are taken away from individual decision-makers in the form of

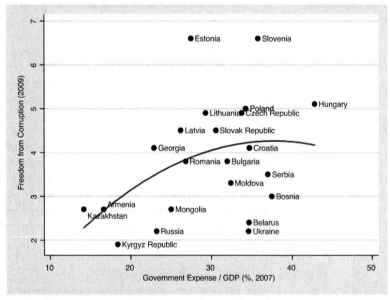

Figure 11.3 Government expenses and freedom from corruption: Transition economies

taxes are to significant extent wasted. From this perspective, a move by Russian Federation to less extensive taxation in early 2000s (i.e. to the left on our graph) was probably a superior short-term policy choice than attempting more extensive redistribution. A move to use a period of high revenue (that coincided with high world energy prices) to limit taxation (and build reserves) instead of boosting government spending was a smart one, given that increased spending would likely to be inefficient.

More generally, we posit that small size of the state sector is more consistent with efficiency where institutions are weak. This efficient policy choice is very clear for high growth Asian economies (see Figure 11.1 above).

12
Anatomy of a Crisis

It is difficult and risky to write about the economic events as they unravel, but the 2008–2009 economic crisis is too important to be ignored. The origins of the crisis were external, but the way different economies responded was determined by the degree to which they are integrated with the European and with the world economy, by the quality of their macroeconomic policies, including fiscal policy, and by quality of institutions that shaped those policies. In this chapter we will ask what could be the lessons from the 2009–2010 crisis. Our answers are preliminary, and open to discussion. However, the discussion can hardly wait, as the answers are needed not only by historians but by policy-makers today.

Introduction: The benefits and costs of economic integration

Gains from trade

As we discussed in Chapter 1, under the Soviet regime, Central Eastern Europe and Central Asia paid a price for its economic isolation and for its weak links with the outside word. Moreover, as the global trade expanded in the second half of previous century, this price for isolationism kept increasing.

It is not difficult to assess the relative cost of economic isolation (and therefore also a corresponding benefit from integration). Thanks to geographical location of the transition economies and accounting for the distribution of the population, which is concentrated in the European part of the region, that is in the West (which relates in particular to Russian Federation), Western Europe remains a gravity centre of trade for transition economies, with a key role played by the German economy thanks both to its potential and its central geographical location. As summarized by Gros and Steinherr (2004), for those countries 'free trade with the EU means effectively, free trade with the only market that really counts'.

Given that the gains from trade are driven by geographic proximity and the economic size of the economies that may be involved in trade, for different countries we may calculate approximate trade potential, estimating so called gravity model based on those factors. Gros and Steinherr (2004) did just that. In effect, they assess that for the transition economies, trade with the old (West European) EU should account for between 60–70 per cent of the overall trade and of 80–90 per cent of trade with different parts of the world. For all transition countries (and separately for all major regions of the Russian Federation) they calculate the periphery gravity index that may be seen as a proxy for gains from free

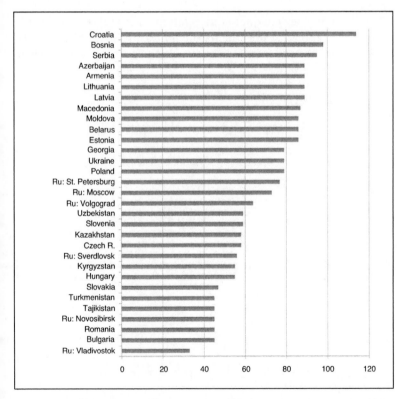

Figure 12.1 Periphery (gravity) index for transition economies, based on 2010 GDP projections and distance

Source: Author's calculation based on Gros and Steinherr (2004).

trade: economies that are located more centrally within the trading area gain more from integration. Figure 12.1 uses their data to present the ranking for the transition economies graphically.

We may note that the ordering of the potential gains from trade do not overlap with the actual integration process. Three Balkan peninsula countries that could benefit most from full integration are not yet EU members at time of writing. In contrast, we find two new EU member states Romania and Bulgaria at the very end of the list. Baltic Republics score high on the ranking, but the countries of Southern Caucasus are not far away. Similarly, potential gains from trade are vital for European part of the Russian Federation. The old capital of Russia, St. Petersburg, located on the Baltic coast, is in relatively short distance from North East Germany and Berlin, far closer from there, than the countries of Southern Europe.

If trade is one key channel of integration, capital flows are equally important. Figure 12.2 documents the increasing share of world FDI flows that has been attracted to the transition economies.[1] If we relate

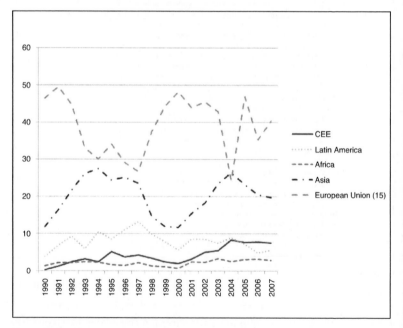

Figure 12.2   Shares in world FDI flows (%), 1990–2007

Source: UNCTAD.

those flows to the overall volume of investment, the significance of FDI becomes even higher. Unlike Far East Asia, transition economies save less, therefore foreign capital inflows play very significant role in their development. Moreover, Sanfey (2010) presents empirical analysis that suggests a casual relationship: capital inflows has been associated with faster growth in transition economies; and interestingly, this relation is more clear-cut that for emerging markets economies outside the transition region. However, at the same time, the price paid for the faster development based on external funding was the growth in current account deficits, increasing risks associated with potential reversals in flows. This factor became important in 2008–2009.

Manufacturing exporters versus resource exporters

While the integration with the world economy progressed in the whole transition region, the pattern of integration differed. In particular, the structure of exports differed considerably between Central Eastern Europe and the Commonwealth of Independent States. While exports from Central Europe are diversified, Russian Federation, Kazakhstan, Azerbaijan, Turkmenistan, and Uzbekistan are rich in energy resources and those dominate in what they sell abroad. That defines a different pattern of integration. Moreover, given the pattern of regional economic links, other CIS countries are in turn sensitive to the development in those countries, and therefore indirectly sensitive to the development on the world energy markets. That implies divergence within the transition countries region, forming two distinctive economic clusters.

Anatomy of the 2008–2009 economic crisis: Fiscal conditions versus monetary conditions

Thus, by 2008, the transition economies were well integrated with the world economy along the dimensions of trade and capital flows, albeit there were important differences in the pattern of this integration as just discussed. The global crisis of 2008–2009 started with the financial sectors in high-income economies, the US in particular, but that did not automatically spread to the financial sectors within the transition countries, as the financial sectors there are relatively less developed and are therefore less prone to internal financial risks. The transition economies were however exposed to the impact of reversals in cross-border financial flows that followed. While direct capital investment is relatively stable and difficult to liquidate in a short run, some more liquid forms of finance, including portfolio investments reversed direction, following the financial crunch in the countries of origin and global crisis of confidence in finance. Similarly, any loans and other financial obligations denominated in foreign currency are subject to currency risk. Anticipations of those risks may trigger currency outflows leading to self-fulfilling prophecies. Those speculative outflows are particularly likely to come early in the crisis in countries that aim to maintain some predetermined level of exchange rate, like for instance Russia.

Parallel to the impact of external financing channels, the key trading partners in the West went into recession affecting exports. At the same time, weak global demand led to sharp downturn in prices of energy resources. While all the transition countries were affected, the scale of those effects was conditional on both structural characteristics of those economies and on the economic policies and institutional set-up.

Below, we will focus the discussion on the four largest transition countries, as measured by population: Russian Federation, Ukraine, Poland and Romania.[2] Figure 12.3 below presents the evolution of econ-

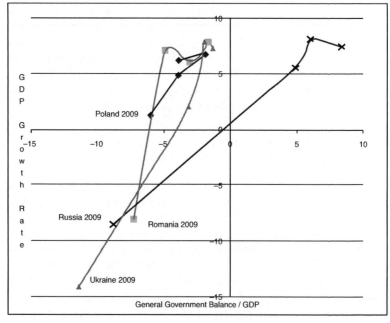

Figure 12.3 GDP growth rates (%) and general government balance over GDP (%), 2006–2009

Source: EBRD; 2009 figures are estimates.

omic performance between 2006 and 2009, along the two key economic dimensions: annual GDP growth rate (vertical axis) and the fiscal position as measured by the ratio of general government balance to GDP (horizontal axis).

As illustrated by the graph, the Russian Federation lost almost 15 percentage points of economic growth between 2008–2009, moving into deep recession. At the same time, its fiscal position shifted in almost parallel way from strong surplus into large deficit. The collapse in prices of oil and gas had dramatic impact on Russia, but the fiscal and, implicitly, the social impact of the crisis was cushioned by prudent fiscal policy pursued prior to the crisis, since 2004. Namely, following the negative experience of the 1998 crisis, in 2004 Russia established the stabilization fund to accumulate reserves at times of high oil prices. It accumulated 157 billion dollars by 2008, despite using some of it for early external debt repayments. To avoid inflationary pressures caused by raw material exports, the funds were invested abroad only. Therefore, despite the external shock, this time Russia avoided a financial meltdown and its economy is likely to bounce back in 2010. Azerbaijan and Kazakhstan created their own sovereign wealth funds even earlier, in 1999 and 2000 correspondingly (Sanfey 2010).

This policy of fiscal responsibility contrasts with the position of Ukraine, which has also some raw materials endowment, albeit smaller than Russia. The impact of the external shocks on Ukraine was as dramatic as in Russia, both in terms of its growth rates and its fiscal position, albeit the change along the latter dimensions was somewhat smaller given that Ukraine's budget was less dependent on income from resource-based exports. However, the fiscal policies in Ukraine differed significantly from those of Russia prior to the crisis and the outcomes were also very different. First as discussed in the previous chapter, share of government expenses in GDP has been much higher in Ukraine than in Russia. Moreover, to finance this large government, Ukraine was running budget deficits prior to the crisis, instead of trying to smooth its time path of government expense, like Russia. Most importantly, it did not accumulate any fiscal reserves, even if prior experience should demonstrate that the Ukrainian macroeconomic cycle had been strongly affected by Russia via economic links and therefore the country is implicitly subject to the same cycles led by international energy resources prices as Russia. As a result Ukraine faced a serious risk of bankruptcy, becoming dependent on financial assistance from IMF. Fortunately, the international response was quick and the support packages were substantial, both for Ukraine, and for Hungary, Latvia and Romania (Sanfey 2010). However, the political cycle in Ukraine implied that none of the major political players was willing to initiate fiscal adjustment. This unwillingness to face reality resulted in fiscal free fall, and strained relations with international donors. Lack of fast adjustment implies that Ukraine is likely to remain dependent on foreign support for longer time, either from Russia, Western international institutions or both.

We now turn to two European Union member states, Poland and Romania. Deterioration in fiscal position was relatively limited in both countries not just as compared with its Eastern neighbours, but also as compared with most of the old EU member states. This lack of counter-cyclical fiscal policy is very typical for middle-income and developing economies (Talvi and Végh 2005); however this contrast was even more striking during this crisis; while a normal pattern is that fiscal policy is acyclical in most developed economies implying smoothing of government consumption over time (*ibid.*), during the 2008–2009 crisis, some of the key Western players were actively promoting larger 'fiscal stimulus' packages, as advocated by United Kingdom in particular. However, despite a similar change in fiscal position compared to Poland, Romania faced a dramatic fall in output, similar to Russia. Moreover, unlike Russia it did not have strong reserves and had to ask for a significant scale support package from IMF. In sharp contrast, the change in the rate of economic growth was relatively small in Poland, and its economy remained growing in 2009, albeit at a slow rate.

Where those differences may be coming from? As indicated at the beginning of this chapter, what we present here is only an exploratory analysis, which will be verified and corrected once all data on the current crisis become available. With this caveat, the author is of opinion that despite all the attention given to fiscal side in the West, it is the monetary conditions that are critical to understand the direct channels that affected the economic outcomes. We may approximate monetary conditions using two key dimensions: movements in the domestic interest rates and movements in exchange rate (as has been used to analyse macroeconomic position in developing countries, e.g.: Hyder and Khan 2007; Kannan *et al.* 2006). Unlike fiscal side, it is along those two dimensions that Polish economic policy during the crisis looks very different. We start with exchange rate, as illustrated with Figure 12.4 below.

Poland not only went through most significant downward adjustment in its exchange rate, but also this adjustment came very early on: the most striking difference between Poland and three other countries is already in the last quarter of 2008. Obviously, adjustment in exchange

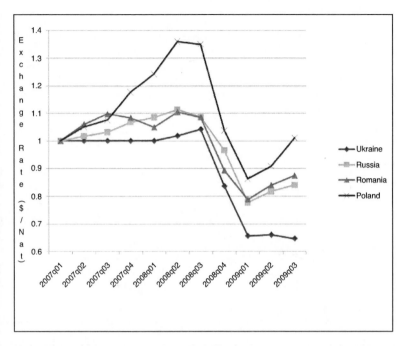

Figure 12.4   Exchange rate index, US dollars/national currency, 1st quarter of 2007 to 3rd quarter of 2009

Source: IMF, International Financial Statistics (December 2009), Calculated on the basis of series 926..AH.ZF.

rate is not a one-fit-all recipe. There are clear-cut trade-offs and risks associated with depreciation, as the latter may get out of control causing financial crisis. However, prior to crisis, Poland kept its foreign-currency denominated obligations under control. Even then, it faced some related risks. Well-timed government intervention to exchange its EU funds for Polish Zlotys played some role preventing the Zloty to slide down into dangerous role, when it was at its low point. Other countries with more significant exposures to foreign funding faced far more difficult dilemmas: either to stimulate exports or to stay away from a risk of mass bankruptcy caused by sudden jump in the burden of external obligations. Latvia could be a prime example of such a situation. Yet, being a small economy, it has been kept afloat by foreign assistance. While Poland is still larger that neighbouring economies, and therefore the role of the domestic market is larger, its exports is still responsible for about 40 per cent of production, so its role remains critical. That implies the exchange

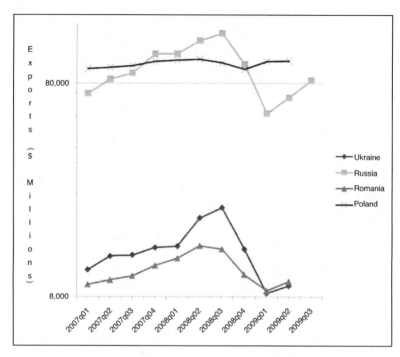

Figure 12.5   Exports, million US dollars, 1ˢᵗ quarter of 2007 to 3ʳᵈ quarter of 2009

Source: IMF, International Financial Statistics (December 2009), series 92670.DZF.

role still plays a significant role. Figure 12.5 illustrates the evolution of exports in the four countries we focus on.

While the size of the Polish economy is significantly smaller than that of Russia, its share in world exports is similar. As discussed above, Russian Federation was hit hard by energy prices, and experienced a dramatic slump in exports in the last quarter of 2008 and the first quarter of 2009. In contrast Poland with a diversified structure of exports suffered far less. With strong currency depreciation already in the last quarter of 2008, its exports increased back to its average 2008 level in the subsequent quarter. The impact of the crisis on exports is hardly visible during the 2009, in sharp contrast to what was experienced by other countries.

Looking closer at the interest rates is equally revealing. Money market rates have been of particular interest during the 2008–2009 global crisis as they reflect shocks to liquidity around the world. The corresponding figures are illustrated by Figure 12.6 below.

Ukraine paid dearly for its fiscal destabilization and macroeconomic destabilization that followed, but the scale of money market shock in interest rate is far larger than the impact of inflation in Ukraine could suggest: the latter never increased beyond 6–8 per cent range in the period we discuss, while the money market rates reached 35 per cent at the beginning of 2009, producing a dramatic liquidity shock. While not comparable with Ukraine, money market rates also kept increasing over 2008 and reached peak levels in the last quarter of 2008 and the first quarter of 2009 for both Russia and Romania. Again, a cycle in Poland looks far weaker and the rates returned to where they were two years before in the first quarter of 2009 already, at the time that both Russia, and especially Ukraine were still facing sharp increases.

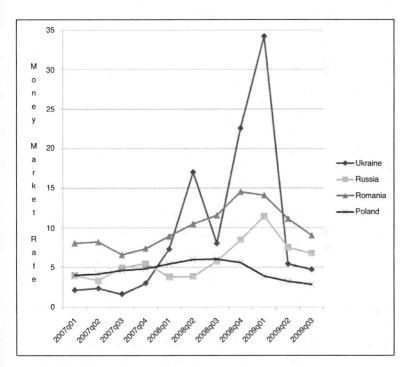

Figure 12.6 Money market rates (% per annum), 1ˢᵗ quarter of 2007 to 3ʳᵈ quarter of 2009

Source: IMF, International Financial Statistics (December 2009), series 92660B.ZF.

Thus, it is not fiscal policy, but monetary conditions, where the difference between Poland and other economies look most clear-cut. In general, in case of transition economies and more general of emerging market economies, old prescriptions for applying fiscal stimulus packages are particularly dangerous. This is because, the critical factor relates to the behaviour of foreign providers of finance. Fiscal destabilization is far more dangerous that any potential negative implications of keeping budget closer to its balance, because the former may destroy the credibility of the government and lead to negative response of international financial markets pushing the economy deeper into crisis.

Beyond the 2008–2009 crisis; the trade-offs between growth rate and volatility of output?

Again, probably the main difficulty in analysing transition economies during the global economic crisis relates to the fact that they now diverge, forming two distinctive groups. Most of the new EU members and those remaining countries in the Balkan peninsula that are still on its way to EU integration are small open economies. They are already integrated with the EU in economic terms, via exports and via cross-border financial flows. In contrast, the major economies in the Eastern part of the former Soviet empire (CIS) are natural resource-based economies, starting with the Russian Federation, but also Kazakhstan and few others. Even the countries of that region, which are not resource rich are still linked economically, therefore tend to follow similar economic cycle as Russia.

Both groups of countries were hit more than advanced market economies, and the CIS group was hit harder than Central Europe. However in both regions, the recovery is also expected to be stronger that in the advanced economies. This is illustrated by Figure 12.7 below.

As it seems at time of writing at the beginning of 2010, the region we are interested in will continue to grow fast, but it is also clear that the cost of this longer-term growth comes in terms of sensitivity to the global economic cycles, therefore oscillations are wider along the growth path. If we accept this view, tensions and crises that characterize both transition economies and some other emerging market economies should be seen as a price of accelerated growth fuelled by integration with world markets. Tornell and Westermann (2005) offer a theory that aims to explain this empirical pattern that characterize countries on the medium level of development (note a contrast between transition economies and both Africa and advanced economies; in both cases the crisis had less serious impact).

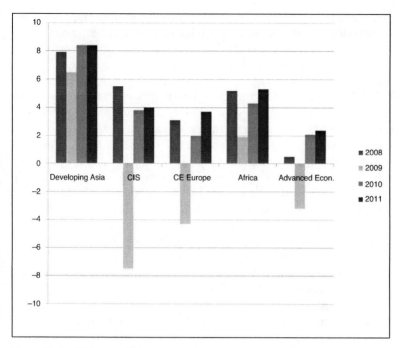

Figure 12.7 GDP growth rates, 2008–2011

Source: IMF, World Economic Outlook (January 2010); 2009 – estimates, 2010–2011 – prediction.

What needs to be explained is that while advanced economies are at least as well integrated with global economy as emerging markets and transition economies, the former are not characterized by the same scale of oscillations. Answering this question, Tornell and Westermann (2005) argue that advanced economies are subject to less serious monetary shocks that work its way through the banking sectors, in line with the monetary channels we accentuated above. Tornell and Westermann (2005) stress differences in access to finance between the internationalized sector of large firms that fully participate in foreign trade and the entrepreneurial sector of smaller firms that have a more local character. Therefore, the latter are far more sensitive to local liquidity shocks, given its finance comes predominantly from the local banking sector. The entrepreneurial sector gets easier access to finance, when foreign funds are flowing into a country during the boom period and are subsequently transferred into lending, often denominated in foreign currency. As a result, in those emerging economies which are exposed heavily to foreign financing, the exchange rate plays a role of economic amplifier. Consistent with this, the exposure to foreign (short-term) financing is a critical parameter. For example, Poland, even if its cumulative growth record since the beginning of transition has been impressive, did pay a price of a slightly lower growth rate at the beginning of 2000s, as compared with those countries where inflow of foreign funds was far more spectacular and so were the growth rates, going up to a region around 10 per cent, especially in the most open Baltic republics. Where the crises were not transformed into longer-term fiscal and debt crises, it is also likely that the recovery may be equally strong.[3]

It is also not difficult to extend Tornell and Westermann's (2005) model to capture a situation of the resource rich economies in the East. The pattern is similar, except that volatile inflows of foreign currency are associated not with international finance but with earnings from resource exports. However, those countries face an additional policy challenge. The cycles they face are even stronger if no effective effort is made to diversify and support the manufacturing sectors not directly related to resource base. Unfortunately, an emerging pattern seems just be the opposite. To understand the underlying reason for the actual policies, we need to consider a political economy perspective. While diversification may be economically efficient, the concentration of gains in the energy sector may lead to political influence of that sector and result in actual government policies that may reinforce imbalances instead of alleviating those. In late 1990s and early 2000s the key energy export countries in the region faced a trend towards less not more diversification: in Russia the share of mining and fuels in export went up from slightly above 60 per cent to above 70 per cent just before the crisis in 2007, in Kazakhstan it went up from about 50 per cent to about 80 per cent and in Azerbaijan from about 70 per cent to over 90 per cent (Sanfey 2010). If there was any diversification effort, it clearly failed.

Crises and institutions

Tornell and Westermann's (2005) argue that the underlying reason behind the dominant role that the financial flows from outside play in development relates to poor institutions. It is inadequate protection of property rights including protection of financial contracts that may be one important factor behind the underdevelopment of the domestic supply of funds and in turn the limited supply of funds to entrepreneurs. This is broadly in line of the 'fourth generation' view on crises (Breuer 2004). According to this, institutional factors are underlying reasons behind the more direct crisis factors that are typically considered – high inflation, loss of foreign reserves, lack of consistency in policies, herd behaviour on the financial markets and lack of prudent fiscal policies prior to the crises (Talvi and Végh 2005). The key issue is that institutions affect expectations, in particular of the foreign and domestic investors. Accordingly, it is not the actual policy, but assessment of the capacity of the government to implement policies that are necessary, that affect the level of trust revealed by the financial markets. Weak institutions may imply that even good government polices are not credible, as they may be easily reversed as a result of instability in government. Similarly, good monetary policy is itself not credible if central banks are under political pressure, their independence is illusory and the objectives of the central bankers are likely to change under pressure in unpredictable way. The same logic applies to fiscal policy. Institutional framework should on one hand leave enough margin to adjust fiscal policy during the crisis (hopefully, to smooth government consumption over the crisis) but even more importantly to generate fiscal reserves prior to the crisis, during the good times. It is the latter that proves particularly difficult in middle-income and emerging economies, where any additional revenues create immediate political pressure to spend (Talvi and Végh 2005). The size of the government becomes inflated during the boom periods, and reversals are costly and difficult politically. In this context, good institutional frameworks relate to fiscal rules limiting arbitrary use of fiscal policy for generating political macroeconomic cycles in a short-term interest of incumbent politicians, to more effective tax administrations, to better control and monitoring of government expenses, and to use of effective tools to manage public debt. Without stronger institutional guarantees, even where 'fiscal rule' is self-proclaimed by the executive branch of the government it is typically not credible. And coming back to the four countries we discussed in this chapter it is a form of constitutional fiscal rule adopted by Poland, where some specific level of debt to GDP ratio triggers adjustment (Benecki *et al.* 2006), that differentiated Poland from the two other economies, helping to support positive expectations by the investors.

Looking further to the East

The issues just discussed – focus on institutional design and institutional quality and related focus on trade-offs between growth rate and oscillations around the trend combined with attention paid to international financing flows may tell us something about the differences between the transition and the advanced economies. Yet, it still does not explain striking differences between performance of emerging Far

East Asian economies of China, Republic of Korea and others, against the rest of the world. While inflow of investment into Far East is high (see Figure 12.2 for illustration), by now those flows are reciprocal; China became the largest foreign direct investor in the world in 2009.

It seems that a clear-cut difference that runs against the mainstream consensus in Western economics, dominant in the second half of last century, is that the savings rates matter. It is savings that are much higher in Asia. The consensus that still dominates the policy-making in the Western world of high-income economies, and was even amplified during the 2008–2009 crisis is that consumption spending, both public and private is good, and saving has negative macroeconomic implications as it withdraws funds from the circular flow. Over the last 60 years the impact of this idea on the design of economic policies, taxes, welfare provision and pensions has been dominant. While consumption credit expanded, real interest rates on savings were both low and the related gains were taxed significantly. So were capital gains and any gains from inheritance, making longer-term capital accumulation strategies of families counter-productive. Saving for pensions and for private health insurance have been discouraged and replaced by (apparently) uniform provision by the government. Thus, both motivation for savings disappeared and gains from savings were eliminated by taxes and by welfare provisions, which in many cases penalized those who save by making access to government services conditional on lack of savings (including old age provisions and other benefits).

As argued in the previous chapter, a striking difference between Far East Asia and European Union relates to the share of government expenses to GDP. In fast growing East Asian economies such as for example China, Republic of Korea or Thailand, this ratio of government redistribution to GDP remains between 10–20 per cent. In France, Italy and UK it has been driven up close to 50 per cent. However, high redistribution by the state that replaces savings[4] is only part of the story. It is not just Western Europe but also the US, with more limited redistribution, that continues to punish its savers and investors via its design of tax policies and welfare benefits. In turn, low domestic saving rates lead to reliance on inflow of funds from abroad, implying that the most developed economies are converging to the similar model of development as some emerging market and transition economies (outside Asia) and are become increasingly sensitive to international financial markets and to the behaviour of their main sponsors.

To reiterate, as a result of economic philosophy that shaped economic policy and institutions for last 60 years, by 2010, even the largest Western economy, the US, is becoming more and more sensitive to inflow of foreign capital, and this comes with not just economic but also political risk. And this effect appears despite the lower size of the US government.

Thus, it may be no longer correct to argue that the transition economies need to learn from the most advanced countries. Apart from Ukraine and Latvia, most of the transition economies weathered the crisis relatively well. As demonstrated by Sanfey (2010), the crisis did not lead to the reversals of the reform process. At time of writing, the attention in Europe is on the Southern European economies, which inflated their public consumption during good times, increasing their debt and where now adjustment is difficult, with the risk of fiscal disintegration in need to be alleviated by external aid.

It may well be time, that the direction of the institutional and policy learning process reverses its direction.

Notes

Chapter 1

1. The command economy was also adopted by Yugoslavia and Albania, yet politically those two countries remained outside the 'Soviet bloc' – i.e. outside 'the sphere of influence' of the USSR, as defined by the lack of a Red Army military presence.
2. The distinction between those four dimensions draws on Gregory and Stuart (1995). See also Kornai (1992), Milgrom and Roberts (1992), Gros and Steinherr (1995, 2004), Temkin (1996) and others.
3. See Applebaum (2003) for an extensive account based on a wide range of sources, many of which became available only after the fall of Communism. Between 1929 and 1953, 18 million people passed through 476 camps scattered across the Soviet Union; at least 3 million perished.

Chapter 2

1. Or for 60 years, if we exclude the initial phases of 'war communism' and the 'New Economic Policy' (NEP) in the Soviet Union (see Gros and Steinherr 2004). At the beginning of the 21st century, the system is still operational in North Korea and Cuba. In addition, China and Vietnam offer two important examples of economic systems which can be functionally described as a unique evolving mixture of a command economy and a market economy, with the balance shifting from the former to the latter over time.
2. 'Why is there an objective price structure in a competitive market? Because, as a result of the parametric function of prices, there is generally only *one* set of prices which satisfies the objective equilibrium conditions – i.e. equalises demand and supply of each commodity. The same objective price structure can be obtained in a socialist economy if the *parametric function of prices* is retained. On a competitive market the *parametric function of prices* results from the number of competing individuals being too large to enable any one to influence prices [on] his own. In a socialist economy, [since the] production and ownership of ... productive resources [apart from] labour [are] centralised, the managers certainly can and do influence prices by their decisions. Therefore, the parametric function of prices must be imposed on them by the Central Planning Board as an *accounting rule*' (Lange 1936: 63, emphasis in the original). Note that the argument used by Lange implies that a market socialist system with free prices and state ownership of capital assets is also feasible, provided that the enterprises are not large – i.e. are unable to inflict monopolistic distortions. Thus, why centralized administrative control over enterprises (including prices controls) is important for the socialist system is not really explained. The answer is that centralized control is crucial, not just because of the monopolistic position of enterprises but

because of the incentive problem resulting from state ownership, which Lange was unwilling to admit. Moreover, importance of capital market is ignored: decentralized enterprises with no transferable property rights to capital assets would still not guarantee that the assets were matched with those who could use them in the most efficient way.

3. All the data correspond to Tables 2.2–2.3.
4. This is the so-called 'ratchet effect'. See Milgrom and Roberts (1992); Roland (2000).
5. High energy use at the end of Communism was accompanied by high pollution and high level of carbon dioxide emissions This had very interesting implications for the international agreements on climate change. In particular, the Kyoto Protocol of 1997 introduced a cap-and-trade system for the so called 'greenhouse gases'. Emissions quotas that have been agreed were based on emissions figures for 1990. Countries that emit less can sell emission permits to other nations. The use of 1990 as a baseline, coupled with the fact that energy-intensive industrial production declined since 1990, left Russia with enormous stock of credits that can be sold to others. Russia is the third largest emitter after the United States and China. Yet as of 2006, its emissions were still 37 per cent below the 1990 levels (*Wall Street Journal*, 23 June 2009).
6. Energy use is affected by the production structure. Economies based on tourism, for example, may be very energy efficient in this respect (see Morocco in Figure 2.3).

Chapter 3

1. Eleven scores were missing; these relate to the former republics of Yugoslavia in earlier years.

Chapter 4

1. One may note that there is no reason to assume that utility possibility frontiers must be concave to the origin, unlike the typical production possibility frontiers (PPFs). The underlying reason is that changes in utility are not necessary proportional to changes in physical quantities.
2. See also the related discussion in Chapter 2, where we argued that one of the main reasons why the later communist governments were unable to introduce the far-reaching reforms considered necessary was because of the undemocratic nature of their regimes, which in turn led to concerns about the implications of potential political unrest (a poor substitute for correcting policies via democratic institutions). The fate of Ceaușescu family in Romania is a good example of the type of risk faced by communist despots, when no forms of democratic mediation were able to serve as a safety valve.
3. However, the price levels in the EU are high because of trade barriers, and the net effect could be different if the EU were open to imports from outside.
4. This is not illustrated here in detail, but data is easily available. For Russia, the time series for both production and energy are readily available from *Russian Economic Trends*.

Chapter 6

1. This delay led to a (now mostly obsolete) discussion of 'gradualism' versus 'big bang', where Hungary was taken as an example of the former, and Poland of the latter. A sampling of that early discussion can be found in Portes (1993).
2. For both Hungary and Poland, the output statistics are as reported by the corresponding Central Statistical Offices for GDP, not for the net material product (NMP). The latter measure, standard under the old regime, excludes a major part of the service sector. The difference is not trivial. For both countries, the use of NMP would show a recession in 1989 (the latter statistic is sometimes confused with GDP and makes its way into some Western reports, in disguise).
3. Here, wage cuts is one mechanism and wage arrears is another. Wage arrears can be seen as equivalent to borrowing from workers. Modelling of this issue is provided by Earle and Sabirianova (2000). See also Desai and Idson (2000, ch. 8).
4. For a general discussion of employee control during the transition, see Earle and Estrin (1996). Empirical evidence consistent with the labour-controlled model is provided in Mickiewicz (1996).
5. When divided by two, it gives a rough measure of the area of output loss, but this additional transformation is spurious – it is just a linear transformation, not affecting the estimation results in any other way.
6. The list of the indicators is not complete. See Campos and Coricelli (2002) for a further discussion.
7. However, a word of caution is needed. Åslund (2001) argues that countries experiencing wars were not only affected by the collapse of output, but also by the collapse of output statistics.

Chapter 8

1. An important omission we do not address is the size of informal sector.
2. Age structure is a crude proxy. It would be better to use data on effective average retirement age (see also previous chapter).
3. In addition, high regulatory barriers are likely to be associated with higher level of corruption. In the transition context, it may be particularly detrimental for job creation by new businesses (Aidis and Mickiewicz 2006).

Chapter 9

1. However, where nominal private owners exist, the systemic change – i.e. a return to a private market economy – is far easier.
2. See Bałtowski and Mickiewicz (2000) and Mickiewicz and Bałtowski (2003) on the discussion, which preceded the privatization programme's implementation in Poland.
3. However, expectations may play the pivotal role here. There is some evidence that the managers of state firms modified their strategy/as a result of privatization expectations, following 'commercialization' ('corporatiza-

tion'), which was the first step in the privatization process (Pinto, Belka and Krajewski 1993). Therefore, slowing down the privatization process is less costly in terms of economic efficiency, where the future privatization plans of the government remain credible.

4. It does not follow that the owner-manager firm is always more advantageous than the incorporated company (where control and ownership are typically separated). As always, there are trade-offs. Concentration of risk is one problem (for a more detailed discussion, see Milgrom and Roberts 1992).

5. Hiring new employees implies that they share rents or quasi-rents with incumbents, thus it is against the interests of the latter. Also, reducing employment by more than voluntary outflows means taking collective decisions which would not otherwise be taken by individual employees. It is likely that those affected can build a coalition blocking the move. Combining those two effects, we get a low responsiveness of employment to output shocks. For other possible implications of employee ownership in the transition context, see Earle and Estrin (1996); for more recent empirical evidence, see Mickiewicz, Gerry and Bishop (2005).

6. See Filatotchev, Wright and Bleaney (1999) for empirical evidence demonstrating that control has been important for managers in Russia.

7. As already discussed, the 'soft' budget is interpreted as a time inconsistency problem. In the context of the discussion here, we have the government that cannot credibly commit itself to bankrupt an enterprise which initiates a negative present value (PV) project, because in the later stage, when some costs are already sunk, the benefits of subsidization will exceed the cost. Knowing that (i.e. expecting future state support), enterprise managers may initiate unprofitable projects (Kornai, Maskin and Roland 2003).

8. Filatotchev, Isachenkova and Mickiewicz (2007) provide evidence on this point.

9. For this reason, with prices on asset markets depressed, the first decision of some privatized companies was to acquire more property, as a prerequisite for access to new investment funding.

10. Another equally unattractive source of capital came from the 'underground economy', which thrived in the final phase of Communism.

11. In some countries, all mass privatization was only via funds, as in Poland.

12. Results obtained by Bennett *et al.* (2007) were in turn challenged by Gouret (2007). However, the latter results may be affected by the idiosyncratic way the privatization variables were coded (see Mickiewicz 2009). A very similar controversy relates to the impact of mass privatization on health, presumably via social effects of induced restructuring. Those negative effects were reported by Stuckler, King, McKee (2009), but challenged later on independently by Gerry, Mickiewicz and Nikoloski (2010), and by Earle and Gehlbach (2010) again based on details of econometric design.

13. Following the classic ('pre-transition') approach (Megginson, Nash and van Randenborgh 1984; Megginson and Netter 2001), three years including the year of privatization are eliminated from pre- and post-privatization comparisons. That research tradition has been typically neglected in the case of transition studies.

14. Unfortunately, accumulating privatization revenues is one issue but keeping government expenses under control is another. Despite its relative success

with privatization programme, Hungary was affected by recurring fiscal crises, as last evidenced in 2008–2009.

Chapter 10

1. An important theme we do not follow up here is that imperfections in the financial markets have more impact on some specific industries, skill-intensive and R&D-intensive ones in particular. Recent evidence on this is provided by Carlin and Mayer (2003).
2. The creditors' rights index was first applied by La Porta *et al.* (1998).
3. One issue we leave aside is the second-best response to the under-developed financial sectors of internalizing financial markets – in particular, the creation of the internal 'credit markets' of the financial-industrial groups (Peroti and Gelfer 2001), but also finance within multinational structures (FDI): both provide new channels of finance and increase credibility, facilitating access to old ones (Filatotchev *et al.* 2007).
4. See also the paper by Gros and Suhrcke (2000).
5. Longer lag structures were attempted, but turned out to be insignificant. More importantly, the magnitude of the first-year negative effect should be treated with caution. It is likely to be inflated in a spurious way, consistently with the phenomenon discussed by Rzońca and Ciżkowicz (2003). See also Mickiewicz (2005, Chapter 10).
6. For all three dependent variables, the impact of the share of foreign banks turned out to be insignificant.

Chapter 11

1. The record belongs to Czechoslovakia, one of the most centralized command economies, where the ratio of revenue to GDP peaked at close to 62 per cent in 1989. Hungary comes next, with 55 per cent in the same year. Three reform laggards – Belarus, Tajikistan and Turkmenistan – still recorded government revenues above 50 per cent for some years during the 1990s (EBRD 1995–2005).
2. Here, we deal with time paths resulting from the reform process. It is worth reminding ourselves that negative social costs in the reforming countries were counterbalanced later by beneficial results from economic growth. In other words, the most dramatic social costs in terms of poverty were experienced by those countries which did not reform (see Milanovic 1998 for evidence). In general, when GDP declines, the poor lose more than the rich (Milanovic 1998: 132). The length and depth of the transitional recession (see Chapter 6) is thus closely associated with the incidence of poverty, and the former was clearly negatively affected by slow reform.
3. In many cases, an increase in expenditure was also linked to the costs of bailout of the banking sector. While a system of direct subsidies to the 'old' sector was relatively easy to dismantle, the 'soft' budget constraint associated with bank lending was far more difficult to eliminate. Given the latter phenomenon, the negative effects of liberalization on enterprise financial positions could trigger banking crises (with some delay).

4. A word of caution. The magnitude of the contemporaneus negative effect is most likely to be inflated in a spurious way, due to the phenomenon discussed in Rzońca and Ciżkowicz (2003). See also the discussion in Mickiewicz (2005), Chapter 10.

Chapter 12

1. I am indebted to Yama Temouri for sharing processed UNCTAD data used here.
2. Uzbekistan should be included as well, but economic data is scarce.
3. Stressing the significance of inflow of foreign, especially short-term capital, and of foreign currency denominated obligations does not imply that foreign ownership of banking played a negative role. In fact Sanfey (2010) demonstrates that foreign bank ownership mitigated capital outflows in the region. Sudden outflows of capital and banking crises were in nobody's interest and international community in Europe proved some capacity for collective action. The Initiative for Coordination of European Banks (Vienna Initiative) aimed to coordinate actions of intentional organizations and private banking institutions to prevent race to the bottom and financial outflows. At the same time, equal treatment of foreign banks by host country governments was confirmed again in exchange.
4. To accept what is claimed here, one has to reject both demand side arguments against positive effects of savings but also so-called Ricardian equivalence, which maintains that people internalize government constraints and will save more in response to increase in government spending, expecting higher taxes in the future (Barro 1979).

Bibliography

Acemoglu, D. (2006) 'Modeling Inefficient Institutions', NBER Working Paper No. W11940.

Acemoglu, D. and S. Johnson (2005) 'Unbundling Institutions', *Journal of Political Economy*, 113: 943–95.

Acemoglu, D. and T. Verdier (2000) 'The Choice between Market Failures and Corruption', *American Economic Review*, 90 (1), 194–211.

Aghion, P. and O. Blanchard (1994) 'On the Speed of Transition in Central Europe', in S. Fisher and J. Rotemberg (eds) *NBER Macroeconomics Annual* (Cambridge, MA: MIT Press), 283–320.

Aghion, P. and O. Blanchard (1998) 'On Privatisation Methods in Eastern Europe and Their Implications', *Economics of Transition*, 6, 87–99.

Aghion, P. and P. Howitt (1994) 'Growth and Unemployment', *The Review of Economic Studies*, 61 (3), 477–94.

Aidis, R. and T. Mickiewicz (2006) 'Entrepreneurs, Expectations and Business Expansion: Lessons from Lithuania', *Europe-Asia Studies*, 58 (6), 855–80.

Aidis, R., S. Estrin and T. Mickiewicz (2008) 'Institutions and Entrepreneurship Development in Russia: A Comparative Perspective', *Journal of Business Venturing*, 23 (6), 656–672.

Åslund, A. (2001) 'The Myth of Output Collapse after Communism', Carnegie Endowment for International Peace Working Paper, 18.

Åslund, A. (2002) *Building Capitalism* (Cambridge: Cambridge University Press).

Åslund, A., P. Boone, S. Johnson, S. Fisher and B. Ickes (1996) 'How to Stabilise: Lessons from Post-Communist Countries', *Brookings Papers on Economic Activity*, 1, 217–313.

Audretsch, D., M. A. Carree, A. van Stel and R. Thurik (2006), 'Does Self-Employment Reduce Unemployment?', *Discussion Papers on Entrepreneurship, Growth and Public Policy* No. 0705, Max Planck Institute of Economics, Jena.

Balcerowicz, L. (1992) *800 Dni* (Warsaw: BGW).

Balcerowicz, L. (1995) *Socialism, Capitalism, Transformation* (Budapest: Central European University Press).

Bałtowski, M. and T. Mickiewicz (2000) 'Privatisation in Poland: Ten Years After', *Post-Communist Economies*, 12 (4), 425–43.

Barr, N. (ed.) (1994) *Labour Market and Social Policy in Central and Eastern Europe* (Oxford: Oxford University Press).

Barr, N. (2001) 'Reforming Welfare States in Post-Communist Countries', in L. Orlowski (ed.) *Transition and Growth in Post-Communist Countries: The Ten-Year Experience* (Northampton, MA: Edward Elgar), 169–217.

Barro, R. (1979) 'On the Determination of Public Debt', *Journal of Political Economy*, 89, 940–971.

Barro, R. (1997) *Determinants of Economic Growth: A Cross-Country Empirical Study* (Cambridge, MA: MIT Press).

Barth, J., G. Caprio and R. Levine (2006) Rethinking Bank Regulation: Till Angels Govern (Cambridge: Cambridge University Press).

Basel Committee on Banking Supervision (2004) *International Convergence of Capital Measurement and Capital Standards. A Revised Framework* (Basel: Bank for International Settlements).

Bell, J. (2001) *The Political Economy of Reform in Post-Communist Poland* (Northampton, MA: Edward Elgar).

Benecki, R., J. Hölscher and M. Jarmużek (2006) 'Fiscal Transparency and Policy Rules in Poland', in P. Jaworski and T. Mickiewicz (eds) *Polish EU Accession in Comparative Perspective* (London: SSEES UCL), 3–28.

Bennett, J., S. Estrin and G. Urga (2007) 'Methods of Privatization and Economic Growth in Transition Economies', *Economics of Transition*, 15 (4), 661–83.

Bentolila, S., J. Dolado, W. Franz and C. Pissarides (1994) 'Labour Flexibility and Wages: Lessons from Spain', *Economic Policy*, 9 (18), 55–99.

Berg, A. (1994) 'Does Macroeconomic Reform Cause Structural Adjustment? Lessons from Poland', *Journal of Comparative Economics*, 18, 376–409.

Blanchard, O. (1997) *The Economics of Post-Communist Transition* (Oxford: Clarendon Press).

Blanchard, O. and P. Aghion (1996) 'On Insider Privatisation', *European Economic Review*, 40, 759–66.

Blanchard, O. and M. Kremer (1997) 'Disorganisation', *Quarterly Journal of Economics*, 112, 1091–126.

Blanchard, O. and T. Philippon (2003) 'The Decline of Rents, and the Rise and Fall of European Unemployment', MIT, unpublished paper.

Blanchflower, D., A. Oswald and A. Stutzer (2001) 'Latent Entrepreneurship across Nations', *European Economic Review*, 45, 680–91.

Boeri, T. (1997) 'Labour Market Reforms in Transition Economies', *Oxford Review of Economic Policy*, 13 (2), 126–40.

Botero, J., S. Djankov, R. La Porta and F. Lopez-De-Silanes (2004) 'The Regulation of Labor', *The Quarterly Journal of Economics*, 119 (4), 1339–82.

Boycko, M., A. Shleifer and R. Vishny (1995) *Privatising Russia* (Cambridge, MA: MIT Press).

Boycko, M., A. Shleifer and R. Vishny (1996) 'A Theory of Privatisation', *Economic Journal*, 106, 309–19.

Brada, J. (1989) 'Technological Progress and Factor Utilisation in Eastern European Economic Growth', *Economica*, 56 (224), 433–48.

Breurer, J. (2004) 'An Exegesis on Currency and Banking Crises', *Journal of Economic Surveys*, 18 (3), 293–320.

Buccellato, T. and T. Mickiewicz (2009) 'Hydrocarbons and Inequality within Regions in Russia', *Europe-Asia Studies*, 61 (3), 385–407.

Calmfors, L. and J. Driffill (1988) 'Bargaining structure, corporatism and macroeconomic performance', *Economic Policy*, 6, 14–47.

Calvo, G. and F. Coricelli (1992) 'Stagflationary Effects of Stabilisation Programmes in Reforming Socialist Countries: Enterprise-side and Household-side Factors', *World Bank Economic Review*, 6, 71–90.

Calvo, G. and F. Coricelli (1993) 'Output Collapse in Eastern Europe: The Role of Credit', *IMF Staff Papers*, 40 (1), 32–52.

Campos, N. and F. Coricelli (2002) 'Growth in Transition; What We Know, What We Don't and What We Should', *Journal of Economic Literature*, 60, 793–836.

Campos, N. and R. Horváth (2006) 'Reform Redux: Measurement, Determinants and Reversals', IZA DP No. 2093.

Carlin, W. and C. Mayer (2003) 'Finance, Investment and Growth', *Journal of Financial Economics*, 69, 191–226.

Christoffersen, P. and P. Doyle (2000) 'From Inflation to Growth: Eight Years of Transition', *Economics of Transition*, 8, 421–51.

Chudzik, R. (2000) 'Banks and the Privatisation of Enterprises in Poland', in E. Rosenbaum, F. Bönker and H. Wagner (eds) *Privatisation, Corporate Governance and the Emergence of Markets* (Basingstoke: Macmillan), 155–70.

Coase, R. (1960) 'The Problem of Social Cost', *Journal of Law and Economics*, 3, 1–44.

Coffee, J. (1996) 'Institutional Investors in Transitional Economies', in R. Frydman, C. Gray and A. Rapaczynski (eds) *Corporate Governance in Central Europe and Russia*, 1 (Budapest: CEU Press), 111–86.

Colombo, E. and J. Driffill (2003) 'Financial Markets and Transition', in E. Colombo and J. Driffill, *The Role of Financial Markets in the Transition Process* (Heidelberg: Physica-Verlag), 1–12.

Conquest, R. (1987) *The Harvest of Sorrow. Soviet Collectivization and the Terror-Famine* (Oxford: Oxford University Press).

Crawford, S. and E. Ostrom (1995) 'A Grammar of Institutions', *The American Political Science Review*, 89 (3), 582–600.

Cullis, J. and P. Jones (1992) *Public Finance and Public Choice* (London: McGraw-Hill).

De Melo, M., C. Denizer, A. Gelb and S. Tenev (1997) 'Circumstance and Choice: The Role of Initial Conditions and Policies in Transition Economies', World Bank Policy Research Working Paper, 1866.

De Melo, M., C. Denizer, A. Gelb and S. Tenev (2001) 'Circumstance and Choice: The Role of Initial Conditions and Policies in Transition Economies', *World Bank Economic Review*, 15, 1–31.

De Melo, M. and A. Gelb (1997) 'Transition to Date: A Comparative Overview', in S. Zecchini (ed.) *Lessons from Economic Transition* (Dordrecht: Kluwer), 59–78.

Desai, P. and T. Idson (2000) *Work Without Wages: Russia's Nonpayment Crisis* (Cambridge, MA: MIT Press).

DiMaggio, P. and W. Powell (1983) 'The Iron Cage Revisited: Institutional Isomorphism and Collective Rationality in Organizational Fields', *American Sociological Review*, 48 (2), 147–60.

Djankov, S., C. McLiesh and A. Shleifer (2005) 'Private Credit in 129 Countries', NBER Working Paper, 11078.

Djankov, S. and P. Murrell (2002) 'Enterprise Restructuring in Transition: A Quantitative Survey, *Journal of Economic Literature*, 60, 739–92.

Drewnowski, J. (ed.) (1982) *Crisis in the East European Economy* (Beckenham: Croom Helm).

Driffill, J. and T. Mickiewicz (2003) 'The Order of Financial Liberalisation: Lessons from the Polish Experience', in E. Colombo and J. Driffill, *The Role of Financial Markets in the Transition Process* (Heidelberg: Physica-Verlag), 13–42.

Earle, J. and S. Estrin (1996) 'Employee Ownership in Transition', in R. Frydman, C. Gray and A. Rapaczynski (eds) *Corporate Governance in Central Europe and Russia*, 2 (Budapest: CEU Press), 1–61.

Earle, J. and S. Gehlbach (2010) 'Did Mass Privatisation *Really* Increase Post-Communist Mortality?', *The Lancet*, 372 (9712), 375.

Earle, J. and K. Sabirianova (2000) 'Equilibrium Wage Arrears: A Theoretical and Empirical Analysis of Institutional Lock-in', IZA Working Paper, 321.

EBRD (1994–2005) *Transition Reports* (London: European Bank for econstruction and Development).

EBRD (1995–2009) *Transition Report* (London: European Bank for Reconstruction and Development).

Estrin, S. and R. Stone (1996) 'A Taxonomy of Mass Privatisation', *Transition*, 7 (11–12), 8–9.

Estrin, S. and T. Mickiewicz (2010) 'Entrepreneurship in Transition Economies; The Role of Institutions and Generational Change', in M. Minniti (ed.) *The Dynamics of Entrepreneurial Activity* (Oxford: Oxford University Press).

European Commission (2003) *Employment in Europe: Recent Trends and Prospects* (Brussels: Directorate-General for Employment and Social Affairs).

Falcetti, E., M. Raiser and P. Sanfey (2002) 'Defying the Odds: Initial Conditions, Reforms and Growth in the First Decade of Transition', *Journal of Comparative Economics*, 30, 229–50.

Falcetti, E., T. Lysenko and P. Sanfey (2006) 'Reforms and Growth in Transition: Re-examining the Evidence', *Journal of Comparative Economics*, 34, 421–45.

Filatotchev, I., N. Isachenkova and T. Mickiewicz (2007) 'Corporate Governance and Investment Finance in Transition Economies: A survey Evidence from Large Firms in Hungary and Poland', *Economics of Transition* 15 (3), 433–60.

Filatotchev, I., M. Wright and M. Bleaney (1999) 'Privatisation, Insider Control and Managerial Entrenchment in Russia', *Economics of Transition*, 7, 481–504.

Fischer, S. and R. Sahay (2000) 'The Transition Economies after Ten Years', IMF Working Paper, WP/00/30.

Fries, S., D. Neven and P. Seabright (2004) *Competition, Ownership and Bank Performance in Transition*, EBRD, unpublished paper.

Fries, S. and A. Taci (2002) 'Banking Reform and Development in Transition Economies', EBRD Working Paper, 71.

Frydman, R., A. Rapaczynski and J. Earle (1993) *The Privatisation Process in Central Europe*, 2 vols (Budapest: CEU Press).

Fukuyama, F. (1995) *Trust* (New York: The Free Press).

Funck, B. and L. Pizzati (eds) (2002) *Labor, Employment and Social Policies in the EU Enlargement Process* (Washington, DC: World Bank).

Gacs, V. and P. Huber (2003a) 'Quantity Adjustment in Candidate Countries Regional Labour Markets', in *Adjustment Capability of Regional Labour Markets*, Workpackage no. 2. ACCESSLAB 5th Framework Project (Vienna: WIFO).

Gacs, V. and P. Huber (2003b) 'Regional Labour Market Problems in the Candidate Countries: A Descriptive Analysis', in *Adjustment Capability of Regional Labour Markets*, Workpackage no. 2., ACCESSLAB 5th Framework Project (Vienna: WIFO).

Gerry, C., B. Kim and C. Li (2004) 'The Gender Wage Gap and Wage Arrears in Russia: Evidence from the RLMS', *Journal of Population Economics*, 17 (2), 1432–75.

Gerry, C. and T. Mickiewicz (2008) 'Inequality, Democracy and Taxation: Lessons from the Post-Communist Transition', *Europe-Asia Studies*, 60 (1), 89–111.

Gerry, C., T. Mickiewicz and Z. Nikoloski (2010) 'Did Mass Privatisation Really Increase Post-Communist Mortality?', *The Lancet*, 375 (9712), 372–4.

Golinowska, S. (2001) 'Welfare State Reforms in Post-Communist Countries: A Comment on Barr', in L. Orlowski (ed.) *Transition and Growth in Post-Communist Countries: The Ten Years' Experience* (Northampton, MA: Edward Elgar), 219–35.

Góra M. and C. Schmidt (1998) 'Long-Term Unemployment, Unemployment Benefits and Social Assistance: The Polish Experience', *Empirical Economics*, 23 (1–2), 55–85.

Gouret, F. (2007) 'Privatization and Output Behavior during the Transition: Methods matter!', *Journal of Comparative Economics*, 35 (1), 3–34.

Gravelle, H. and R. Rees (2004) *Microeconomics* (Harlow: Pearson).

Gregory, P. and R. Stuart (1995) *Comparative Economic Systems* (Boston, MA: Houghton Mifflin).

Gros, A. and D. Steinherr (1995) *Winds of Change* (London: Longman).

Gros, A. and D. Steinherr (2004) *Economic Transition in Central and Eastern Europe* (Cambridge: Cambridge University Press).

Gros, A. and M. Suhrcke (2000) 'Ten Years After: What is Special about Transition Economies', EBRD Working Paper, 56.

Harper, D. (2003) *Foundations of Entrepreneurship and Economic Development* (Abingdon: Routledge).

Hart, O. (2001) 'Financial Contracting', *Journal of Economic Literature*, 39, 1079–100.

Havrda, M. (2003) 'The Czech Republic: The Case of Delayed Transformation', in M. Federowicz and R. Aguilera (eds) *Corporate Governance in a Changing Economic and Political Environment* (Basingstoke: Palgrave Macmillan), 121–43.

Havrylyshyn, O. (2006) *Divergent Paths in Post-Communist Transformation: Capitalism for All or Capitalism for the Few?* (Houndmills: Palgrave Macmillan).

Havrylyshyn, O. and R. van Rooden (2003) 'Institutions Matter in Transition, but do Policies?', *Comparative Economic Studies*, 45, 2–24.

Hayek, F. (1960) *Constitution of Liberty* (London: Routledge).

Hellman, J., G. Jones and D. Kaufmann (2003) 'Seize the State, Seize the Day: State Capture and Influence in Transition Economies', *Journal of Comparative Economics*, 31, 751–73.

Howard, M. (2000) 'The Weakness of Postcommunist Civil Society', *Journal of Democracy*, 13 (1), 157–169.

Hughes G. and P. Hare (1992) 'Industrial Policy and Restructuring in Eastern Europe', *Oxford Review of Economic Policy*, 8, 82–104.

Hyder, Z. and M. Khan (2007) 'Monetary Conditions Index for Pakistan', *SPB Reaserach Bulletin*, 3 (2), 165–90.

ILO (1996) *World Employment 1996/97. National Policies in a Global Context* (Geneva: International Labour Office).

IOSCO (2003) *Objectives and Principles of Securities Regulation* (Madrid: International Organisation of Securities Commissions).

Jackman R. and M. Rutkowski (1994) 'Labour Markets: Unemployment', in N. Barr (ed.) *Labour Markets and Social Policy in Central and Eastern Europe* (Oxford: Oxford University Press).

Jensen, M. and W. Meckling (1976) 'Theory of the Firm: Managerial Behaviour, Agency Costs and Ownership Structure', *Journal of Financial Economics*, 3, 305–60.

Kannan, R., S. Sanyal and B. Bhoi (2006) 'Monetary Conditions Index for India', Reserve Bank of India Occasional Papers 27, No. 3.

Knack, S. (2006), 'Measuring Corruption in Eastern Europe and Central Asia: A Critique of the Cross-Country Indicators', World Bank – Development Research Group (DECRG), World Bank Policy Research Working Paper No. 3968.

Kołodko, G. (1979) 'Fazy wzrostu gospodarczego w Polsce', *Gospodarka Planowa*, 3, 137–43.

Kołodko, G. (1986) 'Economic Growth Cycles in the Centrally Planned Economies: A Hypothesis of Long Cycle', BEBR Faculty Working Paper, No. 1880, University of Illinois at Urbana-Champain.

Kołodko, G. (2002) *Globalisation and Catching-up in Transition Economies* (Rochester NY: University of Rochester Press).

Kornai, J. (1979) 'Resource-Constrained versus Demand Constrained Systems', *Econometrica*, 47, 801–19.

Kornai, J. (1980) '"Hard" and "Soft" Budget Constraints', *Acta Oeconomica*, 25, 231–45.

Kornai, J. (1986) *Contradictions and Dilemmas: Studies on the Socialist Economy and Society* (Cambridge, MA: MIT Press).

Kornai, J. (1992) *The Socialist System: The Political Economy of Communism* (Oxford: Clarendon Press).

Kornai, J. (1995) 'Transformational Recession: The Example of Hungary', in C. Sanders (ed.) *Eastern Europe in Crisis and the Way Out* (Basingstoke: Macmillan), 29–77.

Kornai, J., E. Maskin and G. Roland (2003) 'Understanding the Soft Budget Constraint', *Journal of Economic Literature*, 61, 1095–136.

Kronenberg, T. (2004) 'The Course of Natural Resources in the Transition Economies', *Economics of Transition*, 12, 399–426.

Kurowski, S. (1991) *Polityka Gospodarcza PRL* (Warsaw: Editions Spotkania).

Lange, O. (1936) 'On the Economic Theory of Socialism: Part One', *Review of Economic Studies*, 4, 53–71.

La Porta, R., F. Lopez-de-Silvanes, A. Shleifer and R. Vishny (1998) 'Law and Finance', *Journal of Political Economy*, 106, 1113–55.

La Porta, R., F. Lopez-de-Silanes, A. Shleifer and R. Vishny (1999) 'The quality of government', *Journal of Law, Economics and Organisation*, 15 (1), 222–79.

Lehmann, H. (1998) 'Active Labor Market Policies in Central Europe: First Lessons', in R. Riphahn, D. Snower and K. Zimmermann (eds) *Employment Policy in the Transition: Lessons from German Integration* (Berlin: Springer).

Leontief W. and F. Duchin (1983) *Military Spending* (Oxford: Oxford University Press).

Lindbeck, A. and D. J. Snower (1988) *The Insider-Outsider Theory of Employment and Unemployment* (Cambridge, Massachusetts: MIT Press).

Loungani, P. and N. Sheets (1997) 'Central Bank Independence, Inflation and Growth in Transition Economies', *Journal of Money, Credit, and Banking*, 29, 381–99.

Martín, G. (2002) 'An Overview of Spanish Labour Market Reforms, 1985–2002', *Unidad de Políticas Comparadas* (CSIC) Working Paper 02-17.

McKinnon, R. (1992) 'Taxation, Money and Credit in a Liberalizing Socialist Economy', in C. Clague and G. Rausser (eds) *The Emergence of Market Economies in Eastern Europe* (Cambridge, MA: Blackwell), 109–28.

McKinnon, R. (1993) *The Order of Economic Liberalisation* (Baltimore, MD: Johns Hopkins University Press).

McKinsey (1999) 'Report on Russian Economic Performance', McKinsey Global Institute, http://www/mckinsey.com.

Megginson, W., R. Nash and M. van Randenborgh (1984) 'The Financial and Operating Performance of Newly Privatised Firms: An International Empirical Analysis', *Journal of Finance*, 69, 403–52.

Megginson, W. and J. Netter (2001) 'From State to Market: A Survey of Empirical Studies on Privatisation', *Journal of Economic Literature*, 39, 321–89.

Megginson, W. and J. Netter (2003) 'History and Methods of Privatisation', in D. Parker and D. Saal (eds) *International Handbook on Privatisation* (Cheltenham: Edward Elgar), 25–40.

Mejstrik, M. (2003) 'Privatisation and Corporate Governance in the Czech Republic', in D. Parker and D. Saal (eds) *International Handbook on Privatisation* (Cheltenham: Edward Elgar), 372–401.

Merlevede, B. (2003) 'Reform Reversals and Output Growth in Transition Economies', *Economics of Transition*, 11, 649–69.

Mickiewicz, T. (1988) 'Gra o reforme', *Res Publica*, 2 (12), 112–14.

Mickiewicz, T. (1996) 'The State Sector During Economic Transformation: Employment, Wages and Investment', *Post Communist Economies*, 8 (3), 393–410.

Mickiewicz, T. (2003) 'Convergence in Employment Structures. Transition Countries versus the EU: Reforms, Income Levels or Specialisation Patterns?', in K. Piech (ed.) *Economic Policy and Growth of Central and East European Countries* (London: SSEES UCL), 59–82.

Mickiewicz, T. (2005) *Economic Transition in Central Europe and the Commonwealth of Independent States* (Houndmills: Palgrave Macmillan).

Mickiewicz, T. (ed.) (2006) *Corporate Governance and Finance in Poland and Russia* (Houndmills: Palgrave Macmillan).

Mickiewicz, T. (2009) 'Hierarchy of Governance Institutions and the Pecking Order of Privatisation: Central-Eastern Europe and Central Asia Reconsidered', *Post Communist Economies*, 21 (4), 399–423.

Mickiewicz, T. and M. Bałtowski (2003) 'All Roads Lead to Outside Ownership: Polish Piecemeal Privatisation', in D. Parker and D. Saal (eds) *International Handbook on Privatisation* (Cheltenham: Edward Elgar), 402–26.

Mickiewicz, T. and J. Bell (2000) *Unemployment in Transition: Restructuring and Labour Markets in Central Europe* (Amsterdam: Harwood Academic).

Mickiewicz, T. and A. Zalewska (2006) 'De-industrialisation: Rowthorn and Wells' Model Revisited', *Acta Oeconomica*, 56 (2), 143–66.

Mickiewicz, T., C. Gerry and K. Bishop (2005) 'Privatisation, Corporate Control and Employment Growth: Evidence from a Panel of Large Polish Firms, 1996–2002', *Economic Systems*, 29, 98–119.

Milanovic, B. (1998) *Income, Inequality and Poverty during the Transition from Planned to Market Economy* (Washington, DC: World Bank).

Milgrom, P. and J. Roberts (1992) *Economics, Organisation and Management* (Upper Saddle River, NJ: Prentice Hall).

Mihalyi, P. (2000) 'Corporate Governance during and after Privatisation: The Lessons from Hungary', in E. Rosenbaum, F. Bönker and H. Wagner (eds) *Privatisation, Corporate Governance and the Emergence of Markets* (Basingstoke: Macmillan), 139–54.

Minniti, M., W. Bygrave and E. Autio (2005) *Global Entrepreneurship Monitor: 2005 Executive Report* (Babson Park, MA, US and London: Babson College and London Business School).

Mises, L. von (1966 [1949]) *Human Action: A Treatise on Economics* (Chicago: Contemporary Books/Yale University Press).

Newell, A. and F. Pastore (2000) 'Regional Unemployment and Industrial Restructuring in Poland', Discussion Paper, 194, University of Sussex, Department of Economics.

Nicoletti, G. and S. Scarpetta (2005) 'Product Market Reforms and Employment in OECD Countries', OECD Economics Department Working Papers, No. 472, OECD Publishing.

North, D. (1990) *Institutions, Institutional Change, and Economic Performance* (Cambridge: Cambridge University Press).

OECD (1992) *Economic Surveys: Poland* (Paris: Organisation for Economic Cooperation and Development).

Olson, M. (2000) *Power and Prosperity: Outgrowing Communist and Capitalist Dictatorships* (New York: Basic Books).

Parker, S. (2004) *The Economics of Self-Employment and Entrepreneurship* (Cambridge: Cambridge University Press).

Peroti, E. and S. Gelfer (2001) 'Red Barons or Robber Barons? Governance and Investment in Russian Financial-Industrial Groups', *European Economic Review*, 45, 1601–17.

Persson, T. and G. Tabellini (2003) *The Economic Effect of Constitution* (Cambridge: MIT Press).

Phelps, E. (1994) *Structural Slumps: The Modern Equilibrium Theory of Unemployment, Interest and Assets* (Cambridge, MA: Harvard University Press).

Pinto, B., M. Belka and S. Krajewski (1993) 'Transforming State Enterprises in Poland: Evidence on Adjustment by Manufacturing Firms', *Brookings Papers on Economic Activity*, 1, 213–70.

Pirttilä, J. (2001) 'Fiscal Policy and Structural Reforms in Transition Economies', *Economics of Transition*, 9, 29–52.

Pissarides, C. (2000) *Equilibrium Unemployment Theory* (Cambridge MA: MIT Press).

Porket, J. (1984) 'The Shortage, Use and Reserves of Labour in the Soviet Union', *Osteuropa Wirtschaft*, 29 (1), 8–24.

Portes, R. (ed.) (1993) *Economic Transformation in Central Europe* (London: CEPR).

Radosevic, S. (1999) 'Transformation of Science and Technology Systems into Systems of Innovation in Central and Eastern Europe: The Emerging Patterns and Determinants', *Structural Change and Economic Dynamics*, 10, 277–320.

Rein, M., B. Friedman and A. Wörgötter (eds) (1997) *Enterprise and Social Benefits after Communism* (Cambridge: Cambridge University Press and CEPR).

Riboud, M., C. Sanchez-Paramo and C. Silva-Jauregui (2002) 'Does Eurosclerosis Matter? Institutional Reform and Labour Market Performance in Central and East European Countries', in B. Funck and L. Fizzati (eds) *Labor, Employment and Social Policies in the EU Enlargement Process* (Washington, DC: World Bank), 243–311.

Riedel, J. and B. Comer (1997) 'Transition to a Market Economy in Vietnam', in S. Parker and J. Sachs (eds) *Economies in Transition: Comparing Asia and Europe* (Cambridge, MA: MIT Press), 189–216.

Rodrik, D. (1996) 'Understanding Economic Policy Reform', *Journal of Economic Literature*, 34, 9–41.

Roland, G. (2000) *Transition and Economics: Politics, Markets and Firms* (Cambridge, MA: MIT Press).

Rozelle, S. and J. Swinnen (2004) 'Success and Failure of Reform: Insights from the Transition of Agriculture', *Journal of Economic Literature*, 52, 404–56.

Rutkowski, M. (1990) 'Labour Hoarding and Future Unemployment in Eastern Europe: The Case of Polish Industry', Discussion Paper, 6, LSE Centre for Economic Performance.

Rutkowski, M. (1995) 'Workers in Transition', Policy Research Working Paper, 1556 (Washington, DC: World Bank).

Rutkowski, M. and M. Przybyła (2002) 'Poland: Regional Dimensions of Unemployment', in B. Funck and L. Fizzati (eds) *Labor, Employment and Social Policies in the EU Enlargement Process* (Washington, DC: World Bank), 157–75.

Rzońca, A. and P. Ciżkowicz (2003) 'A Comment on the Relationship between Policies and Growth in Transition Countries', *Economics of Transition*, 11 (4), 743–8.

Sala-i-Martin, X., G. Doppelhofer and R. Miller (2004) 'Determinants of Long-Term Growth: A Bayesian Averaging of Classical Estimates (BACE) Approach', *American Economic Review*, 94, 813–35.

Sanfey, P. (2010) *Transition in Crisis* (London: EBRD, mimeo).

Schaffer, M. and G. Turley (2001) 'Effective versus Statutory Taxation: Measuring Effective Tax Administration in Transition Economies', EBRD Working Paper, 62.

Schroeder, G. (1986) *The System versus Progress* (London: Centre for Research into Communist Economies).

Schwartz, S. and A. Bardi (1997) 'Influences of Adaptation to Communist Rule on Value Priorities in Eastern Europe', *Political Psychology*, 18 (2), 385–410.

Selowsky, M. and R. Martin (1997) 'Policy Performance and Output Growth in the Transition Economies', *American Economic Review, Papers and Proceedings*, 87, 349–53.

Shleifer A. and R. Vishny (1994) 'Politicians and Firms', *Quarterly Journal of Economics*, 109, 995–1025.

Shleifer A. and R. Vishny (1997) 'A Survey of Corporate Governance', *Journal of Finance*, 52, 737–83.

Sirc, L. (1981) 'The Decline in Growth Rates East and West', *Revue d'Etudes Comparatives Est-Ouest*, 12, 63–77; translated into English and published in L. Sirc, *Why the Communist Economies Failed* (London: Centre for Research into Communist Economies, 1994).

Smith, A. (1996) *Russian Foreign Trade in the Transition* (London: Royal Institute of International Affairs).

Stiglitz, J. (1992) 'The Design of Financial Systems for the Newly Emerging Democracies of Eastern Europe', in C. Clague and G. Rausser (eds) *The Emergence of Market Economies in Eastern Europe* (Cambridge, MA: Blackwell), 161–86.

Stiglitz, J. and A. Weiss (1981) 'Credit Rationing in Markets with Imperfect Information', *American Economic Review*, 71, 393–410.

Stuckler, D., L. King, M. McKee (2009) 'Mass Privatisation and the Post-Communist Mortality Crisis: A Cross-National Analysis', *The Lancet*, 373 (9661), 399–407.

Sztanderska, U. and B. Piotrowski (1999) *Background Study on Labour Market and Employment in Poland* (Warsaw: European Training Foundation).

Sztompka, P. (1996) 'Looking Back: The Year 1989 as a Cultural and Civilizational Break', *Communist and Post-Communist Studies*, 29 (2): 115–29.

Takla, L. (1999) 'Privatisation in the Czech Republic', in P. Hare, J. Batt and S. Estrin (eds) *Reconstituting the Market* (Amsterdam: Harwood), 135–54.

Talvi, E. and C. Végh (2005) 'Tax Base Variability and Procyclical Fiscal Policy in Developing Countries', *Journal of Development Economics*, 78, 156–90.

Tanzi, V. and G. Tsibouris (2000) 'Fiscal Reform Over Ten Years of Transition', IMF Working Paper, 113.

Teixeira, P. (2001) 'Labour Market Transition in Portugal, Spain, and Poland', *Faculdade de Economia*, Universidade de Coimbra, mimeo.

Temkin, G. (1989) 'Economic Calculation under Socialism', *Communist Economies*, 1 (1), 31–60.

Temkin, G. (1996) 'Information and Motivation: Reflections on the Socialist Economic System', *Communist and Post Communist Studies*, 29 (1), 25–44.

Tolba, M. and O. El-Kholy (eds) (1992) *The World Environment 1972–1992: Two Decades of Challenge* (London: Chapman & Hall on behalf of UNEP).

Tornell, A. and F. Westermann (2005) Boom-Bust Cycles and Financial Liberalization (Cambridge MA: MIT Press).

Tullock, G. (1967) *Toward the Mathematics of Politics* (Ann Arbor, MI: University of Michigan Press).

United Nations (1995) UN Statistical Yearbook (New York: UN).

Varian, H. (1992) *Microeconomic Analysis* (New York: W.W. Norton).

Voszka, E. (2003) 'Ownership and Corporate Governance in the Hungarian Large Enterprise Sector', in E. Rosenbaum, F. Bönker and H. Wagner (eds) *Privatisation, Corporate Governance and the Emergence of Markets* (Basingstoke: Macmillan), 171–94.

Ward, B. (1958) 'The Firm in Illyria: Market Syndicalism', *American Economic Review*, 48 (4), 566–89.

Wiles, P. (1982) 'Introduction: Zero Growth and the International Nature of the Polish Disease', in J. Drewnowski (ed.) *Crisis in the East European Economy* (Beckenham: Croom Helm), 7–17.

Williamson, O. (2000) 'The New Institutional Economics: Taking Stock, Looking Ahead', *Journal of Economic Literature*, 38, 595–613.

Winiecki, J. (1987) *Economic Prospects – East and West* (London: Centre for Research into Communist Economies).

Winiecki, J. (2002) *Transition Economies and Foreign Trade* (London: Routledge).

Winiecki, E. and J. Winiecki (1992) *The Structural Legacy of the Soviet-Type Economy* (London: CRCE).

Zemplinerova, A. and M. Machacek (2003) 'Privatisation in the Czech Republic: Strengths and Weaknesses', in Y. Kalyuzhnova and W. Andreff (eds) *Privatisation and Structural Change in Transition Economies* (Basingstoke: Palgrave Macmillan), 202–24.

Index